One of Ben's

Born in New Zealand of English, Irish, Welsh and Australian convict ancestry, Maurice Shadbolt has published four collections of short stories, several works of non-fiction, and ten novels. His most recent novel, *The House of Strife*, was the third in a trilogy that began with *Season of the Jew*, winner of the Wattie Book of the Year award in 1987 and selected by the literary editors of the *New York Times* as one of the best books of 1987. The second was *Monday's Warriors*. In 1989, Maurice Shadbolt was awarded the CBE for services to Literature.

'Absorbing and full of surprises.'
New York Times

'Dramatically original.'
Washington Post

BY THE SAME AUTHOR

FICTION

The New Zealanders
Summer Fires and Winter Country
Among the Cinders
The Presence of Music
This Summer's Dolphin
An Ear of the Dragon
Strangers and Journeys
A Touch of Clay
Danger Zone
Figures in Light
The Lovelock Version
Season of the Jew
Monday's Warriors
The House of Strife

DRAMA

Once on Chunuk Bair

NON-FICTION

New Zealand: Gift of the Sea (with Brian Brake)
The Shell Guide to New Zealand
Love and Legend
The Reader's Digest Guide to New Zealand (with Brian Brake)
Voices of Gallipoli

ONE OF BEN'S

Maurice Shadbolt

David Ling Publishing Limited
PO Box 34-601
Birkenhead, Auckland 10

Distributed in New Zealand by Lothian Books

Acknowledgement is made to the following institutions which used material
herein in earlier form: Radio New Zealand, The New Zealand
Listener, Islands (New Zealand), Metro (Auckland) and
Contemporary Authors Autobiography series (Detroit).

One of Ben's

ISBN 0–908990–19–7

First published 1993
This revised and corrected paperback
edition first published 1994

Design by Biggles & Co.
Cover illustration by Jeff Fisher
Typeset by Egan-Reid Ltd
Printed in Hong Kong

It is as if we carry in our make-up the effects of the accidents that have befallen our ancestors, as if we are in many ways programmed before we are born, our lives half outlined for us.

V. S. Naipaul

For my grandchildren, Winston Maurice Shadbolt and Amelia Alice Shadbolt; and their children's children.

Author's Note

As a novelist nears his sixties, he realises he is never going to get his stories told. On his sixtieth birthday he knows it for certain. Often the story of his stories is the best he has to tell. He begins to understand that others might soon misappropriate his tale and communicate it in unrecognisable form. This narrative may be seen as a protective strike. Now and then names or identifying details have been changed for the peace of mind of others. The reader is also advised that a novelist is at work in these pages.

Thanks are due to helpful relatives, Stewart and Catherine Shadbolt, and Judith Gifford, all of Christchurch; Kevin and Ann Shadbolt of Tasmania; Peter Shadbolt of Wellington and Donald Gifford and Yvonne Shadbolt of Auckland; Averil Ford and Kelvin Smythe of Hamilton; and Canterbury historians Gordon Ogilvie, Elsie Locke, Stevan Eldred-Grigg and Norfolk Island archivist Les Brown. It is impossible to overstate the contribution made to this book by two marvellously fervent researchers, Merryl Alley of Hertfordshire and my third cousin Denis Hampton of Christchurch. I am also greatly indebted to the Kearon clan of Arklow. Those named above cannot be held responsible for errors of fact or interpretation. I am also grateful to the staff of the English Department of the University of Waikato for providing me with a fellowship and a room in which to complete the book; and the Literature Committee of the New Zealand Arts Council for assistance in earlier research. Above all I must thank fellow author Elspeth Sandys for her fortitude as the story took form.

Maurice Shadbolt
June 4, 1992

One

A persistent, puzzling and egocentric fantasy threads my earliest years. How it began, why and when, is mystery. The fantasy — fully blown by the time I was eight years old — said the world was a theatrical event designed for my instruction, confusion, and humiliation. As soon as I went to bed, actors were rested and sets refreshed for more make-believe in the morning. I fancied that I might one day surprise my parents in the wings as they wiped away greasepaint and became themselves. Themselves? So who were they? Answers were unnerving. Was my noisy young brother also a participant in this thespian conspiracy? School friends, teachers and relatives had to be party to it too. The extravaganza required a cast of thousands, certainly such of the population of New Zealand as I had seen in city, town and countryside. School, home, not to speak of the main street of my small town, were ingenious fictions. For that matter most of the cosmos must be; even the stars had to be stage managed. This radical interpretation of reality might have been understandable if my parents or other near relatives had a theatrical connection. None did. More, I had never seen a play; the notion must have derived from precocious reading about theatre, or maybe a Hollywood movie. The fantasy failed to serve much useful function after the age of ten, though it returned in flashes for a few years more. To make the world work, I had to assent to the proposition that the place was authentic. It seemed I had been an understudy all along. I was now a trouper too, pushed out from the wings to see how I managed solo. But who was the impresario? And who the author? Whose were my lines?

Looking back, loss of the fantasy now seems a pity. It was a reasonable deduction from the evidence. This is not to say that all performances were flawless. Most of my ancestors and many of my contemporaries have missed their cues, misread their lines, and otherwise failed to make their characters credible. If I lapse, then, I am in respectable company.

'Shut up and listen to me,' my grandfather roared, 'or I'll lock you in the fowl house.'

They were the first words I recall him uttering. Even at the age of three or four years, I saw exile in the fowl house as an unsavoury fate. He wasn't bellowing at me, as it happened, but at my many tall uncles. They were muscular footballers and boxers. When Grandfather Shadbolt laid down the law, however, they shut up and shook like a hayfield in high wind. If an uncle was sufficiently foolhardy to persist in dissent, he risked a fireside log sped in his direction. Grandfather Shadbolt's aim, with firewood or firearms, was punishingly accurate. A champion marksman in his youth, he was still targeting ducks and sons with vigour in his eighth decade.

His favoured subject was justice and its rarity in the human realm; conspicuously in the British realm. This might have been more intelligible to me had I known that his father, my great-grandfather Benjamin, had seeded a sense of large injury in his family for the best of reasons. As a convicted felon he had been domiciled in worse than a fowl house.

The record says that twenty-year-old Benjamin Shadbolt, an English farm labourer, a married man with one child, was hauled before the Hertford assizes on July 10, 1845, and charged with theft. Sharing the dock, facing similar charges, were his older brother, twenty-seven-year-old Johnathan, his twenty-five-year-old cousin George, and his uncle, forty-eight-year-old Solomon Shadbolt. (Solomon was George's father and possibly also a surrogate parent for Benjamin and Johnathan.) A close-knit clan may be inferred.

The four came from the Hertfordshire village of Datchworth, six miles from Hertford and three from Welwyn. Never celebrated by painter or poet, then notorious as a parish which permitted people to perish of starvation in its poorhouse, Datchworth sits in a colourless corner of Hertfordshire among patches of woodland, pasture and ploughed acres. It has two thousand years of history, few of them happy, some of them bloody. A moated fort for Celt settlers of the Bronze and Iron Ages, it was a useful stronghold for conquering Romans too. Such small defended communities, in later centuries, were often able to hold off Danish and Saxon incursions and retain their Roman-Celtic colour. Saxon rule was followed by Norman. For the weathered natives of Datchworth no change of overlord was momentous. They were governed more by months of the year than by masters; animals had to be tended, seed sown, crops won. Winter or summer, sleet or shine, they were people bent beast-like to the brown earth, boulder clay and flinty gravel of their birthplace.

Approached from lush, orderly and open Oxfordshire, today's Datchworth declares itself slowly from austere, rather moody terrain: high hedges and overhanging trees shadow sunken lanes. Even on a mild summer day its ploughed fields and patches of woodland can give off an aloof chill: one can imagine it the residue of lives survived in silent sorrow. The district's largest landmark is 700-year-old All Saints' Church, rather off-centre and apart from the population, showing lonely above trees and fields. The village is all outskirts, with no discernible axis. There are a couple of pubs, a post office, and a small store beside a green where a whipping post still stands. There is nothing fit to be called a village street. Dwellings are scattered. In this respect little has changed: the place always had a patchy character.

In 1845 it had four or five hundred inhabitants, dozens with the distinctive name Shadbolt. A church register dating back to 1570 confirms that Shadbolts have been plentiful there since at least the sixteenth century. Local historians judge that they were likely one of the dozen families resident there, with six ploughs and fifty oxen, when Normans compiled the Domesday Book for tax purposes in 1087. The name Shadbolt derives from archery (a variant spelling is 'Shotboult'; another is 'Shotbolt'). The name is to be found not only in Hertfordshire, but in nearby counties like Bedfordshire, Lincolnshire, and Cambridgeshire. It is a fair deduction that Anglo-Saxon bowmen by the name Shotboult, Shotbolt or Shadbolt battled Norman invaders in 1066. When data for the Domesday Book was gathered, a generation later, they had reverted to the commonplace condition of serfs — or villeins — in an occupied land; they were now chattels of such Norman nobles as Peter de Valognes and Geoffrey of Bec. Serfs the Shadbolts would remain, under one nobleman and the next, for most of nine centuries. Their employment seldom varied from generation to generation. In and around Datchworth — and in the neighbouring parishes of Trewin and Digswell — they ploughed fields for tight-fisted absentee lords and landowners and penny-pinching tenant farmers; they reaped and threshed; they tended flocks. Their toil established Hertfordshire on the London market as a major source of wheat and barley, for the basic British diet of bread and beer; they nourished themselves with the leavings. Where hunger didn't diminish them, disease did. Between 1349 and 1369 the Black Death called on Hertfordshire again and again, leaving some villages eerily empty of life: 'Pestilence came upon us,' wrote one Hertfordshire monk, 'which almost halved all flesh.' Though Datchworth's population was thinned, enough Shadbolts survived to keep the name conspicuous.

Contagion left social stirring. Peasants took over deserted land in hope of becoming free men. Desperate to return them to slavery, landlords used legislation, threats, penalties, poll taxes and prison. Anguish and anger grew. The voice of the egalitarian priest John Ball — a liberation theologian if ever there was one — was heard loud in Hertfordshire. It was Ball's fiery wish 'that there be no villeins nor gentlemen, but that we may all be united together, and that the lords be no greater master than we be. What have we deserved, or why should we be kept thus in servage? We all come from one father and one mother, Adam and Eve.'

Even in twentieth century England, with farm labourers still at the bottom of the social heap, and rural unions resented, that sounds uncommonly like sedition. Ball was imprisoned. Uproar followed. Insurgent men of Kent, led by the peasant leader Wat Tyler, were joined by sympathisers from Hertfordshire, conspicuously by William Gryndcobbe of St Albans. They marched on Maidstone Prison, where they freed Ball, and then on London. In the mayhem following, both Tyler and the Archbishop of Canterbury were slain. The fight then flowed into Hertfordshire itself, with more and more local men declaring for the peasant cause. Among them were the discontented of Datchworth, and presumably more than a few aggrieved Shadbolts. At St Albans, a half-day hike from Datchworth, the rebels were scattered by the lances of King Richard II. John Ball and the Hertfordshire man Gryndcobbe were tried and executed. Surviving rebels limped back to bondage. John Ball's democratic dream seemed aground. *If hope were not*, goes one Hertfordshire saying, *heart should break*. Hope wasn't; hearts did. Yet the revolt sped the end of feudalism. In a generation or two landlords looking to buy loyalty were paying out villagers with money rather than protection and produce. More and more freemen worked their own acres in centuries to come.

Yet for Datchworth families like the Shadbolts it was an

ephemeral freedom. The independence some won was ended by the enclosure acts of the eighteenth and nineteenth centuries, legislation which shut them out from the strips of common land they had long thought their own. Rather than return to the service of rural masters, many moved in dejection to industrial towns. Some Shadbolts became higglers — horse and cart traders — or ostermongers, selling goods from a barrow. Others survived by playing hit and run with rural society, warring with the propertied of Hertfordshire in the way the English peasantry knew best. *He who does not steal from his masters*, argues one rustic proverb, *steals from his children.*

Men in despair of robbing their young sometimes excelled in larger vengeance. In the early 1830s agricultural labourers went on an insurrectionary rampage through the southern English countryside — in the so-called Captain Swing riots — with the desperate poor expressing their grievances by wrecking farm machinery and burning down barns. Retribution was brutal. Prices were put on the heads of ringleaders. Posses loyal to landowners hunted the rebels down. Some two thousand labourers were rounded up, nineteen hung, and five hundred transported to Australia. Uncle Solomon would have been familiar with the Swing riots, perhaps as a sour participant. Most Shadbolts, as always, bleakly accepted what was. 'Hertfordshire hedgehogs', their humble kind was called. They toiled, hungered, and died as human livestock, to be counted with, often bedded with, oxen and horses. Hundreds were born only to fill early graves — some marked, most not — around All Saints' Church.

Though few were affluent enough to purchase family pews, all were reliably Anglican. For the most of their history they had to be. Up to the eighteenth century non-attendance at Sunday service had been a punishable offence in Datchworth. Reluctant participation or resentful posture in the act of worship could also be penalised. The Shadbolt world view was never flawed by Papism or dissent. Biblical family names — Rebecca and Rachel, Samuel and Daniel, Sarah, Joseph, Josec, Johnathan, Solomon, and not least Benjamin — argue a sober respect for the scriptures. Most were not of the kind to be seen intoxicated or travelling irreligiously by horse and cart on the sabbath, further offences against the peace of the realm. Theirs was the faith of their masters. Some saw their fiftieth year; few survived their sixtieth.

No one was to break the Shadbolt mould with more style than the twenty-year-old in the dock at the Hertford assizes on July 10,

1845. On that day in England prices for wheat, barley and oats were average; the hop market was satisfactory; and at meat markets, after a hard winter, even middling mutton was producing a fair return. The Chartists, with their commonplace clamour for the vote, were having a quiet year. There was only one war in evidence. In Britain's new colony of New Zealand, a land of which Benjamin Shadbolt had probably never heard, red-coated troops were engaged disastrously with native rebels among unfamiliar forests and rivers. Queen Victoria was in the ninth year of her long reign.

Presiding over the fate of the four Shadbolts was a Mr Justice Coleridge. Things looked unpromising from the first. Before proceedings began in earnest he drew the attention of jurymen to the increase of crime in Hertfordshire. In ten years the numbers of persons committed for trial had doubled. Was this due to any other cause than moral deterioration of the populace? He urged the citizens of Hertfordshire to watch the progress of crime with more zeal.

Curtailment of capital punishment, he went on, had not been helpful. Crime had increased in the categories for which such punishment could no longer be prescribed. Lawbreaking was not to be checked by increasing the physical comfort of people. Nor did education have a moral effect. The mere power to read and write was of no importance except as a means of amusement. Greater gain might come from religious schooling. Mr Justice Coleridge made no suggestion, however, that the Shadbolts, or any others before the assizes, might beneficially be sentenced to a term of religious instruction.

The delinquent Shadbolts were jointly charged with burgling Widow Priscilla Blindell's drapery store in Little Wymondley, some eight miles from Datchworth, on the night of February 3, 1845. There, it was claimed, they had stolen items to the value of something over £11 — garments, flannel and calico, plus cannisters of tea, eleven pounds of pork meat, and four shillings in the form of half pence and farthings. The charges against them speak for the misery of rural England. Warm clothing and sturdy cloth were craved by the ragged, often half-frozen poor of the English countryside. Any meat short of putrid was coveted by the hungry. Most crime in the English countryside involved theft of food, or food on the hoof, and clothing.

Labourers like the Shadbolts earned between twenty and thirty pounds a year, or a shilling or two a day. That meant daily duels with cold, hunger, landlords and the law; even collecting windfall wood from nearby forest could win a prison term. It also meant a smoky hovel of daub, wattle and thatch, with a mattress of rush and a rabbitskin rug, or merely a hayloft. All four were married, with children. Uncle Solomon had three, cousin George two and brother Johnathan one. Benjamin's first child, a daughter, was born and christened after he was taken into custody. In creeping through snow and forcing entry to Widow Blindell's premises while she and her son slept, in lifting garments and sheets from her shelves, and pork from her larder, the four must have known they were chancing powerful punishment and found it less daunting than law-abiding cold and hunger.

On the face of things, tough, whiskery and villainously tattooed Uncle Solomon, as the senior party, might have been seen as the most culpable of the four; he was also the only one with a prior felony conviction, having served a fifteen-month sentence for theft of the Reverend Drusner's pig and some trusses of hay. Benjamin, on the other hand, might have been judged a misled minor delinquent. But there were few minor delinquencies in early Victorian England; a decade or two earlier the enterprise at Widow Blindell's would have ended with hood, hemp, and hangman. Besides, Benjamin's family had an unedifying history. Benjamin's father (also named Benjamin and when frail and grey in his sixties) was charged in 1841 with stealing a wooden pole, valued at sixpence, from a property occupied by Samuel Sutton. A pole? What kind of pole? A fishing pole? A bean pole? Anyway one missed by Samuel Sutton. The offence was grave enough for justices of the peace to hand down three weeks' imprisonment with hard labour. In 1842, after a village altercation, Benjamin junior, then seventeen years' old, was fined £20 — or most of a farm labourer's annual income — and bound over to keep the peace towards one James Griffiths for six calendar months. Brother Johnathan, cousin George, and uncle Solomon — the kinsmen destined to share the dock with him three years later — were similarly bound over for participation in the same contretemps, but fined only £10. This suggests that Benjamin had standing as a Datchworth rowdy before he turned up at the Hertford assizes in 1845.

It was, however, nothing against Uncle Solomon's reputation. Solomon may literally have got away with murder two decades earlier. On the winter morning of January 7, 1826, the body of Thomas Chalkey, ploughman, was found in moat waters near The Horns public house. The publican reported that the previous evening Chalkey had called into The Horns in the company of Solomon Shadbolt. Chalkey had partaken of one pint of beer and left the premises sober in company with Solomon. Might there then have been a fatal falling out between thieves? After discovery of the ploughman's body Solomon and his young brother Joseph were detained and questioned, but later discharged. Since Chalkey's death could not be established as murder, Solomon could hardly be held as a suspect. He might have had a persuasive explanation of his movements on the evening of Chalkey's demise. If the law had no case against Solomon, Datchworth gossips surely did. Thereafter he was known, fairly or unfairly, as a man lucky to escape the gallows. The mystery would die hard among the hamlets of upland Hertfordshire.

The story could have been informally whispered into a judicial ear nineteen years later; Benjamin and the two other young Shadbolts in the dock may have been tarred by Solomon's brush. It also suggests a reason why Benjamin and his brother Johnathan were represented separately from their relatives. A trio of lawyers appeared for the Datchworth quartet. Why not one for all four? And how, one has to ask, was their defence funded? Solomon and his son George may have financed their lawyer with ill-gotten cash — with, for a start, Widow Blindell's missing stash of halfpennies and farthings. But how could Benjamin and Johnathan, indigent farm labourers, afford a lawyer apiece? Who put up the money in an attempt to stop the brothers going down with Solomon and George? There is something here which should meet the eye; it doesn't. One might surmise a moneyed well-wisher. It is certainly possible to see a divide in the family.

As it happened, however, the servant of the law presiding over the assizes that midsummer morning in 1845 was not of a mind to distinguish one melancholy felon from another. Blue-eyed, brown-haired, and clean-shaven Benjamin — the only one of the four defendants literate — pleaded not guilty along with his older kinsmen. No defence of youthful folly could therefore be put to the court. The evidence tendered was fairly compelling, though much of it devolved on goods recovered from the prisoners in early April, two months after the burglary. Two pickle jars filled with tea, for example, had been found behind the chimney in Benjamin's cottage. There were new calico sheets and pillow cases on his bed. Benjamin had also been wearing a new flannel jacket, only a little soiled, of the kind Widow Blindell sold. Similar items had been recovered from Solomon, George and Johnathan. On the other hand a defence lawyer succeeded in establishing that the flannel shirts were of the common sort worn in Hertfordshire; and that the tea found was of the dark kind generally consumed in rural communities. Moreover, Widow Blindell was unable to make positive identification of some of the property.

Much of the evidence presented looked similarly suspect. One Isaac Croft, labourer, testified — half a year after the event — that on the early morning of February 4, hours following the robbery, he had seen Benjamin and Johnathan walking toward Datchworth from the direction of Little Wymondley. Benjamin appeared to have his pockets filled and Johnathan seemed to have something bulky under his smock. This was hardly incriminating. The lacklustre lawyers acting for Benjamin and Johnathan might have asked Isaac Croft how religiously he studied the calendar and congratulated him on an immaculate memory; they might also have asked how he knew that morning of a robbery eight miles away. In the event they failed to. (There was no newspaper report of the felony; that week's *Hertford Mercury* considered the theft of twenty turnips and farm labourers' unnatural practices of more interest to its readers.)

A police constable named Hawkes claimed to have overheard a conversation between Benjamin and George Shadbolt after they were taken into custody. Benjamin, according Hawkes' testimony, said 'I suppose we shall be transported for seven years this time'. And George was supposed to have replied, 'I suppose we shall, but if the buggers had not been at home that night they would have had a pretty job to watch us.' So far as meaning may be won from it, this has the smell of many dubious police 'verbals' — evidence designed to prejudice jurors and to stitch up a case less than convincing. It doesn't make sense either. Why should Benjamin, on his maiden appearance before the assizes, talk of being transported 'for seven years this time'? This time? Only Solomon had a record; and could have such a fear. If the words *were* spoken, then they sound more like Solomon's.

A good deal was made of price tickets found in association with the allegedly stolen goods — three or four marked to the sum of three shillings and eightpence. Widow Blindell testified that her flannel jackets were priced at three shillings and eightpence. Under cross examination, however, she admitted this was the price charged by other drapers in Hertfordshire; she further admitted that it was not always her practice to remove price tags when she sold garments. This raises an interesting question. The Shadbolts may not have been innocent; but they appear to have been remarkably unprofessional. Even a novice shoplifter would know better than to leave a price tag on or about a stolen article.

Three sets of footprints — two barefoot and one shod — had been found in the snow outside Widow Blindell's store. (The feet in shoes presumably belonged to Solomon.) Anyway this indicated more than a family short of footwear. It also implied that one of the four had not been party to the burglary, and might be guilty only of receiving stolen goods from a relative. Young Benjamin, perhaps? No suggestion was offered. The lawyers acting for Benjamin and Johnathan made a case on behalf of the brothers, but the *Hertford Mercury* recorded no storm of eloquence. Nor did they make much of the distance the alleged burglars must have had to cover — an improbable sixteen miles there and back in the hours of dark. The ground between Datchworth and Little Wymondley is hilly; it was also slippery with snow that long midwinter night in 1845. Even in moonlight such an excursion would have been madcap. The lawyer acting for Solomon and George asked jurors to dismiss from their minds the relationship between the prisoners and allow each to stand or fall on the evidence against him alone. Better that a hundred guilty men escape, he argued, than one innocent person should suffer. Were Solomon and George — and particularly desperate Solomon — trying to shift guilt on to Benjamin and Johnathan? It sounds suspiciously like it. If so, the Shadbolts at this point would not have been looking at each other; bitter exchanges would have followed in the cells.

The jurors were not impressed by defence pleas. They took only ten minutes to return guilty verdicts against all four. Mr Justice Coleridge wistfully reminded the prisoners that many a criminal had paid the penalty of his life for an offence far less heinous than the burglary for which they stood convicted. There were no mitigating circumstances. Nor had anyone come forward to speak to their character. They consequently merited the most severe punishment.

After 1815, Britain had ended the transportation of first-time offenders to the Australian colonies. Though three of the four fell into the first-time class, they were seen as deserving of long absence from Datchworth. They were sentenced 'to be transported across the seas' for fifteen years. Older Solomon, with his prior conviction placed before the court, was banished for twenty years. Given his forty-eight years, that surely meant he would never see Datchworth again. They thus all became privy to Britain's bizarre social experiment, begun in 1788, which condemned some 160,000 convicted men, women and juveniles to bitter Australian exile. Benjamin later received an additional month's transportation for assault committed in the course of protesting his confinement. It is inconceivable that this bonus dismayed him much. Bad could hardly be worse.

Mr Justice Coleridge congratulated the police on their intelligent work on the case. The efficient prosecution meant Hertfordshire was now rid of a family of notorious thieves who had baffled the best efforts of police for several years past. This surprisingly venomous judicial outburst suggests that the police case against the four might indeed have been manufactured to put them behind bars — with the less than languid collaboration of Mr Justice Coleridge. It also confirmed that a family — or a reputation — had been on trial; and that Benjamin and Johnathan had never had a chance of being considered separately from Solomon and George. The shameless Shadbolts, condemned by the decent of Hertfordshire, all went down together.

If expulsion from England was designed as a deterrent to the clan, it seems never to have curbed them. Australian records say there were two Shadbolts resident in the convict colony of Norfolk Island in the 1830s. They were not necessarily felons; they could have been among the hundreds of farm labourers dispatched to Australia after the Captain Swing riots. Either way transportation was nothing new to the family — or indeed to many rural families. It was said that English villages, in the first half of the nineteenth century, 'sleep by the shores of Botany Bay'. (For Botany Bay read Van Diemen's Land and Norfolk Island too.)

As I write this another piece of information floats across my desk. Six months after Benjamin and his relatives made their appearance there, a George Shadbolt, aged sixteen, was convicted at the Hertford assizes for stealing a loaf of bread from a baker's cart.

Was Mr Justice Coleridge, allergic to the name Shadbolt, presiding that day too? If so, he was in no mood for second thoughts. This Shadbolt was likewise sentenced to transportation and served two years in the labour gangs of Port Phillip, Victoria, before winning a pardon in his nineteenth year.

I look for, and find, this adolescent on the family tree. He was Benjamin's cousin. So much for deterrence.

Recriminations spent, the Datchworth four were transferred from Hertford Gaol to Millbank Prison, near London. There they had a month of confinement in which to familiarise themselves with each other again, perhaps to forgive each other. Finally, on August 29, 1845, at the port of Woolwich, they were bundled aboard the 600-ton Sunderland-built convict transport *Mayda* for the sweaty, lice-ridden and sometimes lethal four-month voyage to Australia. Did they know their destination at this stage? Possibly not. But they would fast have learned from the crew of the *Mayda*. They and their two hundred fellow passengers were bound for the most dreaded of all England's penal colonies in the South Sea: Norfolk Island, a settlement built to bring men to their knees with despair. Men assigned there had, in the words of one bureaucrat, 'forfeited all claim to the protection of the law.' Which meant they were subject to the whims of their warders, no matter how vicious. It was explicitly designed to promote pain and kill hope. For the most part it did.

What of the families of those transported? Benjamin may have had the chance, before the *Mayda* carried him away, to farewell his tearful and destitute wife Caroline, his months-old daughter Rachel too; he was never to see either again, or Hertfordshire.

Two

On January 8, 1846, the *Mayda* made landfall. The Shadbolts' first sight of the steep cliffs and wooded heights of Norfolk Island would have left them with mixed feelings. On the one hand the shore promised relief from the rancid *Mayda*, the bruising Atlantic and brawling Indian Ocean, the wormy biscuit and sea-fouled salt beef, the slow deaths and short burials at sea, and their shipboard shackles. On the other hand there was the reputation of the place. Might it be as bad as rumour reported? The convict grapevine left little leeway for optimism.

The penal colonies of Australia had never been busier. In that decade, due to efficient law enforcement in Britain, Van Diemen's Land alone took in 26,000 transportees. Two thousand filled the prisoners' barracks and cells of tiny, remote and surf-lashed Norfolk Island. The loneliest suburb of suffering on the antipodean convict circuit, it specialised in subduing the pick of the crop, in lifers and long-termers like the Shadbolts.

The Shadbolts' first glimpse of the abyss came when the *Mayda* stood off the reef at Kingston Town and unloaded its chained human freight into whaleboats. The newcomers were rowed across the violent surf of the reef. That was the least of their introductory ordeals. Dumped dizzily on land, they stumbled up a white beach. There, while trying to wash away the filth of travel, they were set upon brutally by veteran convicts. The new arrivals were beaten up and their few possessions plundered. The men of the constabulary were passive spectators to this initiation rite. Given their characters, especially rambunctious Benjamin's, it is possible that the Shadbolt four fought back for a time. Given the odds against them, it is equally possible that they didn't. Anyway they finished their first day on Norfolk Island bleeding and bruised, stripped of all that they wore. If nothing else they learned that their fellow prisoners were as formidable a proposition as their callous guards.

Four hundred miles north of New Zealand and nearly a thousand miles from the Australian mainland, Norfolk was mysteriously left unsettled by the restless voyagers of Polynesia. Though evidence says they brushed with the island, leaving adzes, a midden or two, and rats and banana trees to mark their passage, it was one of the few lumps of land in the South Pacific on which they failed to pitch permanent camp. Why they didn't defies understanding. Might they have diminished themselves with feuding, pronounced the place inhospitably jinxed, and sailed off to larger and cooler New Zealand? Might some tohunga, or tribal priest, have been afforded some visionary glimpse of the island's dire future — men shuffling nightmarishly in chain gangs, whips carving the backs of captives down to the bone, pinioned men hung helpless by the neck until dead? Whatever the reason Polynesians inexplicably judged the place undesirable, which it is not; they left one of the world's most benign islands to men of another colour.

For British penal purposes the place was near perfect, virtually impossible to escape. With its distinctive pine trees, dramatic coast, rich soil and half-tropic climate, it had once been a welcome landfall for mariners wearied by the Pacific's long sealanes; Britons had since laboured mightily to make it an 8500-acre meadow in hell. The prevailing rationale of the institution was simple: the labour gangs of Norfolk Island were meant to dull the spirit of long-term prisoners and make them sensitive to discipline before returning them as cheap labour to Van Diemen's Land. One favoured device for diminishing men, far more effective than hard labour in chain gangs, was the human-powered crankmill which sat near the landing place at Kingston Town. Designed to grind maize, it was manned by a hundred shackled convicts in two shifts of fifty. When the first fifty slumped exhausted, the second took over. 'The labour,' one observer noted, 'appears to be exceptionally severe; the yells and screams of the unfortunate criminals as they heave at the cumbersome machine almost induces a belief that the spectator is listening to the cries of lost souls.'

Seldom was thought given to improving their characters. 'Their sunken glazed eyes, deadly pale faces, hollow fleshless cheeks and once manly limbs [had] shrivelled and withered up as if by premature old age,' said one judicial observer.' They looked less like human beings than the shadows of gnomes who had risen from their sepulchral abode. What man was or ever could be reclaimed under such a system as this? 'There were up to two thousand of them — condemned, as the prospectus put it, to 'punishment short of death'. Which meant living death, with literal death an often welcome caller. Feuding and sodomy were their favoured diversions. The depraved nature of the place even caused soul-searching in Britain's House of Commons. On the whole, however, it was judged that not only should Norfolk Island be richly rumoured as terrible; it had to be terrible too.

It was. Its only rivals since have been Adolf Hitler's Auschwitz and Joseph Stalin's gulags. One earlier commandant of the island thought nothing of overseeing the administration of 1500 lashes on five recalcitrants before taking breakfast. The ground about the triangles, to which flogged men were tied, wasn't merely saturated; witnesses recall blood running in shiny streams. The drive to punish, again and again, was fanatic. Prisoners may have gone mad, but so sometimes did their persecutors. Insanity was built into the system.

Orange trees flourished in Norfolk's kindly climate. One deranged commandant cut the orchards down, arguing that oranges were too large a luxury for the convicts in his care. They might pick and eat them when they should be at hard labour. Besides, foul prison diet — one pound of salt beef and one pound of maize mash daily — was part of their punishment.

This episode was characteristic. Humanitarians who found themselves there were never permitted to disturb the even tenor of terror for long. One literate captive mourned: 'Let a man's heart be what it will when he comes here, his Man's heart is taken from him, and he is given the heart of a Beast'. On the gallows condemned Norfolk men were known to kiss the feet of the hangman in thanks for pending release from pain and despair; others wept when they heard of their reprieve.

On July 1, 1846, six months after their arrival, the Shadbolts were witness to the most dramatic event in the island's penal history. It began as a food riot and finished in slaughter. As always on Norfolk Island, food was short and mostly foul; convict diet seemed to underline the contempt in which they were held by their native land. Sixty starving convicts, enfeebled further by dysentery, hurled themselves at their guards with makeshift weapons. It was a despairing act. 'Follow me and you follow to the gallows,' promised one ringleader. It was not a prospect to inspirit any but the boldest and most bitter, and certainly not the Hertfordshire four. The mutineers slew four soldiers before they were scattered by British bayonets. By nightfall all were in irons and awaiting trial, fourteen on capital charges. As soon as a judge and a reliable ex-convict hangman could be fetched from the Australian mainland, they were found guilty of murder and abetting murder by a jury of five military officers. No one appeared for their defence. Twelve of the fourteen were sentenced to death.

The Shadbolts were witness to the hangings too. With other comrades in calamity, they were paraded to watch the last minutes of twelve hymn-singing mutineers, hung in two sets of six. When the corpses of the first six were cut down, dumped in coffins and borne off by bullock cart, the second six were unshackled, pushed to a trapdoor, fitted with hood and rope, and dispatched. Aside from the hymns, and the crashing trapdoor, the affair was tolerably quiet; no voices were raised and no last statements from the scaffold allowed.

Death didn't take the men quickly. Nineteenth century hangmen were notoriously inefficient. A decent interval was necessary before convulsions ceased. Did Benjamin try to look away? Did Johnathan and George? Hard-bitten Solomon may have mustered the courage to gaze upon a likely future. For good measure, in the following week, they were assembled to witness five further convicts hooded and hung too. It was the busiest week for the hangman in Norfolk Island's history. The Shadbolts were a long way from the fields and woods of Datchworth.

Horror hadn't finished with them. The hangings heralded the regime of John Giles Price on the island. The original of the sadistic Maurice Frere in Marcus Clarke's celebrated nineteenth century novel *For the Term of his Natural Life*, the bull-necked and bespectacled Price is one of the most repellent figures in Australian history. Seen as the man to put the island to rights, he began zealously flogging his way to infamy. He had no belief in reform. His one penal principle was retribution. It was ensured by an insanitary ring of informers and confirmed by the cat of nine tails and the gallows. He enjoyed selecting brutal convicts to serve as overseers. Told that a newly arrived convict was 'an inoffensive man with fine feelings', Price replied 'We'll soon take *them* out of him'. Subordinates showing sympathy for convicts were sent packing. Men were flogged for keeping tame birds, for losing their shoe-laces, for speaking without permission, for collecting herbs to heal their festering wounds, and especially for trying to escape by way of suicide. Price's vengeance continued beyond the punishment triangles. He had flogged men tied down in strait-jackets until their mangled flesh began to rot and reek; he turned robust prisoners into men grateful for a grave. Plainly insane, Price earned his death long before being pulped by a hundred Victorian convicts in 1857. Across Australia thousands of men toasted those who mustered the courage to kill him.

The bad luck of the Shadbolts had its limits after all. As rural labourers of competence, rather than run of the mill pickpockets and embezzlers of urban England, they were more useful on a prison farm than in the hellish cells of Kingston Town. They were transferred to the upland community of Cascade. It was the one location on Norfolk about which observers had good to say. Though toil was hard and hateful in the fields, the station at Cascade, said one diarist, had 'a neat and cheerful appearance, contrasting favourably with the settlement below. It stands high, backed by picturesque hills, thickly wooded, from whence the land falls rapidly to the sea, whose blue waters bound the view...There is a profusion of vegetables and fruit.' Prisoners' barracks were built of homely weatherboards and shingles rather than stern stone. Guards were few, overseers occasionally tolerant, and military presence light. Prisoners were sometimes allowed small gardens of their own. As a place of confinement it was something short of paradisial, but it suggested that the Shadbolts might, with a little cunning and craft, last the distance.

Benjamin was first to stumble. He was given a flock of sheep to tend, a task familiar to a former Hertfordshire hired hand. In January 1847, after a year on Norfolk, he was found guilty of leaving his livestock unattended. Was he seen asleep under a tree, while the flock wandered, or was that the least of his sins? In the proximity of Kingston Town and Commandant Price such dereliction of duty would surely have won a flogging and possibly a spell in the feared crankmill. In the easier-going Cascade community he was merely awarded three months' hard labour in chains. Cousin George was to have harder. Evidence suggests that George was soon deep in Norfolk's lively black market, trading fresh meat and vegetables to famished soldiers in exchange for tobacco. (Tobacco was forbidden to all but privileged prisoners.) Discovered in possession of unauthorised mutton — perhaps, who knows, from Benjamin's unattended flock — George got four months' hard labour in chains. Then he was found in possession of pipe and clandestine tobacco: that was worth another five months in a chain gang.

Worse followed. A weary fifty years old, unhinged and homesick for Hertfordshire, Uncle Solomon curled up and died. Under the Price regime the three young Shadbolts would have been lucky to have been allowed a prayer before his corpse was covered. Any protection prison-seasoned Solomon might have given them was gone. The fetid prisoners' barracks of Norfolk, with some twenty inches between hammocks, were notorious for predatory sodomites. To put it mildly, 'unnatural practices' were endemic — even Commandant Price was famous for an attachment to a whip-wielding convict henchman. Young Benjamin, Johnathan and George would now have been easy prizes. There is no reason to suppose they went unravished.

By the beginning of 1848 the surviving three had their probationary passes. Now broken in as workhorses, they had the right to leave the Norfolk pit for the more modest afflictions of Van Diemen's Land. A probationary pass meant a prisoner could work for wages for a reputable settler, or build roads and bridges for Van Diemen's Land's local government. It didn't mean freedom; he was still under legal rein and a curfew. He couldn't wander. If good behaviour earned it, the next stage out of bondage was a ticket-of-leave, which meant a convict could choose his own master. Conditional or absolute pardon might follow. Such was the prospect before them when their ship hoisted sail for Van Diemen's Land; they would not have looked back upon Norfolk Island with more than a shudder. At least, unlike Solomon, they were not there to stay.

A century and a half after its last chain gang was unshackled, peaceful Norfolk Island is one of the most pleasant places in the South Pacific. More than temperate, less than tropical, it has an amiable all-year climate; the population is small and tourism modest and controlled. The surf bangs spectacularly up basalt cliffs. The idiosyncratically graceful pines grow as high. Yet a few yards from golden beaches, where Australian and New Zealand visitors sun themselves, the ruins of the convict colony stubbornly persist. Within the crumbling walls the ground is grassed; there are picnic tables where the punishment triangles and the gallows stood. (The thirteen stone steps to the trapdoor are now shadows on a fragment of wall.) The atmosphere, all the same, is crushing.

Nearby the elegant Georgian buildings where commandants, administrators and clergymen lived and worked have been handsomely refurbished. They overlook the surviving stonework of the convict quarters. There has been no attempt to restore that place of suffering. Yet eroding ruins still take the eye more than discreet renovation. Nowhere in the Pacific is there a location more eloquent of man's inhumanity to man. Norfolk Island's history will befoul it forever.

The one dissonant note, in a place otherwise sensitive to its history, is in the island's lone travel agency. Arrowed convict suits are on sale to visitors — $20 new, $15 second hand. For those so disposed, there are jolly 'convict evenings' at which such garments can be worn. There is a word for this: obscene.

Three

On Van Diemen's Land, soon to be renamed Tasmania, the three surviving Shadbolts laboured for free settlers and local government, as prescribed, until their tickets of leave turned up. Johnathan was first to put his in peril. In 1850 he was charged with threatening to raze the house of a flinty employer named Thomas Peckham. (Which suggests that the Shadbolts may indeed have been disciples of the incendiary Captain Swing.) Johnathan was sentenced to four months' hard labour, the sentence to be served at a distance from Thomas Peckham's dwelling.

For the first year or two Benjamin's life had less drama; he found himself at home in a district where scarred survivors of Norfolk Island were thick on the ground. Theirs was a brotherhood not easily forsaken. Nor was he inclined to disavow it; some of these friendships, born of mutual misery, would last his lifetime. Possibly he tried the straight and narrow for a time; or perhaps he was just lucky with the law. However, his prospects for a ticket-of-leave and eventual pardon were not improved when, in 1851, he was charged with being absent from his place of employment without permission and sentenced to a month's hard labour. And again, in 1852, at Launceston, he was charged with being out after the curfew prescribed for the holder of a probationary pass. Another spell of hard labour followed.

Benjamin's real sins, however, were of a carnal kind; he possibly reckoned a little rock-breaking and road-building worth it. His absences and late hours are explained by the fact that in 1851 he had begun wooing Somerset-born Elizabeth Perham, the seventeen-year-old daughter of a respectable settler family. The Perhams were then in large disrepair. Father Thomas hadn't prospered in Tasmania. Leaving his wife and eleven children behind, and hoping to better himself on the goldfields of Victoria, he had shipped off to the

Australian mainland. Then he vanished, thought murdered by a bush-ranger. There was no longer a man of the house. Benjamin saw advantage in the vacant post. On his best behaviour, he harboured in the Perham family and bedded innocent Elizabeth. The beleagured Perhams had another problem; in 1852 there was a Shadbolt cuckoo in their nest, a son born to Benjamin and Elizabeth. They christened him Linden. Dismay must have been mighty. There was no question of marriage. Benjamin still had a wife and child in distant Datchworth.

The following year burly Benjamin won his ticket-of-leave, giving him freedom to choose his employers, and to spend more time with his antipodean paramour and son. Before long, like Hertfordshire Shadbolts before him, he was at work as a hawker, travelling from settlement to settlement, with one eye on buyers and the other on booty. In 1855 a second child, a daughter christened Emma, was born to Benjamin and Elizabeth. It was a mixed decade for the couple. Unreformed Benjamin was beginning to look less a lightweight of crime than a promising middleweight. First there was a larceny charge in Launceston. For spiriting away two dozen of Joseph Breadew's geese, valued at six pounds, he won a four-year sentence in the newly built prison of Port Arthur. Out again in two, he was charged with horse stealing in Hobart in 1857. He lost his ticket-of-leave and finished with hard labour back in Port Arthur. The intervals between his prison terms were distinguished by Elizabeth's pregnancies. During his time in Port Arthur, another daughter, named Amelia, was born.

Designed as an 'abode of misery' — in the words of its founder — Port Arthur's sadism was institutional rather than random; it made even the Norfolk Island of John Giles Price look playful. Beatings were informal and frequent. A difficult prisoner, as Benjamin proved to be, lived much of his day in darkness and silence, deprived of all sensory stimulation. Outside his cell he wore a hood so he could not recognise fellow inmates or be recognised. To have served time in Port Arthur, it is said, was to be durably marked. Some claim that it surpassed even Norfolk Island in the number of men it left lunatic. The Hertfordshire hedgehog named Benjamin Shadbolt was a hardier proposition. With miraculously loyal Elizabeth in wait outside he survived Port Arthur sane.

On November 19, 1858, a depleted and surely more sober Benjamin was given to understand that he had finished serving his time; that he was now a free man. It was thirteen years since the Hertford assizes sent him to the southern hemisphere. His brother Johnathan and cousin George, years free, were digging into Australia and industriously disguising their origins. Benjamin's recidivism had become an embarrassment. Johnathan put his difficult young brother behind him by hiking off to Western Australia; he disappears from the record, his progress now only to be tracked by a trickle of presumed descendants.

Cousin George, on the other hand, stood his ground. He established himself in Tasmania as a prosperous house-builder, blacksmith and wheelwright, bigamously wedding a worldly Londoner named Jane Whitton who, with a couple of unlawful marriages behind her, was no stranger to bigamy (and a convicted thief and prostitute besides). George and Jane, exemplars of Christian virtue from the day they exchanged vows, were to breed five daughters and two sons. Though illiterate, George was soon a commanding figure in the newly settled Sassafras district, instrumental in establishing the first state school there. Surrendering the abject faith of his fathers, he was also reborn a formidable Methodist, superintendent of his community's Sunday school.

George's rising star suggested to Benjamin that there was something to be said for a lawful life. Elizabeth also had a powerful case to state. After Benjamin's terms in Port Arthur he was a stranger to his offspring, especially to his seven-year-old son Linden. After their reunion thirty-three-year-old Benjamin and twenty-year-old Elizabeth passionately set about making up for lost years. In weeks Elizabeth was with her fourth child.

Benjamin's gaze turned to the Tasman Sea. Earlier in 1858 a fellow ticket-of-leave man named James Wilson had sailed off to New Zealand. He reported back on a promising Anglican settlement by name of Canterbury, and a richly forested place called Banks Peninsula. Whalers had been based in its harbours for years; sawmills were newly at work there. Men with a will could licitly better themselves overnight. Men with a past could put it behind them. Indeed the first European settlers on Banks Peninsula, in the 1830s, had been graduates of Van Diemen's Land and Botany Bay; the place had long been a beachhead for veterans of Australia's penal colonies looking to launder their reputations and make good in a kinder land. Wilson had teamed up with another old Tasmanian hand, a shipwright named Barwick; they were building schooners to transport Banks Peninsula timber around the New Zealand coast. There were few policemen to be seen in New Zealand and fewer prisons. Insensitive magistrates were even less in evidence. That meant freedom. It certainly meant Benjamin had nothing against timber.

On March 4, 1859, four months after his release from Port Arthur, Benjamin and his brood boarded a Hanoverian brig named the *Amasis* in Hobart Town. It was bound for the New Zealand port of Lyttelton with a cargo of sawn timber and a complement of twelve passengers, nearly half of them Shadbolts. There was also a Perham — Elizabeth's young brother, twenty-two-year-old Luke, looking for prosperity in partnership with Benjamin. What might have been a brisk week's journey became a seven-week test of stamina and stomachs. The voyage began inauspiciously. The modest 216-ton *Amasis* hit heavy seas, sprang leaks, and seemed due to disappear in Tasman deeps. Elizabeth had reason to be fearful about the New Zealand enterprise from the first. Benjamin had still to display any talent for virtue. How could New Zealand improve matters? How survive with four children and a feckless spouse in a strange and forested land? Awesome seas, seasickness, and seriously suffering children confirmed her apprehensions. Finally the *Amasis* quit the unequal battle with storm and listed back to Hobart. The shaken Shadbolts were shepherded back on to Tasmanian soil again; the leaky *Amasis*, it transpired, now required a four week refit before it could pit itself against the Tasman a second time.

At this point it seems that Elizabeth, four months' pregnant, made her misgivings known. Her infant daughters, four-year-old Emma and two-year-old Amelia, were in indifferent shape; her son Linden looked to be hanging to life by a thread. The boy might not survive another bout with vicious seas. Possibly Elizabeth struck a heart-breaking bargain with still undaunted Benjamin. Emma and Amelia were too young to be left behind; Linden could be. The upshot was that sickly Linden was delivered into the care of righteous George Shadbolt and his reliable wife Jane before the *Amasis* hoisted sail again on April 9. At least Linden would have a wholesome household until the time came to rejoin his family. The decision had a painful logic. Benjamin had been walled away for much of Linden's life; the child was far closer to George than to his father. He was also to be the sacrificial lamb in Benjamin's New Zealand sortie.

The *Amasis'* second attempt on the Tasman was no large improvement on the first. But on April 26, 1859, after nineteen sickening days, the vessel finally lurched into view of the misty coast of Canterbury and, after a day's indecision on the part of its skipper, put into harbour. Thanks to the Almighty were loud. To starboard was the salty village of Lyttelton, gateway to Christchurch and greater Canterbury, crammed between harbour and hill. On the port side bulked the wooded and mountainous peninsula Captain James Cook named for his indefatigable botanist Joseph Banks. Cook wrongly deduced it to be an island, one of the few mistakes the navigator ever made.

Peninsula or island, it was all the same to Benjamin: he was looking at his future. His travel-weary trio of females, on the other hand, must have been less visionary about the prospect before them; Elizabeth, for one, was never known to chance the Tasman again. 'The *Amasis* [has] met with severe weather,' *The Lyttelton Times* recorded tersely. 'She brings no mail and no news.'

But she had brought Benjamin Shadbolt, late and little loved of Datchworth, Norfolk Island and Port Arthur. His beginnings in New Zealand remain indistinct, on faded shipping lists, and altogether enigmatic. For some reason Benjamin's voyaging wasn't done. Hardly had the family landed in Lyttelton, and taken temporary residence over the hills in the muddy plains town of Christchurch, than Benjamin set off north, apparently to Wellington. He was back again in Lyttelton, on a vessel called *Lord Worsley*, on May 26. In short, he makes himself a narrative nightmare: for two or three weeks, after the most critical move in his life, he frivolously goes missing. The most abstemious author, faced with this inconsiderate behaviour on the part of a protagonist, would go hunting for whisky. Yet this solo episode has to be significant; he was hardly an enthusiast for sea journeys after the anguished Tasman crossing. Was he checking out the North Island as against a Banks Peninsula base, and finding it less promising? (Land was scarce there, and war with Maoris likely.) Or did he have a rendezvous to keep with some old associate in Wellington? It seems the latter. For alongside his name as passenger on the *Lord Worlsey*, is a 'Wilson'. This has to be none other than James Wilson, loyal ally in adversity and now the boat-builder of Banks Peninsula; the man who promised Benjamin a better life in New Zealand. In the light of later events, one thing is sure. The jaunt must have been to Benjamin's advantage: it must have had more than a little to do with money. He had no discernible means of support. His incomprehensible excursioning, on arrival in New Zealand, must have finally emptied his wallet of what little it held. His old convict acquaintance James Wilson could have rescued Benjamin with ready cash; it is difficult to see who else might have.

Domestic matters were also pressing. Twelve weeks later, on September 8, 1859, in Christchurch, a fourth child, another girl, was born to Benjamin and Elizabeth. They called her Tamar, after the river which flows through Launceston, and near which, perhaps beside which, she was conceived. It was their last gesture toward Tasmania. Was Tamar an omen of better things to come? Perhaps. Thereafter New Zealand was home, and that robust corner of the colony called Banks Peninsula.

Four

*T*hereafter, however, begins in murk. When we meet Benjamin decently lit in the record again, soon after 1860, he is a reliable, respected and even revered citizen of Canterbury, New Zealand. He is a prosperous farmer; an affluent sawmiller; a well-heeled storekeeper, butcher and publican, owner of a smithy and stables, a dealer in cattle, proprietor of a billiard parlour, provider of public transport, promoter of worthy causes, owner and breeder of winning racehorses, and not least a dedicated churchman. Where did he get the capital to fund his awesome social standing? It is improbable that Benjamin had enough time in the four months between his release from Port Arthur and his arrival in New Zealand to make a quick fortune on the Victorian goldfields. Might he have won it in a poker game with high stakes? Later in life he was a spirited gambler, but it is difficult to see how a Port Arthur pauper could have bought into a game played for more than pennies. There is a more colourful possibility. After his apprenticeship in lesser crime, he might have tried a little bush-ranging on Tasmania's roads before decamping fast to New Zealand, as many Australian fugitives then did. Canterbury politician and sometime New Zealand Premier Henry Sewell recorded his fears in his journal in 1855: 'Immigration from Melbourne is beginning,' he lamented, 'but not of the best class. People frighten us by saying a mounted patrol will soon be necessary. Blessings on the transportation system, which has filled the colonies with convict labour, to their common terror.' In other words, Van Diemen's Land was alive and well in virtuous Canterbury.

Despite such signals from diarists of the time, New Zealand historians have been all but mute on the subject of the former convicts who shook off Australia of joyless memory and made New Zealand a home in the nineteenth century. Anxious to distinguish

New Zealand from Australia socially and physically, chroniclers have turned a blind eye to the inconspicuous contingents of ex-convicts who saw the Tasman Sea as a highway to opportunity; and were to pioneer much of the new colony. Aside from the few who turned to crime again, they have not been seen as worth recalling. New Zealanders know rather more about such law-abiding minorities as the Chinese, Bohemians, Scandinavians, and Dalmatians who struck root in New Zealand in the nineteenth century. Yet there were thousands of less celebrated settlers in New Zealand's first decades as a colony, especially when Australia's footloose stormed ashore by the tens of thousand in the gold rushes of the 1860s, or were recruited by British regiments to fight rebel Maori in the same decade. Ex-convicts and their progeny may well have outnumbered the official settlers set ashore by skippers of the entrepreneurial New Zealand Company between 1840 and 1850. Beginning a new and healthier life, these informal migrants were not anxious to announce their presence in the colony; nor did their immediate descendants publicise their background. They left, it seems, no journals or memoirs. Benjamin's story may stand for those of the unremembered many.

The chances are that Benjamin sighted more than a few familiar faces ashore after the *Amasis* berthed at Canterbury's port of Lyttelton. How many other once shaven heads were soon residing under Canterbury's top hats, how many corrugated backs under the laundered linen shirts of Christchurch? Anyway Benjamin is distinctly and suddenly a man of means. I am tempted to surmise that there might, after all, be something to the family legend that Benjamin received a substantial legacy at about the time of his arrival in New Zealand. But a legacy from whom? That hypothetical well-wisher who furnished lawyers for Benjamin and his brother at the Hertford assizes?

The legend says a legacy from an English landowner who fathered Benjamin in exercise of *droit de seigneur*. The problem with this is that New Zealand has a surfeit of such family tales; the Shadbolts seem merely to have been following fashion in feeling the need to freshen up an unimpressive pedigree. A little light banditry looks more plausible: Benjamin hot-footing it from Tasmania to New Zealand with the law breathing down his neck. Is there a clue in the puzzling journey Benjamin made to Wellington soon after his arrival in Lyttelton? And what of James Wilson? Might he or some chain-gang colleague in Wellington have been holding loot to

Benjamin's credit? The fact is that, within a year or two of his first sighting of Banks Peninsula, Benjamin took up land at Duvauchelle, at the head of Akaroa harbour. He bought and refurbished a pub called The Traveller's Rest and soon built a solid homestead. He also launched into business. Seeing the small communities of Banks Peninsula unnecessarily sequestered by wilderness and water, he began a shipping service which fortnightly ferried mail and passengers from settlement to settlement.

He also took over the local store, which his devoted friend Wilson was running at a loss, and put the place in profit. Wilson looks to be the wild card in Benjamin's story. 'A very peculiar character,' judges one local chronicler. 'Very mean in scraping together all he possibly could, and very generous in giving the shirt off his back to the first man who asked him.' Benjamin seems to have been the recipient of Wilson's trousers too; his sometime partner was soon judged bankrupt. By then the first of Benjamin's several sawmills was gutting the forest.

To be fair, there is no evidence to suggest that his assets came his way unlawfully. On this premise hard-headed, holy and increasingly prosperous cousin George, in Tasmania, might be seen as the prime candidate for the role of Benjamin's angel. He may have been in a position to back Benjamin's move to New Zealand, with a few pounds thrown in for past favours. Or might the motive have been remorse? After all George and his father Solomon, more than anyone else, were responsible for Benjamin's transportation. There could have been a debt of conscience. George would also have been killing two birds with one stone — ridding himself of an undesirable relative, and performing his Christian duty. Whatever the price of seeing Benjamin's back, it could have been worth every penny.

Otherwise Benjamin didn't win his wealth with other than brute effort and pioneer sweat. Giddied by freedom, and with a new and powerful sense of family purpose, he seems to have worked as a man possessed to establish himself in New Zealand in a sensationally short time; he would certainly have seen no future in being another forlorn mill-hand. Perhaps there was an enriching tree-felling contract. Perhaps old Tasmanian hands helped him fast up the colonial ladder. He made every rung a winner. At no point does Benjamin appear to resemble the description the colonist chronicler Alexander Bathgate gives of ex-Australian convicts he encountered in New Zealand: 'One could almost tell from his manner,' Bathgate claimed in his book *Colonial Experiences* (1874) 'that a man had been a convict. Your thorough convict is often cringingly civil, and has a sneaking hang-dog look which betrays him. He is so different from the colonial mechanic or miner. He wants their sturdy independent air and blunt manner [and knows] that there is no use in denying that they belong to the fraternity of old hands, even though they are loathe to speak of their dark days, and no wonder.' Benjamin was not notable for cringing civility or famous for a hang-dog look. And he was never, so far any New Zealand neighbour knew him, less than independent and blunt: never other than a model colonist.

In a land of lovely harbours, Akaroa is one of the most luminous. From almost every Banks Peninsula height it looks to be a lake locked between the eroding rumps of long-spent volcanoes. It had been a valley until liberated ice-age waters leapt over barricading rock and lapped inland; those waters left a place of haunting grace behind. It was to inspire one of New Zealand's most reverberant landscape poems, Ursula Bethell's 'The Long Harbour'. Writing much of a century later, Bethell celebrates plant, flower, hawthorn, hedgerow and pastureland — the man-sweetened peninsula the pioneers left behind. The unexpected last stanza has always left me breathless:

> *It would not be a hard thing to wake up one morning*
> *to the sound of birdsong in scarce-stirring willow trees*
> *waves lapping, oars plashing, chains running slowly,*
> *and faint voices calling across the harbour;*
> *to embark at dawn, following the old forefathers,*
> *to put forth at daybreak for some lovelier,*
> *still undiscovered shore.*

Such sentiments were a luxury for later decades. Benjamin and Elizabeth had no intention of putting forth for elsewhere; they had their lasting shore. When they arrived the harbourside hills had still to know pasture and hedgerow; they were gloomy with primeval growth. At the tidal head of the harbour, Duvauchelle was isolated, linked to the rest of the South Island by unkind tracks, and a little less uncomfortably by schooner. The nearest community of substance was Akaroa village, founded by a French whaling skipper turned coloniser in 1840. Sixty French and German colonists had arrived in that year, a little late in the day, to find the Union Jack fluttering ashore. They settled all the same, marooned in a Britannic tide. They planted walnut, chestnut, vines and herb gardens; much of Akaroa's early architecture had a frisson of France.

At untamed Duvauchelle, named for a French settler who never took up the land, timber trees like matai and totara grew wild to the water's edge, and birdsong was dense. The vegetation was so murderously matted that unseasoned travellers could be lost forever; and sometimes were. It was also a place with an unhappy history. Local Maori had mostly been extinguished by ruthless musket-bearing tribesmen from the north; there had been a human smorgasbord on Benjamin's land, as bones underfoot still testified, with flesh surplus to festive requirements salted and borne back to the North Island in baskets. Surviving Maori on Banks Peninsula considered Benjamin's first acres cursed. Familiar with places more manifestly luckless, Benjamin was not one to dwell on such intelligence; birds rose grieving to the sky as trees began toppling. He had clients for his timber at hand. Ex-Tasmanians Wilson and Barwick and their ship-building team of thirty, among them other soul mates and cell mates, were rewarding customers.

Some of these sweaty and calloused refugees may have looked back longingly to Van Diemen's Land. Existence in Duvauchelle was cruel, dangerous and short on comfort. Sawyers and mill workers camped in rough huts along the foreshore. Few earned enough to buy or lease a patch of land they could call their own, or to build durable dwellings. Crippling accidents — from falling trees, runaway trollies, mill machinery — were commonplace; fatalities were frequent. There was no compensation for injury. Some found it expedient to call a halt to their cheerless lives with gunshot or a rope slung from a tree.

Benjamin's and Elizabeth's first year in Duvauchelle, with three infant daughters and soon a second son, must have been as miserable and fatiguing as it was for the men Benjamin began to employ. A correspondent in *The Lyttelton Times* said of Duvauchelle's industrious residents that they had their sleeves rolled above their elbows 'from early morn to dewy eve'. Benjamin was at it still longer. After dark he shook the sawdust from his hair and took up duty as host of The Traveller's Rest. He won his money's worth from his men by day; and recouped his outlay by night. That is to picture him as ruthless. On the other hand old Banks Peninsula residents still recall him — more than a century after his death — as a fair and compassionate employer. They recollect their fathers and grandfathers telling them so. Charitable or calculating, Benjamin made himself memorable.

In perhaps the most piquant twist of all, he became the arm of the law in his neck of Banks Peninsula. As a condition of holding the licence of The Travellers' Rest, he was sworn in as local constable, obliged to assist magistrates and police, and responsible for keeping the peace and bringing burglars, rustlers and other undesirables to book. Before long, retired robber Benjamin was arresting neighbours caught in the act of lifting his livestock. Never enthusiastic about dispatching men to prison, he preferred to play magistrate and see malefactors on their way with a thrashing. The Hertfordshire housebreaker and Hobart horse-thief was not only a pillar of propriety in his rough-cast colonial community; he was squire of Duvauchelle too.

The ebullient son of Datchworth milled timber right and left for the dwellings, bridges, boats and post-and-rail fences of the new colony; he pushed his timber tramways and mills ever higher, following the forest as it retreated up the volcanic spine of the peninsula, and even then gave it no quarter. He harried it until it retreated down the other side of the summits to the sea.

Meanwhile two more children were born to still unwed Benjamin and Elizabeth. Another was lost. Benjamin liked to ride with his cherished four-year-old Tamar sitting doll-like before him in the saddle. He had been slow getting the hang of his Australian-born children. New Zealand-born Tamar was different, an affectionate substitute for the baby daughter left behind in Hertfordshire. To win Tamar's laughter, he pushed his horse too lustily on a summer day in 1864. She slipped from the saddle and shattered. Benjamin and Elizabeth raced their child down harbour to Akaroa, to a surgeon who failed to revive her. Stricken Elizabeth and devastated Benjamin buried her in the Anglican cemetery there. Benjamin found a local craftsman to inscribe the slate plaque they set on Tamar's grave. The crude wording remains legible thirteen decades later. It does not speak of death: it records only that tiny Tamar was 'disbodied' in February 1864.

Nine-year-old Emma and seven-year-old Amelia, still in the flesh, stepped into the breach; especially and lastingly Amelia. As she grew she remained the most cherished chip off Benjamin's block. Bewitchingly beautiful, an elegant horsewoman and accomplished musician, she was seldom to be seen out of her father's company, leaving hopeful suitors in despair. Loyal to his memory, unwilling to settle for sentiments more commonplace, Amelia was never to marry.

There is a photograph of Benjamin in his pioneer heyday. It shows a solid citizen indeed: tidily bearded, thick-built, fleshy and faintly Falstaffian, with a good head of hair showing under his top hat; there is humour in his mouth, but his eyes are shrewd. His expression — perhaps the boredom of a long photographic sitting — is patient and faraway. What is on Benjamin's mind as he waits for the fool of a photographer to finish? His farm, his mills, his horses? Surely his horses. He found it more rewarding to race them than steal them.

One pioneer memoir recalls that as early as 1860, hardly a year after his arrival in New Zealand, he was engrossed in the notion of bettering himself on the colony's racetracks. Might he have once been a stable hand, or apprentice groom, in Hertfordshire? Anyway his career as an owner, breeder and trainer of fast horses began in earnest at Banks Peninsula picnic meetings — which he first organised on Boxing Day 1861 — with a beast called Comet. Publican Shadbolt raced Comet against brewer George Haylock's horse Lucifer for a purse of £25. Lucifer took the first heat. The second was judged a draw. In the third and fourth heats, however, Comet began to sparkle, with Lucifer labouring far to the rear. A loud and lively ball followed at The Travellers' Rest. There was no looking back. Peninsula picnic meetings were soon too modest a venue. Benjamin's beasts, bred in his paddocks and trained on the beach below his homestead, began distinguishing themselves on racetracks the length of New Zealand.

His holdings of forest and his noisy steam-driven timber mills gave him standing in the brawny and boisterously egalitarian frontier world of Banks Peninsula — a society distinct from that of conventional and class-bound Christchurch and greater Canterbury. By 1864 he was running the first public conveyance on the peninsula — a buggy pulled by two horses which picked up well-watered passengers at his pub and delivered them down harbour to Akaroa. In 1865 he was elected chairman of the Akaroa and Wainui Road Board, thereby ensuring highways were fit for his conveyances.

Roads crept across the peninsula, linking settlement after settlement, with Benjamin's buggies banging lucratively behind.

Local politics, however, were puny beside his real passion. Love of horseflesh allowed him to put on his top hat and mix with the pastoral gentry of Christchurch. In their company Benjamin was always the best of good fellows, a lavish entertainer with an open wallet. It was a world away from The Travellers' Rest where he unbuttoned in the company of poker-playing cronies. Canterbury was then the capital of horse-racing in New Zealand, home of both the Canterbury Derby (later the New Zealand Derby) and the New Zealand Grand National. In pursuit of both prizes Benjamin bought, reared and trained horse after horse. Among his long line of aspirant winners were Rob Roy, Lord of Erin, Noble and Sunshine; and not least Miss Fleet. In a triumphant return to the land of past pain and punishment he even travelled to Australia with his beloved Amelia in search of better bloodstock. In Melbourne he didn't think twice about buying up the distinguished and prize-winning stallion Eclat — 'a handsome brown horse with great bone, muscular power and faultless symmetry' — for three hundred guineas, rather more than he could have earned in ten years as a Hertfordshire labourer, even with theft on the side. As things were, he charged out Eclat's services at five guineas per mare.

Even his sheep were champions. He astonished the populace of Banks Peninsula by producing a two-tooth sheep which, when killed and dressed, weighed in at 106 lbs. 'It shows what the enterprise of our settlers can do with highly bred stock,' boasted *The Akaroa Mail*, 'and what the grazing qualities of the peninsula are.' Or, perhaps, what an emancipated Hertfordshire peasant might do.

Another look at Benjamin's photograph suggests a man not given to thinking long about sheep and in need of a drink. He was seldom far from one. According to a local history Benjamin made The Travellers' Rest a 'popular and profitable' watering hole. Which means rough, rowdy and enriching. 'In [Benjamin Shadbolt's] time there were high jinks at the Head of the Bay,' says the same chronicle. 'Sawyers made their money very easily, and spent it as freely as they got it.' Among those filling Benjamin's pockets were former residents of Van Diemen's Land with whom he could quietly, in a back room over a few hands of poker, recall his less liberated years. When his horses became demanding he handed management of the pub back to his old acolyte Wilson. (Faithful to his last breath, Wilson would eventually even be buried beside Benjamin: of such loyalty was Australia's post-convict mythology of mateship made.)

When Benjamin lost his first pub to fire, he built a large and luxurious replacement — 'second to none in Canterbury' claimed the local press — named The Somerset, after Elizabeth's birthplace. He had less joy as a publican elsewhere. He leased the Commercial Hotel in Akaroa and there crossed swords, and certainly words, with the most noxious of the South Pacific's freebooters, buccaneer and blackbirder Bully Hayes. It appears that Benjamin worsted Hayes in a high-risk poker game. Otherwise it was not a contest of equals. The piqued and predatory Hayes had his revenge by abducting Benjamin's prettiest waitress, a sixteen-year-old Irish orphan named Helen Murray, and dumping her on a northern shore when he had taken his piratical pleasure.

Might there have been something else to this episode? Might pretty Helen have been more to Benjamin than an attractive employee — so making Hayes' vengeance more comprehensive? Suspicion isn't evidence. There is not a line of print or fragment of family lore to suggest the squire of Duvauchelle was less than a faithful mate. Besides, his two teenage daughters, Emma and Amelia, were there to ensure he never strayed far from the path of marital fidelity.

Benjamin moved to put other matters right. By 1866 he and Elizabeth had bred seven children out of wedlock. This was not common knowledge in their neighbourhood; most settlers around Akaroa harbour had no reason to see the couple as other than man and wife of long standing. The squire of Duvauchelle was now forty-one years old, and his lady thirty-one. Perhaps in that year he had news of his wife's death in Hertfordshire. If not, he may have decided her silence was as good as the grave's. The probability is that he was, like cousin George and brother Johnathan, adding bigamy to his list of misdemeanours. With so many unsanctioned children on show there was no chance of a church wedding. He took Elizabeth tactfully over the hills to Christchurch, well away from neighbours, and wed her in the city's registry office. Ceremony didn't slow the production of children. He set about siring another eight.

There was one conspicuous truant as their family grew. Their first born, Linden, left behind in Tasmania, chose not to join his parents and siblings on Banks Peninsula. He remained in George

Shadbolt's austere Sassafras household, prospering on his own account as blacksmith, wheelwright, and farmer. Perhaps Benjamin was still seen as too raffish a proposition as a father; better godly George. It was 1876 — almost twenty years after he had last seen his parents — before Linden turned up on Banks Peninsula. By then he was a married man with two sons. He set up as a blacksmith, presumably failed to prosper, and sailed home to Tasmania to take over George Shadbolt's workshop and become the employer of twenty tradesmen. Cantankerous Linden may have clashed with his equally forceful father. He may even have extracted conscience money from his parent. If nothing else, Linden's short stay allowed Tasmanian Shadbolts to put the taint of transportation still further behind them. They now claimed an unblemished origin in New Zealand.

Rachel, the daughter left in Datchworth, also remains a mystery. Perhaps she was dead too; or perhaps married with children and reluctant to leave Hertfordshire. It is difficult to imagine Benjamin not wanting to bring her out. For otherwise his generosity is on record. Down and outs, old lags and struggling neighbours found him a soft touch; there was always a meal, a mattress and maybe work for drifters who failed to find kindness elsewhere in Canterbury. He fetched Elizabeth's luckless family from Tasmania, and set her scapegrace, frequently bankrupt brother Luke up as a farmer on acres neighbouring Shadbolt land. (It failed to improve Luke's character or his luck, though he managed to father two husky sport-loving sons for the Boer war).

Benjamin also sent a message home to Hertfordshire urging siblings to join him. His young brother Peter took up the challenge and arrived in 1864 with his wife and seven children. What Peter — an honest, modest and illiterate Datchworth labourer — made of his tearaway brother's success in the South Seas may be left to the imagination, as much in this narrative must. By Peter's humble measure Benjamin was scandalously prosperous, a walking testimonial to Britain's transportation system. Was this unbridled life-lover the brother he had last seen, nearly twenty years before, as a miserably chained felon? Benjamin may have offered Peter the store, pub, or even a sawmill to manage. All that interested gentle thirty-eight-year-old Peter was land he could call his own, with no overseer to please, no landlord to oblige. That had never been more than dream in Datchworth. Banks Peninsula, for God-fearing Peter, was a Biblical promise fulfilled: *The Lord thy God bringeth thee into a good land, a land of brooks and water . . . a land of oil, olive and honey; a land where thou shalt eat bread without scarceness.*

In putting rural England behind him Peter had slipped chains too. Banks Peninsula's pioneer hardships seemed frivolous. Benjamin helped his brother find pasture, at nearby French Farm, on which to prosper; his descendants there still do. Peter was to father another seven children before age called enough. The difference between these twin trunks of the family tree was evident to observers. Benjamin's were the wild Shadbolts; Peter's were the sober. Benjamin's people were improvident, reckless with land and money; Peter's were frugal and canny. (Within a decade — in this land which promised peace and plenty — Benjamin's sons were feuding with Peter's so ferociously that they finished up in court.) The contrast in character seems still to colour the family thirteen decades on.

Benjamin was no slouch as a farmer either. Tipping his hat toward his dour birthplace for the last time, he named his thousand-acre spread Hertford Farm. At the first Banks Peninsula agricultural and pastoral show in 1870 he was by far the largest prizewinner. His horse Quick Step took the first prize in the equine section. He had the best ewes, the best fat sheep, the best bull. His bullocks were highly commended, likewise his bacon and ham. (According to *The Lyttelton Times* a 'pleasant and convivial' evening followed at his pub, as well it might.) Later in the decade his cheeses became as celebrated as his livestock. He also harvested up to a thousand sacks of cocksfoot seed off Hertford Farm annually — seed needed to rejuvenate mediocre pastureland elsewhere — and used the proceeds to finance the purchase of faster horses. The lusty lieutenant of Mammon, however, remained a sober aide of the Almighty. He was by far the largest benefactor of Duvauchelle's little Anglican church, designed by the celebrated colonial architect Benjamin Mountfort, in which increasingly pious Amelia Shadbolt was to play the harmonium for thirty years or more. (In the secular world the Misses Shadbolt, Emma and Amelia, were well known for their musical evenings, especially for their Christy Minstrel turns.)

With more and more rooms needed to house his offspring, the Shadbolt homestead grew. Hedges bordered it, and beds of bright flowers; there were fountains and lily ponds. The park-like grounds were shaded by trees — cherry, apple, plum, peach and walnut — with a bold show of blossom in spring. There was a maid; there was a gardener. The living room boasted two pianos. Life-size oil paintings of Benjamin, Elizabeth and their children hung on the walls. A young salesman travelling in ladies' finery reported, after staying a night at the homestead, and doing good business, that the place was palatial enough to do the Governor of New Zealand proud. Even the family carriages were regal. The visitor was especially bewitched by the number of wealthy and most marriage-able young women fluttering around. All that deterred him from pursuing one of these lively young Shadbolts, he said, was that their father was an old convict, 'which I do not like'. That imperfection was soon to be remedied.

Somewhere over the years, somewhere in this sedate setting, intelligence of the family's felonious beginnings was circumspectly interred. Perhaps musical Amelia composed the new lyrics. It was said that the Hertfordshire Shadbolts were a landed family with aristocratic connections; that Benjamin was actually a gentleman adventurer in the antipodes, one who would some day return to take up ancestral estates. The fantasy was an article of family faith for more than a century, and for that matter still is.

Five

In life, Benjamin was as large and lavish as righteousness and respectability allowed. Any excuse for a party was a good excuse; he enlivened Duvauchelle with celebratory dinners on the least provocation — for the new extension of a timber tramway, for a racetrack triumph. One posthumous verdict is that he was a man who 'seemed never to miss a chance'. His confrontations with fortune weren't always in his favour. In 1870 his open wallet, high living and stable of horses all but undid him. With the country in depression, and prices for farm produce low, he came within fifty pounds of being declared bankrupt. Might he have called on solvent brother Peter for help? Or did he see merit in running a tighter ship? Anyway he survived fiscal shoals to sail through another decade.

That he had firm views on justice may be inferred from his frequent courtroom appearances — more often than not in pursuit of bad debts, and at least once in connection with bad dogs. By differing recklessly and rowdily with a magistrate he managed to add contempt of court to his miscellany of convictions; he was sentenced to an overnight stay in the Akaroa lock-up. For a man familiar with lengthier confinements this was no humiliation. Next morning, distinctly undiminished, he shook the wrinkles from his suit, tipped his hat to curious locals, and drove his buggy back to Hertford Farm at high speed. Said one memorialist: 'Obstinate, foolish, pig-headed — sometimes he was all of these.' His energetic genes and active libido ensured that the lives of his children and grandchildren would lack little in obstinacy either; some would surpass him in folly.

Perhaps it was more good luck than good management that he had only one other large difficulty with the law. As publican he was charged with serving a gravely intoxicated sawmiller named Billy Webb with spirituous liquor — in other words, with a pint of raw gin. To win a bet with a neighbour, Webb quaffed the pint and promptly perished on the floor of The Somerset. Benjamin's regular customers trooped loyally into the court to testify that Webb had not seemed drunk to them. The judge nevertheless reprimanded Benjamin for allowing such 'a disgraceful exhibition' in his public house and dismissed the charge with a caution. Benjamin had reason to mop his brow with relief: he hadn't lost his good standing, but it had been a near thing.

Benjamin himself finished serving his time in 1882. Britain's academies of hard knocks had left him constitutionally frail. In November 1881 he stood again for local office but was too infirm to present himself at public meetings. In December, even more ominously, he was the most conspicuous absentee at the Banks Peninsula picnic race meeting, though several of his horses were running, and one or two winning.

As his flesh weakened, his mind wandered. Drifting toward his last day, he had cause to look back on his life. It had been a misty path through the woods, with more than a few man-traps, but the barefoot burglar from Hertfordshire hadn't done badly. The chains, whips and gallows of Norfolk Island hadn't subdued him; Port Arthur's solitary cells hadn't robbed him of reason. But he now had a summons to a companionless prison notorious for invisible warders who threw the key away. He began paying off debts, settling accounts in more ways than one. Days before his death he busied himself destroying personal papers; he was so thorough — or impulsive — that he even managed to tear up his will. When Elizabeth, his one beneficiary, drew this to his attention, he instructed her to paste the will together again. This she did to his satisfaction. 'As good as ever it was,' he pronounced.

What of the other documents destroyed? It is not difficult to guess at their nature; there may have been a crumpled ticket-of-leave among them. He saw no need to burden his children with his story, or for that matter his grandchildren and great-grandchildren. Nor would he.

In April 1882 the esteemed citizen, loved husband and father and loyal mate finally collapsed with an intestinal obstruction. Kitchen-table surgery failed to save him. He was a modest fifty-seven. The Canterbury Derby and the New Zealand Grand National had escaped him. Though his estate was worth a reasonably impressive £11,000, his legendary English fortune remained a lovingly polished rumour, likewise his aristocratic connections; ancestral lands made no showing on his final balance sheet. His horses had begun to lose, with Sunshine failing to glow, Miss Fleet reluctant to fly and Eclat's offspring winning no glory; his poker hands had been indifferent for years; the timber had been cut, his mills shut, and the price of cocksfoot seed had fallen. It seems he sought uplift in liquor, though he was seen sober — 'a gallant sufferer' — at a Presbyterian tea party in the last week of his life.

Two Anglican priests and four hundred slow-moving mourners — many in buggy and coach, others on horseback — followed his coffin to the diminutive cemetery on the skyline above Duvauchelle. All Banks Peninsula's communities were represented; some in the procession had made the long overland journey from Christchurch. Among the many bare-headed at the graveside were men who had known Benjamin in his unruly youth. 'Those whom his cheery laugh gladdened, and his kind hospitality cherished,' said *The Akaroa Mail*, 'will follow him with saddened heart to his long last home beneath that soil which he found a wilderness and left a cultured garden'. *The Lyttelton Times* mourned the passing of a model citizen, one who 'gave his time willingly and ungrudgingly to the public weal, acting honourably and honestly in discharging the functions of public office'. The rhymester of the *The Akaroa Mail* grieved:

He wasn't a saint, God bless him!
We liked him better for that.
Like us he'd his faults and his follies,
And he never in judgement sat
On the weaker ones who had fallen
In the weary battle of life,
But would cheer his stricken brothers,
And fit them again for the strife.

When he came here, the forest primeval
Spread over the face of the land,
And each acre had to be wrestled
From that forest's giant hand.
Twas a hard and a weary struggle
To reclaim the obstinate ground;
But now, where all was the wild wood,
A smiling village is found.

In those early days roads were scanty,
Or rather there were none at all,
And ofttimes the travelling swagger
Was weary and ready to fall;
But of one thing he always was certain,
And that was, he'd be all right
If somehow or other he managed
To be near to 'Old Shad's' at night.

I have seen his kind face soften
At a tale of want and woe,
At the thought that some poor creature
Should be born to suffer so.
All I can say is, he loved his fellows,
And gave them a helping hand,
And the man who sincerely does so
Is as good as the best in the land.

Old Shad's pub didn't outlive him. It was razed by a diligent temperance activist — perhaps an embittered relative of the lamented Billy Webb — in the year of Benjamin's death. Or such is the story. There is another as startling. At an inquiry it was hinted powerfully that it might have been torched by Elizabeth to remove an unreliable manager; or that the manager might have fired it to inconvenience her. Either way it suggests a desperate feud. Small wonder that Benjamin's teetotal spectre was soon said to be roaming Duvauchelle; he may still be loitering melancholy there. For the Shadbolt story thereafter is one of riches to rags: no top hats were inherited. The one lasting relic of the Shadbolt heyday is his elegant grave above Duvauchelle, recording the birth and death of a buoyant and benevolent giant among men. Elizabeth garnished the headstone with porcelain roses. The grave is also possessed of an initialled footstone, such as only the resting places of Canterbury's original gentry were. Was that his wish? Anyway it was what he got. Justice, of sorts, was served. His life made those of most New Zealand founding fathers seem feeble.

Legend says that widow Elizabeth killed herself with grief. If so, it has to be added that it took her two decades and a dramatic intake of alcohol. She rebuilt The Somerset and proved as wholehearted a host as Benjamin had been. Her daily diet included a bottle of brandy. Religion was a reliable solace too, though she had reservations about the Bible. On Banks Peninsula they still tell the tale of the Anglican cleric who asked if she read the gospels. 'Not often,' she confessed. 'I like stories with a happy ending.'

She was often seen in search of one. Dark-dressed, and with sprays of flowers in season, she daily climbed up the steep road to the Duvauchelle cemetery to converse with Benjamin. She also claimed to have seen him shadowy about the Shadbolt homestead, waiting on their reunion in the world of the spirit. In the material world she resourcefully held their family together and tried, not always successfully, to pilot it past temptation and transgression. Her last years were frequently shadowed by loss; five of her fifteen children predeceased her. She died of cirrhosis of the liver, at the age of sixty-six, in 1903. Bravely, it was said. 'Full of hospitality and human kindness,' *The Akaroa Mail* mourned, 'she leaves behind a void that will be difficult to fill.' On her deathbed she professed no interest in flying into the arms of Jesus; she had business with Benjamin first.

The year 1886 signalled an early end to Benjamin's Eden. The antipodean Adam was just four years dead. Hills he had incautiously left treeless began rumbling down on Duvauchelle. Scores of Shadbolt acres soared down harbour, likewise the last of his prize-winning cattle and sheep. High ground was scoured; low ground was buried under boulder, rubble and slush. The sins of the father were lustily home to roost. Too late to unseat Benjamin himself, the insubordinate land unsaddled his sons and daughters. They would soon scatter this way and that, twig and leaf shaking free from the family tree. One thing they did uncommonly well was breed. They never let up on it, year in and year out. Their children excelled too. At last tally Benjamin and his brother Peter had three thousand descendants. There are Shadbolt offshoots with Maori complexion and others with Asian and Samoan shading. The family has begun to take on the colour of the Pacific. Most have lived, and still live, irreproachable lives. Shadbolts soldiered at Gallipoli and the Somme in World War I; in African desert, Italian mountains and Pacific jungle in World War II. Many farm, fish, and turn forest into timber as their forbears did. There are doctors, nurses, accountants, lawyers, photographers, carpenters, mechanics, journalists, teachers, academics, and even a promising literary critic. For what it is worth, more than a few have been policemen.

On June 4, 1990, one descendant thought to find Benjamin in Datchworth. I had now outlived him by a year. It was my 58th birthday, and I wanted to share it with my elusive predecessor. In England for publication of my ninth novel, I was also trying to make sense of my surname and rescue my ancestral story. On the other side of the world New Zealand was celebrating the sesquicentennial of its beginnings as a nation. The climate was rich with racial controversy, with liberal apologias, and Maori oratory. Making the acquaintance of forebears seemed a more useful project than joining in the din. If nothing else it might confirm that no race resident in New Zealand had loss, hardship and heartache on its own. Searching Benjamin out, however, was a demoralising endeavour. His life refused to present itself as my tenth novel; it insisted on shaping as the histrionic stuff of television soap opera, indifferently scripted, intemperately acted and showily shot. How trim truth of excess? Life is always larger than life-size. It is certainly under no obligation to make existence easy for novelists.

On a sunny afternoon a friend with her own claim on my day drove me through Hertfordshire toward Datchworth. We parked outside All Saints' Church, where thirty generations of Shadbolts have knelt dourly in prayer and farewelled their dead.

Datchworth has been judged the most haunted village in Hertfordshire. Once a celebrated medium was called in to investigate the place. She reported an unusual concentration of distressed spirits in the churchyard. Apparitions — presumably of the six thousand villagers interred in the churchyard and anonymously in neighbouring fields — have often been reported there.

There were no shades abroad that day. There were spring flowers in the churchyard and Shadbolt names chiselled in stone. While my companion listed them I looked inside the church. Begun in the thirteenth century, finished in the fourteenth, All Saints' has a robustly simple Norman form. It owes nothing to a distinguished outside architect. It rose slowly, over decades, built by local people who gathered flint rubble for its walls from the fields of Datchworth. Its interior is modest. No names of noble families grace the walls. There are no elegant tombs; no sleeping crusaders. The names honoured here are humble. An organist was rehearsing; otherwise I had the place to myself. I knelt with a prayer of sorts. Benjamin, however, failed to make himself felt.

There are still Shadbolts in Datchworth. I found one, a gentle and hospitable man by name of George, pulling weeds from a well-groomed vegetable garden. He had rough country hands; his face was disconcertingly familiar. He could have passed as my grandfather's brother, or my father's. Nearly eighty years old, he had begun adult life much as Benjamin, as a farm labourer. The difference was that hard-working George had respectably remained one. He recalled bad years and better as we talked. He marvelled that Shadbolts of Datchworth should have found a home in a far land of which he knew next to nothing. The only Shadbolt travellers George knew had been those who left Hertfordshire to fight Britain's battles. Those who survived had returned gratefully to their native shires, seldom to move outside again. He knew of Shadbolts in Oxfordshire, over in Buckinghamshire too. He had even heard of one or two in London. But in New Zealand? He shook his head again in wonder.

'How have the Shadbolts done out there?' he asked cautiously.

'We're still there,' I explained.

'Then you must be glad of New Zealand,' he decided.

'We must,' I agreed.

Literary essayists had told me that folk memory died hard in the English countryside; that the past still lived on in greying heads. I steered George toward family history. My hope was that somewhere in the village a memory of four transported felons might survive. But that would have been too rich a bonus. At the least I might be able to establish blood connection with George. What did he know of his predecessors? He knew his father's name, he said. His grandfather's? No; he was afraid not. Not? Not. So much for literary essayists; so much for the magic of folk memory. I let George return bemused to his garden.

I looked for the dwelling where Benjamin, Peter and their eight brothers and sisters had been born early in the nineteenth century. A map made in 1829 showed the location of their parents' cottage in Hocuts Lane, on 240 square yards of land set in orchard. I peered over brick walls and through iron gates. The orchard was gone; the cottage too. There were new houses, shiny BMWs parked in their courtyards. Datchworth is now in London's commuter belt, more suburb than village. Land which once turned to Shadbolt ploughs is on the rise in value. Nearly two thousand newcomers, largely urban professionals, now call it home. If there was a whisper of lowlier lives once lived there, it wasn't audible to me.

Finally I tried a Datchworth pub, a likelier place to look for

Benjamin. There were two on offer. The Inn on the Green was large and upmarket, The Plough small and unpretentious. We decided on the The Plough. Perhaps the wrong choice, given Benjamin's social-climbing character. He wasn't there either.

The friendly young publican eyed us as we looked over a map of the district. 'Tourists?' he asked.

'Visitors,' I explained.

'Looking for someone?'

'A relative.'

'Can I help?'

'It seems he's gone,' I said.

'People here never move far.'

'He did,' I said.

I toasted Benjamin with the pub's best bitter.

There are two mischievous items of coincidence or synchronicity here. Several times in my adult life, while still unfamiliar with my ancestry, I have become involved with long-term prisoners such as Benjamin. I have even had some hand in securing freedom for two or three of them. This may, of course, mean nothing. Rather more disquieting, there is the matter of my first short story, or the first I recall writing. It was artlessly titled 'A Good Man'. I was fourteen years old and the story took a school prize. A family saga in four pages, it told of a man convicted of theft in England and transported cruelly to Norfolk Island and Tasmania. Finally he escapes to New Zealand, makes good, and dies a respected citizen. Beyond his name I knew little of Benjamin then, still less of his story; it would be another forty years before I found him fluent in my life. 'Imaginative if a little too fanciful,' judged my English teacher. So who dreamed up that improbable schoolboy narrative? Had Benjamin, on his best behaviour in the grave, won a ticket-of-leave authorising him to dream me? And does he still?

Six

Benjamin's death heralded the end of the Shadbolt regime in Duvauchelle; Elizabeth's confirmed it. As age, melancholy and alcohol overtook her, her head for business grew misty; debts began mounting. All the same her estate was valued at more than £13,000, a useful sum in 1903. With ten beneficiaries, though, it looked leaner; it amounted to not much more than £1000 for each surviving son and daughter. Soon after she kept her assignation with Benjamin, Hertford Farm was auctioned off in twenty-five modest lots, in many cases to Benjamin's former employees. That might have pleased him. Other things might not have. The vacated homestead, the centrepiece of his estate, fell into the hands of strangers; the once lovingly groomed grounds grew weeds. Some lots of land were bought by Benjamin's sons — by Benjamin junior (born 1860), the equestrian dandy of the family, and by Ernest Francis (born 1873), my grandfather. With the exception of lonely Amelia, who had moved from the homestead into a modest cottage, other sons and daughters picked up their money and looked for fresh territory to tame.

Ernest's holdings included a part share of that picturesque volcanic outpouring, warred over by the Maori, now green with English grass, called Onawe peninsula; the most distinctive feature of Akaroa harbour. Ernest failed to turn the picturesque to profit. Farming proved even less lucrative as cocksfoot seed prices continued to fall. Ernest began contemplating prospects elsewhere.

No longer living in the manner to which he was accustomed, his elegant brother Benjamin, after a couple of impecunious years, grew restless with life as a smallholder too. He shook paternal dust from his feet, picked up his riding boots and saddle, and headed north to Hawke's Bay — there to do his father credit by founding a small and respected dynasty of horse-breeders and trainers. Ernest was left flying the Shadbolt flag in Duvauchelle, with seldom a sibling in view.

In 1898 Ernest married a fellow worshipper at the Duvauchelle Anglican church, a lively-eyed nineteen-year-old named Ada Shaw. Her parents, William and Annie Shaw, had arrived in New Zealand in the 1890s. They were mistily middle class, with a private income and pretensions. William, a bookish Englishman, was constitutionally frail; he migrated on the advice of a doctor who suggested Canada or New Zealand might suit his health better. New Zealand, from a distance, looked the more desirable prospect. Told that migrant Englishmen felt most at home in Canterbury, with its Gothic architecture and Anglican trimmings, William made it his choice of domicile. Christchurch proved much as promised, but nearby Banks Peninsula, where lemon trees grew, had a kinder climate; he shifted to Duvauchelle, and took up light employment as village postmaster. This move was a mistake. Minus most graces, populated by persons of doubtful lineage, rugged Banks Peninsula had little in common with the rest of Canterbury; it was distinctly no place for a gentle reader of Jane Austen and Anthony Trollope. The Shaws lived aloof from the community, behind lace curtains, mixing socially with neighbours mainly at Anglican service. William looked with distaste on rough and rowdy colonial pursuits — drinking, gambling, pig-hunting, fishing, sculling, horse-racing. He also looked down on colonials. He was determined that his precious daughter Ada would never marry a New Zealander. Ada, among other ladylike pursuits, painted watercolours and wrote verse; she shared her father's love of literature and read aloud to her parents on winter evenings. She could do better for herself, William insisted, than wed a rural roughneck. Uproar therefore ensued when the apple of his eye announced herself besotted by sheep farmer Ernest Shadbolt. She wanted, so help her, to marry him.

Marry Ernest Shadbolt? The son of a publican and gambler? Ada's suitor was William's nightmare made flesh. Athletic Ernest had captained both cricket and rugby teams at Christchurch Boys' High School. He was also a boxer, an oarsman, an axeman, a champion runner and rifleman, and not least a hard-riding member of the Canterbury Yeoman Cavalry — altogether the kind of uncouth and outdoor-loving colonial William most disdained. More, it was rumoured in Duvauchelle that the Shadbolts were even less than they looked. William might even have heard it muttered that Ernest was the son of a transported criminal. That would have made the proposed liaison seem an even larger social catastrophe. William bitterly refused underage Ada permission to marry. Tumult in the Shaw household was such that agitated and weak-hearted Annie Shaw, fearful of her husband's rage, frantic at the thought of losing her daughter, collapsed and died. Bereft and remorseful, William no longer had the strength to withhold consent to the marriage.

Eight weeks after Annie's death nineteen-year-old Ada and twenty-five-year-old Ernest exhanged vows. It may have been some solace to William that his son-in-law soon afterward kept elevated company. Ernest's powerful physique and distinguished record in the Canterbury Yeoman Cavalry won him a place in a four-man colonial bodyguard provided for the future King George V of England when he toured New Zealand as Duke of Cornwall and York in 1901. It was the loftiest moment of Ernest's life; in later years he frequently invited his family — not to speak of magistrates and politicians — to recall that he had ridden alongside George V in his prime. Thereafter, and for fifty years, Ernest was in free fall.

In the same auspicious year the union of Ada and Ernest produced my father Frank, their first child. Or did it? A more piquant version of his origins survives on Banks Peninsula after nine decades — that my father was not the son of his ostensible parents, but the illegitimate child of his Aunt Amelia, then forty-two years old. Local lore asserts that Amelia had the one amorous fling of her long spinsterhood, perhaps with a passing stranger, perhaps with someone nearer home, before her spectacular beauty faded. According to this narrative my father was compassionately claimed as their own by Ada and Ernest. Who knows? My father's birth certificate is uninformative. In any case the birth certificate could easily have been adjusted to suit Shadbolt circumstances; Ada's post-master father, William Shaw, was in charge of details of birth, death and marriage in Duvauchelle. A small slip of William's pen might have named Ada rather than Amelia as Frank's mother. Later events rather take rumour's side. Whether his mother was Ada or Amelia it seems agreed that he was born premature, less than three pounds in weight; that he was abandoned for dead by a doctor and revived miraculously by a midwife; that he was christened hastily within five days of his birth; and that he remained a sickly infant. And whoever his natural parents, my father was a grandson of Benjamin.

Ernest finally quit his dwindling stake in Duvauchelle. That left Amelia the last of Benjamin's line conspicuously in residence. Now revered locally for the sweetness and light she shed, she baked shortbread for children, nursed the ill and the aged in her neighbourhood, and never failed her musical chores on the sabbath. Elsewhere on the harbour Peter's Shadbolts were dug in deep; Benjamin's were in flight. Most put the past behind them by moving to the North Island; some loitered in Canterbury to materialise as citizens of Christchurch with an immaculate bloodline.

Ernest first moved no further than Little River, in the hinterland of Banks Peninsula. A railhead to serve the peninsula had arrived there in the late nineteenth century, bringing neglected territory to life. Timbermen had levelled enough forest to leave fifty farms in production. Filled with pioneer fervour, the district's population had doubled and then tripled after the arrival of the railway — to a giddying five hundred souls. Duvauchelle was a fading coach-stop by comparison.

Expecting the area to prosper still more, and property values to rise, Ernest made a speculative leap to Little River. He sank some £1600, all he had, in property beside the busy railway station. There was an accommodation house, a family dwelling, a billiard saloon and a general store. There wasn't much more to the township. For a time it may have seemed Ernest was destined to be squire of Little River as Benjamin had been of Duvauchelle. Ernest, however, failed to notice that the momentum engendered by the arrival of the railway was gone; Little River's heyday lasted less than two decades. The district, like Banks Peninsula as a whole, was becoming what it rustically remains — a backwater coloured by its Victorian origins. As sawyers cleared the last fragments of forest, there was less and less milled timber to rail out to Christchurch. Most of the freight carried away was farm produce, with sacks of cocksfoot seed in season, just enough to justify the existence of the railway. Otherwise the village's largest distinction was as a junction for travellers. At Little River rail passengers disembarked and met the coach service to Akaroa, or vice versa. Often they stayed overnight, thus making Ernest's accommodation house a seemingly safe proposition.

On the other hand he may soon have noted that too many of the passengers boarding the train at Little River had one-way tickets and their worldly goods bundled; they were putting Banks Peninsula behind them to look for prosperity elsewhere. Family after family was selling up and moving out; communities were shrivelling. It was not a promising base for an ambitious businessman or aspirant squire.

Ernest may have got the message. Metaphorically and literally he had leapt deep into dung. The drama of the King's excrement followed on his move to Little River — the monarch being (in 1906) King Edward VII of England, and the wastes of his loyal New Zealand subjects the point at issue. Soon after occupying their Little River property in October 1906 Ernest and Ada became aware of offensive smells. So did their employees. The stench mounted in the summer months following. There was something of an epidemic. Sore throats were common. There was dysentery and diarrhoea. Ernest himself suffered more than most, with fainting fits and fevers (or so his doctor would testify) and appendicitis to boot. Intestinally distressed guests complained and vacated the accommodation house. A friend of the family, coming to stay, dramatically took ill and died. The cause may not have been poisonous emissions, but the death was seen as suggestive. Unwholesome atmospheric conditions cut custom in the store. Ernest's commercial kingdom was collapsing around him; Little River, in short, got up his nose. It had once been home to a considerable Maori population, though there were few brown faces near now. Was there an old curse on the place? Was it an ancient burial ground?

If a curse, it was not of a pagan kind. Excavation turned up not forgotten human bones but festering human faeces. The source of Ernest's woe proved to be the Little River railhead itself. For the comfort of travellers, and railway employees, urinals and water closets had been provided at the station when it was built. In theory a piped drain carried these wastes away across Ernest's land to a downhill stream. In fact the drain had been forgotten. Pipes had long collapsed, leaving Ernest's empire becalmed in a sea of sewage. His doctor pronounced the property dangerous to health and told him to leave; Ada and their three children had already flown back to Amelia at Duvauchelle.

When all was revealed after fifteen ruinous months, Ernest didn't cry hallelujah; he went to a Christchurch lawyer. With hindsight, it looks to have been the largest mistake in a life of many. He brought suit against the crown as the nominal owner of the railway station (*Shadbolt versus the King 1909*) for nuisance done to his premises, and claimed damages of £1000. Ernest's barrister was the distinguished Danish-born advocate Oscar Alpers, later to become a judge of the New Zealand Supreme Court. Alpers thought the sum claimed a little large, but fought the case effectively. The jury returned with a finding that Ernest's complaint against the Railway Department had been proven; it awarded £100 damages. Honour seemed to have been satisfied.

Mr Justice Denniston, presiding over the case, took a dimmer view. In a surprisingly vehement intervention, after the jury had given its verdict, he argued that the court was giving Ernest a free ride from Little River, making the sly and possibly pertinent observation: 'Whether owing to the plaintiff's [Little River] venture not proving successful, or from some other reason, he was anxious to get out of it, and took advantage of the excuse of the insanitary surroundings to do so, trusting to get damages from the Crown.'

To the shock of all present, Mr Justice Denniston set the jury verdict aside on the grounds that damages awarded were excessive. Had it been left to him, he said, he would have awarded Ernest £20 at most. Lawyer Alpers was furious. So was fraught Ernest. Winner of the war, he had bewilderingly been robbed of the rewards of triumph. He might have retired from the fray there and then, picking up the miserly £25 which the Railways Department promptly offered in full and final settlement. He had no money to pay jury fees or the witnesses' expenses of a second trial. But barrister Alpers had his blood up, likewise Ernest's solicitors. The legal fraternity put together a fund for Ernest to fight the case again.

The evidence presented to the court was the same; the judge was the same. The impatient Christchurch jurymen knew from their newspapers that they were wasting their day; that it had all been heard before. Retiring to the jury room, they thought to teach Judge Denniston a lesson for having interfered with the verdict of good men and true. They found for Ernest and resolved to award him the same sum of damages as the original jury. The problem was that no one in the room could recall the figure. They guessed £200, twice the first jury's award. Denniston was frosty. Alpers was delighted. Denniston asked why Alpers was not moving for judgement. Why was he waiting? 'In the hope that your Honour may set aside the verdict again,' Alpers insolently explained, 'so that I may double my client's damages once more.'

That might have been the end of it. It wasn't. Vindictive Judge

Denniston refused to award costs to Ernest. Reeling away from the legal duel, Ernest found himself still insolvent. His seemingly sympathetic solicitors were making off with most of the damages awarded. Deciding to sue them, on the score of general negligence, he found no Christchurch lawyer willing to crusade against one of his own; the legal profession cannily closed ranks and Ernest was left to conduct his case solo. Tripped on points of law, floored by judicial procedure, he made a graceless showing; he retired bloody and bowed. Finally and desperately he began firing off petition after petition to Parliament asking for sums ranging up to £5000 to restore him to fiscal and physical health. Politicians, persuaded that something was gravely amiss in the affair, took pity. Four years after the foul vapours emptied the Shadbolts from Little River, they awarded Ernest £100 from the public purse.

Out of pocket, out of countenance, Ernest was not conspicuously placated. So much for justice, especially that of the British kind. 'British justice?' he said, surely echoing his father. 'It's like snakes in New Zealand. There are no snakes in New Zealand. There is no British justice.' Duvauchelle was behind him; Little River a sour lesson learned. Adrift, he had a spell as a travelling salesman in the tradition of Hertfordshire Shadbolt hawkers; and another as a reporter for the salacious weekly journal *Truth*, which specialised in messy divorce proceedings, bestiality in the back country, and depraved Bible Class teachers. If nothing else, Ernest's hours in court, waiting for sensation to materialise, may have sharpened his irreverent feelings for the law and its failings; Mr Justice Denniston, for one, would not have welcomed the sight of Ernest on the press bench. Nor would Christchurch lawyers. At length Ernest saw no future in listing the indiscretions of the citizens of Canterbury. He wanted his own stage. Like Benjamin, he looked to the land. That, in the twentieth century's second decade, meant looking north.

Seven

In common with many younger men in Canterbury of large families (he was now touching forty) Ernest was tempted by Maori-owned bush country being bought up by the government and balloted for settlement in the heart of the North Island. He won 268 acres in a ballot. With what was left of his money he might better himself yet. He and Ada packed and sailed north with their children. There was one enigmatic exception — Frank, my father, a still delicate thirteen-year-old. They deposited him at Duvauchelle in the care of his Aunt (or birth mother) Amelia. It is difficult to make this episode intelligible. The explanation I inherit is that my father looked unlikely to survive the rigours of life in dank North Island hill country; it was therefore thought better to leave him with Amelia in Banks Peninsula's tranquil climate. Nevertheless Ernest was mysteriously duplicating Benjamin's performance as a parent. Benjamin and Elizabeth had left their seven-year-old son Linden behind when they quit Tasmania for New Zealand. Ernest and Ada left Frank behind when they left the South Island for the North. Might relinquishing first-born children have been a time-honoured Shadbolt ritual, a quaint Hertfordshire custom? Anyway my father's return to Amelia and Duvauchelle tended to confirm all that village gossips said — that young Frank was Amelia's child, not Ada's. But by whom? Amelia's affections seem to have been reserved for family members, first for her father, then for her brothers and sisters. It is difficult to see how she could have found time for anyone else.

Ernest's colonial Odyssey took him by steamer, rail and riverboat into the North Island's heartland, the darkly forested region still known as the King Country. The Maori King and his retinue of rebellious tribesmen had set up shop in the territory after the New Zealand wars of the 1860s. Until a few years before Ernest's arrival the territory had been a powerful Maori enclave through which pale-skinned adventurers and surveyors journeyed at risk. By the turn of the century, however, tribesmen had decided that the day of distancing themselves was past; they began suicidally parting with their land, not at the point of a bayonet, but for pounds and pence.

Ernest's land, all precipitous hills and hollows, neighboured the misty Wanganui River, the traditional Maori canoe route which leaps one hundred and fifty spectacular miles to the sea from the North Island's volcanic heart. The newly risen settlement of Taumarunui was a dozen miles upstream. The railway had recently reached Taumarunui; it suggested that the long isolated region had a future. There were still Maori craft abroad on the river, their occupants watching with wonder as impassioned and often hungry pioneers, willing to part with good money for bad land, began attacking their territory. Wisely they kept a distance. Fools flourishing banknotes were not to be discouraged.

The century was still in its spring when Ernest, Ada and four children scrambled ashore from a riverboat. The prospect before them was ferny and formidable. When the riverboat hooted off downstream, they were left with not a fellow human in sight. There was a stiff upland hike ahead to locate their acres. Meanwhile they raised tents, lit a fire, and survived their first downpour. Presently a lone and curious horseman made an appearance. He was a man named Herlihy, an Irishman tree-felling nearby. He looked at Ernest and Ada and their whimpering infants, the oldest nine years old, the youngest barely two. He was aghast.

'My God,' he said. 'Are you serious about this?'

'About what?' Ernest said.

'Bringing a woman and children in here,' Herlihy said.

'What does it damn well look like?' Ernest said.

Next day compassionate Mr Herlihy was back at first light. 'The river's in flood,' he shouted. 'Get to higher ground.'

He was just in time. Minutes later the risen river was storming across their campsite and carrying away such of their property as they failed to heave to high ground. So ended their first full day in the King Country; the two or three thousand ahead were no more stylish.

Eight

At first, as Ernest felled and fired forest, ploughed fern under, and fenced his territory, his family persisted in tents. He was soon scattering grass seed, and stocking the devastated land with sheep. Then storm left their tents a few fluttering shreds. Conceding that weatherproof accommodation was necessary for the survival of offspring, he hammered up a hut to which he added rough rooms as his family grew, one child hard on another. My father, until his late teens in the care of Aunt Amelia by the tides of Akaroa harbour, came north now and then on holiday. Ernest would ride out of the wilds to meet apprehensive Frank at Taumarunui railway station.

'Is there another one, Dad?' my father would ask.

'Of course there bloody well is,' Ernest told him.

'A boy or a girl?'

'One or the other,' Ernest said in poor humour. He had difficulty in getting their sexes right, also their names.

My shattered father would sob. There was more nightmare ahead. His muddy brothers and sisters made his visits a torment. This Little Lord Fauntleroy in fashionable check cap and knickerbockers was a freak from a far planet. They circled him menacingly, teased him, tugged off his cap, messed his hair, and dumped him in deep puddles. When he tried to woo them by judiciously handing out sweets from a bag, they grabbed the entire bag away. It was as dizzying and dismaying as a collision with a rogue tribe in dark Africa. If his Aunt Amelia accompanied him, as she sometimes protectively did, there was no mention of new offspring; she believed Ernest and Ada had bred too many for their own good. The latest addition to the family would therefore be loaned to kindly Mr Herlihy and his wife for the duration of Amelia's visit.

My father was glad to get back to the serene South Island again.

Conditions in the North Island bush were ferociously uncomfortable. Illness — in the form of colds, influenza and fevers — was rampant. There were also septic lacerations and broken limbs in consequence of war with the wilderness. Much of the living area was taken up by a vast fireplace backed with sods and sheets of corrugated iron. The fireplace was virtually a room in itself. Logs glowed there yearlong, an iron kettle steamed, and clothes hung to dry. Pigeon, duck and wild pork comprised much of the family diet. If Ernest's marksmanship faltered, or his hunting knife failed to bury itself in one of the wild boar he battled, there were eels boiled in a billy-can. As formidable a gambler as his father, but far from a race track, Ernest pitted himself against the powerful Wanganui River. He wagered that he could sail a tin bath tub from Taumarunui ten miles downstream to Otunui Landing. Why a bath tub? Why not? With no more than a paddle for propulsion he survived breathtaking rocks and rapids to win the wager.

'I wouldn't make a habit of it,' Mr Herlihy warned.

Though he had hung up his boxing gloves, Ernest still found use for unpadded fists. In World War I anti-German feeling washed into even the wildest New Zealand back country. Two loyal locals suspected the name Shadbolt Germanic in origin and planned an ambush on a bridle path to put the bush-burning Hun in his place. Ernest, forewarned, kept the rendezvous. The overwrought patriots finished in hospital with concussion and fractures. Thereafter Ernest let it be known he welcomed all comers. They were slow to show themselves.

Ernest was less impressive whipping land into shape. The isolation was killing. Neighbours were few and mostly far. There was storm, flood, and landslide. At best his farm was charred stumps and scraps of pasture. At worst it was a sodden desert of clay, patched faintly with grass, overstocked and overrun with hungry beasts.

The largest woe, however, was access. The government had promised a road within three months of balloted land being taken up. It was more than four years before a road arrived. Meanwhile there was a pack track of sorts crossing private property; but gates were nailed up and notices menaced travellers with prosecution. There was no riverboat landing in easy ride. Other possible routes were greasy, hazardous and mostly impassable in winter. Speeding Ada to hospital, when she went into labour again, was an annual ordeal. They once made it with only a minute to spare. On another excursion to town Ernest's horse reeled down a gully and rolled crushingly over its rider. That left him physically impaired, with even less competence as a farmer. Sons attempting the same route were injured by rolling rocks and slithering packhorses dragging them downhill. One boy was carried half-dead to hospital where medical folly, in the family's view anyway, all but finished off his remaining half.

With school miles away, along a slippery bridle path, few of their children had more than a passing acquaintance with education. Some never met up with it at all. Infant Stanley went down with pneumonia when winter was at its worst. With mud in high tide between the farm and town, it was impossible to get him to hospital. Stanley died in Ernest's arms one bitter midnight, with storm roaring around. When the weather cleared Ernest roped his son's tiny body to his back and rode into Taumarunui for inquest and burial.

From that day forward Ernest farmed sorrows rather than sheep. Grievances grew faster than his flock. Ripe to war with the world, he started with a skirmish. He refused to pay hospital bills totalling £45 between 1916 and 1919. In his view that debt was best met by the government which had promised much, delivered little, and de facto killed his son. Moreover, in his view, the hospital was domain of deranged killers disguised as doctors. It was not his intention to subsidise medical ineptitude in any shape or form. Lest things turn sour, however, he placed the farm in Ada's name, thereby allowing him to plead penury.

What follows is reconstruction. The difficulty with facts is that they are under no obligation to make sense. Ernest certainly isn't. The story, with facts for foundation and filled out with family lore, goes something like this.

Just as he was struggling to his feet as a farmer the district was hit by a freak local drought. Neighbours dispatched their flocks and herds over the hills to greener pastures. Ernest too thought to cut his livestock numbers. He struck a deal with a shipping company to barge away his distressed and skinny sheep. The company's vessel failed to appear. Most of Ernest's animals perished for want of feed.

His hour had come. Fools and frauds of lawyers had hardship ahead. All other alleged servants of justice, magistrates, judges and bailiffs likewise. There would be no replay of the Little River debacle. He would not only sue for breach of contract himself; he would do it with authority. He bought up law books and began scanning them with fervour. They went to his head. Along the way he discovered a gift for courtroom oratory. After he had disposed of the delinquent shipping company, if not to his entire satisfaction, he began firing writs at anyone who broke cover. Men wise in the ways of Ernest Francis Shadbolt — stock and station agents, bank managers, civil servants, lawyers, doctors, contractors and storekeepers — kept a wary distance.

For the next thirty years, almost literally to his last breath, law was the unrequited passion of his life. As a bush lawyer — as advocates with never a day in law school were commonly called — he was to fight more than forty actions before he died, even then presumably hoping to plead his case in a higher court. Most were theatrical rather than judicial events; he played to full houses, with spectators having ridden in from miles around, and standing room only at the rear of the court. He was soon more eye-catching than ever Benjamin had been. Fifty years later I met a man who, as a young law clerk, had looked in on one of Grandfather Shadbolt's longer litigations; he still remembered it with wonder. 'Murderous rhetoric,' he said.

When Ernest ran short of wrongs, he made do with those of others; he is said to have freed a man unjustly convicted of robbery and rape. Though he managed to rise unhumbled from many long and inscrutable litigations, possibly by driving temperate magistrates and judges to drink, he failed to become milder in mood. Farming, on the whole, seems to have been beneath him. He was indifferent to pastures slipping away to river and sea so long as there were lackeys of the law to battle. For twenty years he was also Parliament's most persistent petitioner, pleading that inequities be righted and the iniquitous punished. Parliamentarians found urgent business elsewhere when they saw Ernest bearing down on them. The flamboyant Labour politician John A. Lee, though decorated for his courage on the Western Front, made a point of never letting Ernest get between him and the nearest door.

Nine

By 1917 Ernest and Ada had sold their original property and bought another nearby, this one handier to the Wanganui River; they could now take the riverboat into Taumarunui rather than risk their lives on rough tracks. According to Ernest this deal left them destitute. According to the New Zealand Lands and Survey Department, however, they realised better than £600 over their original outlay. Thinking to build a sturdy dwelling at last, Ada called in some timber. Stacked carelessly close to the river, it was carried away by flood. That called for another courtroom contest, with honours to Ernest but damages light. Disillusioned Ada and Ernest sold up again and bought an upriver property free from flood. According to Ernest this was another pecuniary disaster. According to the New Zealand Lands and Survey Department, they were better off to the amount of £700. The third property, after being profitably cleared of timber, was finally sold too. All in all, claimed one civil servant, they had netted something like £1800 from the three transactions with their original outlay intact. 'Mrs Shadbolt is simply speculating in property,' this official claimed. (For Mrs Shadbolt read Mr.)

Where, then, did the proceeds go? Possibly into funding more extravagant courtroom dramas; possibly on the backs of slow horses. Anyway it trickled away without trace.

By this time the Shadbolts were tiring of Taumarunui, and Taumarunui more so of them. Leading citizens flinched and fled when they saw Ernest approaching. His dispute with the Taumarunui Hospital Board, in the matter of unpaid bills, was in its third or fourth year and promised to become even longer-running. A change of scene and a break with the recent past began to seem desirable. They looked further north and found a farm outside Matamata, in the more benign Waikato region. They took it up in

1921. That move, however, only heralded even more judicial travail.

In his absence, the Taumarunui Hospital Board struck. The secretary of the hospital board unkindly summed up Ernest as follows: 'He is a man with a grievance and spends the greater part of his time in ventilating his troubles while his wife and family do farm work. My board is determined to bring this man to book. Leniency is wasted on him.' The magistrate appears to have judged so too: he was painfully familiar with Ernest Francis Shadbolt and had lately seen him at race meetings, gambling rather liberally for a man claiming no means.

Anyway leniency was not in evidence on a winter morning of 1921, when officers of the law descended on the Waikato farm, arrested Ernest, and bore him away from his wife and weeping children to serve a two-week sentence in the stark Victorian fortress of Auckland's Mount Eden prison. (Ex-convict Benjamin may have been heard sighing on high as the prison gates clanged behind his son.) There, at least in his version of events, Ernest was kept among long-term, dangerous and disease-ridden prisoners and in insanitary conditions. Prison authorities claimed that he had a clean cell, clean blankets, and had raised no objection to mixing with long-term inmates. Discharged, and back on the farm, Ernest began pressing for a royal inquiry into the circumstances of his arrest and confinement. He claimed, among other things, that his health had been permanently affected. The hospital board, the presiding magistrate, the arresting police, and the officers of the prison service, were all to rue the day they first heard the name Ernest Shadbolt. As he pressed petitions on Parliament, their paperwork became more and more mountainous as they attempted to counter his allegations.

That, though, soon seemed a side issue. Ernest not only looked for trouble. Trouble also came hunting for him. How else explain that the Shadbolts came to buy their new Waikato farm from a crooked farmer and through a fraudulent land agent? Before the Shadbolts took up residence the farmer switched 'an extra choice' dairy herd — part of the deal — for a collection of decrepit beasts best fitted for dog food. That was bad enough. There was worse. They found, after close to £3000 changed hands, that they didn't even have clear title to the land. That fight would enliven Ernest through the 1920s. The land agent went to prison, in the end, but that was no help to Ernest and Ada. This time they *were* ruined.

Aunt Amelia had died in 1920. She had just travelled up to the North Island with my nineteen-year-old father with the notion of returning him to his family. 'It's time to make a man of him,' Ernest had announced. Amelia, however, remained unimpressed with Ernest's capacity as a farmer and a father. His farm was in tatters; his unruly children remained in rags. It was no place for her darling Frank. Even more disastrously Amelia took a chill in the autumnal mist and damp of the King Country. Within a week or two of arriving back in Duvauchelle with my father she succumbed to pleurisy. She was interred beside Benjamin and Elizabeth in an unmarked grave, one sign of how far the fortunes of Benjamin's flock had fallen; most of his sons, after one failed venture or another, seem to have finished in bankruptcy proceedings. The little money Amelia left in her will provided for an altar in the Duvauchelle Anglican church. There was the sum of £200 for my father. His peaceful Banks Peninsula adolescence was at an end. Pampered to the last, he was never to recover from Amelia's maternal attentions; she might have taught him to tie his shoe-laces, but even that is not certain.

Thereafter he was loose in a rough world. He was soon looking back on his cloudless Banks Peninsula beginnings wistfully, more and more so as he aged. Never having written or perhaps even read a line of poetry in his adult life, he composed a soulful ballad on his Duvauchelle boyhood which he read aloud at family functions. He recalled netting flounder with his French cousins when Akaroa Harbour seethed with mighty fish; he remembered gathering cocksfoot seed under everlasting summer skies. There were also Amelia's musical evenings, her tennis parties in the simmering summer twilights of Banks Peninsula. (Aunt Amelia had kept up pretences, and seemly social occasions, long after the family's indigence was plain.)

A half century on, my father began urging me to return there, buy back the Shadbolt land, and refurbish Benjamin's homestead. I pointed out that I was in no position to do this, financially or otherwise. Nevertheless he remained insistent. And this notion that I might reclaim the land, *prima facie* at least, was to persist beyond the grave. Not long after his death, pursuing an interest in psychic research, I sat anonymously with a talented medium. My father soon hove into hearing, as deceased parents are prone to do in a respectable seance, and began hammering on about Banks Peninsula,

Duvauchelle, and my buying back the family land. It was necessary
for my nerves, he told me; I should never find tranquillity until I did.
Perhaps; perhaps not. I had never seen my father as omniscient in
life; I didn't see that death necessarily made him wiser. Eden remains
lost.

After Aunt Amelia's death he joined his five brothers and four sisters
in their trek from the clammy gorges of the King Country into the
swampy plains of the Waikato. That was one shock. The next was
loss of his precious legacy. Ernest snatched it up as fast as Frank's
siblings had grabbed away his bags of sweets. Ernest argued that
with further legal combat looming all hands were needed at the
pumps to keep the family afloat; young Frank's pounds were
indispensable in lubricating the pumps.

While Ernest pondered his law texts his sons drained land,
fenced pasture, milked the herd and saw the cream off to dairy
factories. Sometime in the 1920s Ernest was moved by the notion
that he might serve his long-term interests best by determining the
laws of the land rather than deciphering them. He decided to stand
for Parliament. There was no election due, but no matter. With my
father — no longer a sickly juvenile, but the eldest son, with
responsibilities — he drove his buggy into the town of Matamata.
There my father was presented with a large bell. For his part, Ernest
had a stepladder.

'What is the bell for?' my father asked.

'To ring,' Ernest said shortly.

My father remained baffled and fearful.

'You ring the bell,' Ernest explained with impatience, 'and I
address the voters.'

He set up his stepladder, straightened his tie, consulted his notes,
and otherwise made ready for his election campaign.

Meanwhile my father marched up and down the main street of
Matamata ringing a bell and announcing to bemused citizens that
they had a new Parliamentary candidate on show. When a curious
crowd gathered to hear, Ernest proved as innovative a politician as
any in the history of democracy. He made no promises. Far from
wooing the wondering electors, he denounced them as complacent
fools; they deserved all they got from their corrupt and imbecilic
political leaders. He, Ernest Francis Shadbolt, could yet show them
the way and the light.

There was light heckling, then a storm of colourful language. Ernest gave no ground. Besides, his voice was louder.

When the last heckler was hoarse, and listeners thinned, Ernest descended from his stepladder and considered my father.

'How was the speech, son?' he asked.

'Good,' my father said carefully. 'Only one thing wrong, so far as I could see.'

'Wrong?' Ernest roared. 'Wrong? What the hell are you talking about?'

'You're winning no votes,' my father pointed out.

In the end Ernest must have seen it too. He thought better of a humiliating show on the hustings, and of losing his deposit. After one fast circuit he retired from the political arena before the nation knew he was there.

In the mid 1920s Ernest thought to call quits with the land too. Butterfat prices had fallen; there was no profit and less joy in farming; above all there was no future for his large family. Perhaps he was spurred by Ada's concern for the education of their ten children. In tiny Duvauchelle, my father had never progressed beyond primary school; his brothers and sisters had met up with even less learning in the backwoods. There was still hope, however, for children further down the line. Of all the characters in this chronicle, Ada Mary, Ernest's wife, my grandmother, remains the most enigmatic. Wispy, gentle and intelligent, she followed her headlong husband — with no audible complaint — from one faulty farm to another; from one legendary litigation to the next. In harness to a perambulating fumarole, her serenity was astonishing. Perhaps her feelings were saved for the verse she managed to write amid family hue and cry. She also continued to read widely and well. When she felt moved to lift the level of family argument she quoted George Bernard Shaw, Upton Sinclair, H.G. Wells, Aldous Huxley and Bertrand Russell. These names made no impression on Ernest. Given the chance he would have locked this cackling contingent in the fowl house too.

Perhaps funded by a courtroom coup, perhaps by a winning horse, Ernest abandoned his last bona fide farm and moved his family to a scrubby patch of land on the western outskirts of Auckland, between New Lynn and Green Bay. With potteries, brickworks and a tannery, New Lynn was embryonically industrial;

Green Bay, lapped by the tides of the Manukau Harbour, was grassy and rural. He was then in his middle fifties. When depression began darkening the country, Ernest braced for the worst. He cleared the land, dug out a large vegetable garden, ran one or two cows, and raised chickens; duck shoots and fishing trips further replenished the family larder. He even managed to graze a losing racehorse or two on his land. His sons might have been jobless; he saw that they were never idle. Anyone seen staring pensively into the middle distance soon found a spade or a pitchfork thrust into his hand. 'You, whatever your name is,' he would roar. 'Make yourself useful.' His problem with his children's names was lifelong. The arrival of his children's children made matters worse. He couldn't distinguish them from his own. And they had names too. Whoever they were, on the other hand, they could be productively employed weeding his garden, digging his potatoes and raking his hay.

There was another harvest. Across the road from the family home was Auckland's largest golf course. Through the worst of the depression the city's affluent were on show there, seemingly indifferent to the distress around them. Sometimes misdirected golf balls lobbed into the road; sometimes they flew into the family flower beds. Ernest saw a means of rearranging the wealth of the nation. He gathered up the balls where they fell, pocketed them fast, and later sold them second hand at the clubhouse. With his youngest sons he also began stealthy forays along the perimeter of the golf links. Balls bouncing wide of the green, into the rough or patches of pine, were from that time in double hazard. A young Shadbolt would break cover, pounce, flee, and Ernest would have another ball for sale.

He was never impressed by the twentieth century. In the nineteenth men had been men and women didn't argue. He had a large suspicion of technology. He wouldn't have a telephone in the house, but reluctantly admitted radio after he heard his first race commentary. From that point the shelf where the talking box sat was a shrine. Toward electricity his feelings were mixed. He couldn't see it or hear it; it made no sense. He suspected it stopped his chickens laying and blighted his potatoes. On the other hand it was necessary to power the radio and keep him abreast of the sport of kings. A compromise was necessary. Ada could have the infernal stuff in the house provided she kept it on a firm leash — that is, switched it on and off.

For the life of me, I should like to find him an endearing rogue: rather more like the crusty patriarch who roams post-pioneer New Zealand with his runaway grandson in my first novel, *Among the Cinders*. That story derived from an intense and moving liaison between Ernest and a grandson left fatherless by World War II. In the last years of his life Ernest got one relationship right. Elsewhere the record frustrates me. He may have been a rogue. He was never endearing.

Lacking legal projects worth his time and talent, Ernest finally aspired to authorship. He composed lengthening tracts about his litigations, his life, New Zealand society, and the universally miserable condition of mankind. 'The meek will never inherit the bloody earth,' he announced with authority. (He failed to notice that the vociferous aren't necessarily heir to it either.) Almost as ambitiously, he laboured upon a chronicle called 'Shadbolts by Land and Sea'. With no publisher interested in his fearless patrols into the republic of letters, Ernest rented empty shops — of which there were many in the depression — and used their windows to display his manuscripts a chapter at a time for the enlightenment of passers-by. Each day he changed a chapter. (Did anyone ever read them? Perhaps Ernest, like many authors, wrote with an ideal reader in mind. I never qualified. Years later, when he was still at it, I recall crossing the street with embarrassment when I encountered a shop window filled with Ernest's prose.) Though they were subversive in nature, calling for most human institutions to be levelled, and society to be shaped as Ernest saw fit, these documents were not essentially political; they paid no dues to the art of the possible. Ernest was an insurrection of one.

Ten

*E*rnest's children began to go their own way. The most public, in the 1930s, was his daughter Renee, known in the family as Aunt Sis. Tall, angular and acerbic, she trained as a nurse after a useful apprenticeship seeing to the survival of siblings in the back country. Early in the decade she was impressed by the number of working men's heads needing repair after police batons terminated marches of the unemployed. She was even more astonished by the number of doctors and fellow nurses reluctant to treat such injuries. Though more interested in theosophy than political theory, feeling that mystics like Krishnamurti and Rudolf Steiner offered more to mankind than Joseph Stalin, she moved as far to the left as her lifelong suspicion of fellow human beings allowed. That suspicion precluded her from allying herself with a political party. The most ringing party manifesto had no remedy for human suffering. In her view it was here to stay. The destiny of the human race was to dwell in cruel muddle. No cause was worthwhile unless based in compassion.

That belief was tested in July 1936 when civil war began in Spain. General Franco's right-wing revolt against the elected government of the country became a lethal rehearsal for World War II. Squadrons of German bombers and regiments of Italian fascists raced to reinforce Franco. Fighting was fierce from the first, and casualties mounted. Idealistic young men of many lands, including a few footloose New Zealanders, joined an indifferently equipped and hastily trained International Brigade to defend democracy and the Spanish Republic. In New Zealand a Spanish Medical Aid Committee was formed, with branches the length of the country. Many thought to disparage it as a communist front. Communists were apparent on the committee, but so too were liberals, members of the Labour Party, clergymen, and old-fashioned humanitarians.

By early 1937 enough money had been raised to send a team of three nurses to serve with republican forces in Spain. Twenty-eight-year-old Sis volunteered. With twelve years' nursing experience behind her, she was appointed leader and spokeswoman of the team. Too late, she learned that one of her companions, an excitable young woman named Sharples, though experienced in nursing, was something short of qualified. This lack had not been noticed by lay people putting the team together. Sis was alarmed. She judged Sharples an adventuress, unfit for the strenuous job in hand. But she remained silent, as she put it, for the good of the cause. The cause was to demand that Sis kept silence often in the months ahead. But an Auckland newspaper reporter, pressing her for her political sympathies, won the reluctant admission that she was probably on the side of the beleaguered democrats of the Spanish Republic: 'I don't know whether any great question of political adherence is involved,' she protested. 'We feel that we can be of some service to people in need.'

Others were less enthusiastic about a project to give aid and comfort to the wounded soldiers and savaged citizens of the Spanish Republic. The issue might prove a platform for home-grown extremists. On the day of their departure for Spain the three were detained by police at an Auckland farewell function and taken in for questioning. There was a three hour interrogation to determine their political sympathies. Nurse Isobel Dodds was informed that she was only going to Spain to escape an unhappy love affair and even more fancifully accused of recently having given birth to an illegitimate child, though what relevance this had was unclear. Nurse Sharples was told she was politically naive; it was suggested she turn around and go home. But the big guns were trained on Sister Shadbolt. She was accused of being the secretary of a communist cell; and of insidiously misleading the others about her role in the enterprise. 'I've never been even a secretary of a tennis club,' Sis argued.

Harassment failed to divide or break the three. They sailed on schedule for Spain, leaving political uproar behind. The then Labour Minister of Police, Peter Fraser, disclaimed all knowledge of the inquisition of the nurses. Finally he admitted that the police had exceeded their brief. Calls for a full inquiry into the affair were ignored. It was plain that the New Zealand government was panicky about the prospect of three dedicated revolutionaries flying New Zealand's flag in Spain, in violation of Britain's non-intervention agreement with other European powers. In practice this agreement meant that, but for military aid from the Soviet Union, Spain was abandoned to General Franco and his German and Italian allies. In New Zealand, remote from the war, the last-minute intimidation of the nurses made the cause of the Spanish Republic a large political issue. The struggling Spanish Medical Aid Committee was deluged by donations and declarations of support; the fate of the three nurses became a national concern.

Indifferent to commotion behind them, the three arrived in Spain in July 1937, travelling across the French border into Barcelona with a convoy of ambulances provided by American sympathisers. Most personal effects had to be abandoned beforehand; they were allowed to carry only one small suitcase each into the war zone. First they were stationed in Huete, in central Spain, 350 miles from Valencia. Their makeshift hospital, a commandeered monastery with 2600 beds, took in serious casualties from field hospitals close to the conflict. The monastery beds filled as fighting neared. Most of their patients were republican; some were General Franco's nationalists. Suffering had no political colour. In other respects, especially after indiscriminate bombing, it was impossible to remain neutral. The nurses found themselves answerable to martial discipline and enrolled in the republican army with military rank. They were also paid according to rank and on army rations. This was not as they supposed their situation would be — or as their New Zealand sponsors and well-wishers still imagined it to be. It was, however, how things were.

Rather than quibble and assert their independence, they carried on nursing men mangled and dying. The wounded came in daily by the truckload; ambulances were few. Most were left to die. Taught to save life, doctors and nurses found themselves in uneasy collaboration with death. Each day began with decisions on who should be allowed to perish. Amputation was the favoured method of treatment for those selected to live; and the amputations went on around the clock, or until limbs needing removal exceeded the supply of sterile instruments. Death lost meaning in Huete as patients by the hundred were carried off for burial. In a delirium of exhaustion, the New Zealand nurses grew indifferent to the danger in their situation.

Medical teams were handicapped not only by a heartbreaking

shortage of food and medicines, but by language difficulties. It was more than a matter of knowing little of the Spanish language; the men of the International Brigade spoke several. There was another, more urgent problem. German aircraft were beginning to bomb and strafe the district; the nationalist army was soon imperilling the road link with Valencia.

In early 1938, during the Jarama offensive, the nurses were hurriedly evacuated without baggage. Hours afterwards their hospital was levelled by swastika-marked bombers. It was a near thing. So was their escape through Spain to Barcelona. Their train was the last to cross the remaining bridge across Ebro River. Under artillery fire, the train was hidden in a siding until dark; and then driven at high speed across the river. Hours later the bridge was debris.

They were not to escape unscarred. Increasingly anarchic Nurse Sharples, wandering off on her own to drive an ambulance, was wounded by artillery shrapnel. Sis was soon obliged to warn New Zealand sponsors that Sharples was ill-disciplined and irresponsible, a trial to those who worked with her. Doctors found her of no use; her real ambition, it seemed, was to fly a republican plane, not to nurse at all. An Australian nurse's verdict was that she was 'nuts'. The evidence suggests that she might have been unstable all along. Sis seems to have suspected as much in New Zealand.

In the relatively safe haven of Barcelona Sis and her more sober colleague Nurse Dodds helped establish a new hospital for the wounded of the International Brigade. By this time ideological divisions on the republican side were apparent. Great power isolation of the Spanish Republic, allowing Franco, Hitler and Mussolini their way, also meant that communists had the upper hand behind republican lines. In the Soviet Union Stalin was purging enemies real and fancied and shooting his generals; he demanded his pound of flesh in Spain too. Internecine strife was at its deadliest in Barcelona, with gunfire in the streets and non-Stalinists, anarchists, socialists, Trotzkyites and others of impure belief being herded into prison or pushed before firing squads. This war within a war did nothing for the morale of the New Zealand nurses. Fissures in the republican coalition became apparent in the tiny New Zealand contingent too.

For tactical reasons — to ensure that New Zealand donations

kept coming — they were still required by their sponsors to pose as neutrals in Spain. Nurse Sharples, finding Spain headier than ever, thought it time to end the pussy-footing. They were in the uniform of the republican army, and what of it? Whose side were they on but the republic's? It was no longer a civil war, Spaniard fighting Spaniard. Spaniard was now battling Italian and German; the world must be told.

Challenging Sis's authority to speak for the three, she damned New Zealand's Spanish Medical Aid Committee for its faint-hearted fund-raising — and its lack of political integrity — and refused to acknowledge them until they declared shamelessly for the republic. The cautious committee was left with no option. Nurse Sharples was recalled to New Zealand in early 1938. Over her protest, she was told there was no prospect of her being returned to Spain. She was judged too wayward for further service. Her confused public pronouncements suggest this may have been true; but it is difficult not to sympathise with her stance. Whether equally committed Sis did is another matter. She kept up the pretence of taking instructions from New Zealand and reported back regularly in apolitical prose.

As rifts grew on the republican side the two remaining New Zealand nurses found themselves under suspicion. Their mail was rigorously censored or confiscated and destroyed. The few mutilated letters reaching New Zealand were incoherent. Only conventional phrases and ideologically sound sentiments suited the censors; frank discussion of the situation in Spain was out of the question, let alone information about their personal plight. They grew uneasy and bewildered, more and more isolated. For their pains the fatigued and fearful pair were allowed a furlough in London. This allowed Sis to send off an uninhibited letter to New Zealand sympathisers explaining their difficulties; and why their communications with New Zealand were so stilted. 'One has to be so careful with the [republican] censors it hardly seems worth writing at all,' she warned.

Always frank-spoken otherwise, Sis may have been tempted to signal that their woes were worse than verbal; that happenings within republican ranks left them increasingly insecure; as army personnel they might find themselves facing a court martial too. At all events she chose not to send such a message. Nor did she suggest that they were ready to quit and go home. The cause with which they were allied — the fight for survival of a democratic Spain —

remained a just one, regardless of the Stalinist ideologues beginning to muddy it. In her words, it was a 'war for civilization [against] the creeping monster of fascism.' What she saw on her London furlough was dispiriting. 'British complacency,' she wrote, 'makes me want to tear out my hair in despair'.

They returned to Catalonia, to a hospital near Mataro, and the victims of the war. Despite her reservations about unsavoury events on the republican side Sis involved herself in propaganda work, travelling to Madrid to join other voices in radio broadcasts directed vainly at the conscience of the international community. It is difficult to imagine her broadcasts as other than formidable. Hers was not the fashionable war which literary camp-followers of the Spanish Republic publicised. (She later read Ernest Hemingway, and was not impressed.) There were no gallant stands against the fascist foe in her account of the war; she spoke with authority only of makeshift hospitals, shredded human beings, shortages of food and medicine.

There is an explanation for her increasingly fervent commitment. It is personal. From the first Sis found fellow spirits among the dedicated and often doomed young men of the International Brigade. One she nursed was a young anti-Nazi German named Willi Remmel, an elegant, eloquent and wispily bearded officer in the Ernst Thaelmann battalion of the brigade. He and Sis were soon lovers. Finally, with sirens sounding around Mataro, there was a quick civil wedding. She now had a husband at risk in the conflict; her doubts went by the board. Willi might not have been impressed by them anyway; he was an impassioned communist. They may have spent a night or two together; there was nothing in the nature of a honeymoon. Sis went back to patching up people, and Willi back to battle. She was now literally wedded to the republican cause. Yet she was discreet to the last. Her New Zealand sponsors were never to learn of her marriage to Willi Remmel of the Ernst Thaelmann battalion. Her family knew only the little she saw fit to confide.

In late 1938, for tactical reasons, the International Brigade was disbanded. 'Its work is now complete,' Sis reported to her sponsors. The republic wished to demonstrate that it stood defiantly alone against fascism. (The gamble failed: the world remained indifferent to Spain's anguish.) Sis and fellow nurse Isobel Dodds arrived back in New Zealand in January 1939. In Auckland there was a mayoral reception for the two heroines. There were heartfelt welcomes elsewhere too. Attempts to belittle them as communist dupes failed. Sis did an exhausting stint as a lecturer up and down New Zealand, speaking at rallies to raise money and medical supplies for the republic. Duty demanded no less. If people wanted to celebrate her as colourful and courageous — as a local counterpart of Spain's dashing La Passionara — it had to be suffered for the good of the cause. Her heart wasn't in that script. She had her own. Spain had had merely confirmed her poor opinion of the human species.

What, then, of soldier husband Willi? The story grows shadowy. Sis seldom brought herself to talk about Willi for the remaining decades of her life. For years I was content with the notion that it had been a passing wartime passion, ended by my aunt's departure from Spain. It is true that history unravelled them, but not without a fight. When the International Brigade disbanded, young Americans, Britons, Scandinavians and Frenchmen returned home. German and Austrian members of the brigade, however, had no haven. Nazi Germany and its satellite Austria would offer them only a concentration camp. They had to take their chances with the Spanish, or cross the Pyrenees and throw themselves on the mercy of the French. That meant an internment camp until they found a country ready to give them refuge. That was the best fate could do for Willi Remmel. A cache of heartbreaking letters in Wellington's Alexander Turnbull Library, in a file devoted to New Zealanders involved in the Spanish Civil War, tells me the rest.

With her lecture tour finished, Sis took a job nursing in a small rest home near Wellington. Every pound she could afford was sent, via Spanish Medical Aid channels, to interned Willi. She also began battering on bureaucratic doors to win him asylum in New Zealand. To her contact she wrote: 'Was so pleased Willi Remmel received that money. Received a letter from him and he was overjoyed. Are you sending any money over to Paris again in the near future as I perhaps could include another pound or two to help him on his way. He is sharing the money with some of his Spanish comrades who are in another [French internment] camp a mile or two away whom we all knew while we were in Spain. I am endeavouring to get a permit to get Willi out to New Zealand but have no luck. [I was told] I should have word in 7-10 days and it is 17 now. Am wondering if it would be possible to pay his boat fare from this end as of course he has no money and it will take everything I have to bring him out here but feel perhaps it will give one of these poor unfortunates a fresh chance in life again. To be behind that barbed wire with no hope for months on end is enough to drive men mad and the French authorities are doing everything in their power to persuade the Germans and Austrians to join the Foreign Legion and have been ill-treating some of their officers who warned against joining to fight under a capitalist flag and in many cases against their negro brothers to guard capitalist interests . . . Life goes on in the same old way. All my energies are concentrated on getting Willi out.'

Not once in this communication does she concede her personal interest in Willi, let alone acknowledge marriage to the man. She did not admit as much to Wellington civil servants and politicians either. Despising human weakness in any manifestation, she loathed it in herself above all; the world was never going to see her vulnerable.

A week or two later, toward the end of August 1939, she is writing with ill-concealed despair: 'Willi Remmel's permit [to enter New Zealand] is refused and I feel that nothing much matters in life at the moment, although I realize one's private feelings matter very little in this world. Everyone is talking and thinking of war.'

She was right. Private feelings now mattered very little. A few days later Hitler stormed into Poland; Europe was at war. Sis must have known her marriage doomed. She wrote: 'Life goes on much the same and I'm afraid I have been very upset about Willi's permit being refused. He is such a fine man and I cannot bear to think of him when he knows he is still condemned to remain behind the barbed wire on the Pyrenees and now the war is on God knows what sort of treatment he will be receiving. Enclosed you will find another £5 that I hope you will be able to send out with your draft [to Paris] to be sent on to Willi. I was fortunate enough to be able to buy a few English pound notes that I sent over to England to be sent on to him but have not heard whether he has received them yet. Of course there is always the chance that their camp has been shifted or that they have been forced into the Foreign Legion but that is the luck of the game.'

The last of these letters records her sending still more money to Willi. 'He should have enough to carry him on for a month or two,' she judges. 'He sent me one or two pictures of his camp and said as they look over the barbed wire they think how long, how long before we are free.'

There the correspondence ends. There too their marriage.

Eleven

Never at a loss in the making of legend, the Shadbolt family had several versions of subsequent events. The likeliest said Willi escaped French internment and made his way to the Soviet Union. This tale has two endings, neither of them edifying. One finale has Willi perishing in a Stalinist purge. The other has him surviving world war to become a Party functionary in East Germany. There is evidence for the second. A cousin remembers Sis receiving letters addressed in a distinctively Gothic hand, with a German postmark, after hostilities had ended. Letters from Willi? Who else? Anyway Sis hid them away or burned them. Finally they stopped coming. It was said in the family that triumphant Franco had annulled all civil marriages contracted in Spain in the years of the republic; that the marriage of Sis and Willi no longer had legal standing. (If true, this would explain why Sis was never known to get a divorce. If not, she was to become another Shadbolt bigamist.)

Even if her marriage had no existence, Sis did; she had most of her life left to live. When the republic fell in late 1939, and Franco's firing squads became busy, she locked herself away with her grief. Elsewhere, one of her colleagues in Spain found suffering in silence no solution. Unable to shake off the experience, Millicent Sharples took her own life. Public events thereafter were never seen to move Sis much. Other than on occasions when she had a glass of sherry too many, Spain was seldom mentioned; even close colleagues never learned she had been there. And next to none knew about Willi Remmel.

Life would be poor without postscripts. At Sis's funeral in 1977 there were to be no flowers by her own request. But there were. On her coffin there was a lone bouquet of red roses, placed there by a sister who knew her story. The attached message read: *With love everlasting from Willi.*

After her return from Spain she had difficulty finding employment. Many in her profession didn't want to know her. It might have been professional jealousy. It may have been political. 'Sister Shadbolt' remained an uncomfortably conspicuous figure. In World War II, with Spain's civil war now recognised as a nobly premature attempt to halt fascism, she was called in to nurse maimed men returning to New Zealand from the battlefields of Greece, Africa, Italy and the Solomon Islands. The men she nursed remember her as a tender tyrant.

At the war's end she married a small, wrinkled, violin-playing retired bank manager named George McLennan, owner of a citrus orchard in the then remote Bay of Islands. George had no interest in politics or her past. If he had any passion at all it was reserved for perfecting his home brew and scraping a recognisable tune from his violin. Other than in respect of his advanced age and small stature — more than twenty years her senior and about half her height — he appeared well placed to offer her relief from the world. After two weeks of watching oranges ripen, and listening to George's melancholic melodies, she left him. Why then the marriage? 'Such a funny little man,' she later said vaguely. 'I imagine I must have felt sorry for him. I didn't know his damn violin would drive me mad.'

There is another explanation for the marriage. It gave her a new name. When she returned to nursing it was as Sister McLennan, later as Matron McLennan. Sister Shadbolt was gone, and Spain exorcised. Did she ever reply to those mysterious letters in a distinctive Gothic script? I begin to think not.

In the late 1940s she began a long reign as queen of the Hokianga hospital in the sandy, subtropical far north of New Zealand. Her headquarters was an eccentrically wandering wooden building on a hilltop site high above the sea-lapped village of Rawene. The busy maternity ward looked out on the local cemetery: the place was rich in reminders of first and last things. The clientele, like the region, was mostly Maori.

Sis remained childless with no regrets. 'I see no virtue in reproducing myself,' she said. 'It's all vanity.' So she mothered nephews and nieces who met with her approval and some who didn't, and also children who came her way as matron of the hospital. Overburdened mothers often left superfluous and altogether healthy children in her care; the hospital resembled a noisy kindergarten. It was also a happy one. At breakfast with nurses she often demanded to know where they had slept the previous night, and with whom. If she didn't approve of their companions, she made it known. She terrorised doctors who turned up now and then to administer the hospital. More often than not they resigned and fled the district. 'Fools,' she said. 'They aren't going to tell me how to run this place.' Visiting specialists got short shrift too. When she discovered one shirker furtively attempting to leave before seeing his full quota of patients, she pushed him back into the surgery, locked the door, and refused him freedom until he undertook to perform a fair day's work.

Her collisions with Maori custom were equally informal. Helping deliver a baby on a heaving hospital-bound launch one wild Hokianga night, she casually tossed the afterbirth overboard. No Maori fished the harbour for three months. Sis didn't notice. And, though she complained about the absence of fish from the hospital kitchen, no one dared tell her.

She had larger problems with Rawene townsfolk who thought to take the moral high ground in respect of her staff. There were complaints that the nurses' home, in the hospital grounds, was little better than a bawdy house; nurses were shamelessly having their boy friends on overnight stay. When prudish complaints became a bitter chorus, a public meeting of townfolk was called. Citizen after citizen mounted the platform to plead that the nurses' home be purified, all male visitors banned. Twitchy Sis listened with impatience. Finally she took the stage. She didn't hide her contempt for those who preceded her.

'I value my staff,' she announced icily. 'I value their health even more. I would sooner they were tucked up warm with their men friends on a Saturday night than catching cold on damp ground under a dripping tree.'

There was an awed silence as Sis departed. No more was heard in the Hokianga of the love lives of her nurses.

After most of two decades, and a couple of matrimonial near misses, Sis handed the hospital over to a niece, confirming it as a family enterprise for another five years. She was then something over sixty years of age. She never managed retirement. She made herself available for family disasters, of which there were many, and offered much merciless advice to any relative — brother or sister, nephew or niece — who crossed her field of fire. For young female members of the family she had a cryptic message: 'Don't worry what a man is like under the blankets. What's he like under the bonnet of a car?' Moving from emergency to crisis, she never encumbered herself with possessions; they never filled more than one world-weary suitcase. That was all she carried into Spain. 'Travel light,' she explained, 'and you're never disappointed.'

She was surely explaining her emotional life. She never admitted illness or fatigue. Her one apparent weakness was insomnia; her bedroom windows were thickly blacked out and seamlessly taped to prevent dawn light leaking in. I once risked asking what worry kept her awake; my suspicion was that it might be nightmarish memories of Spain, perhaps the marriage she made there. If so, she wasn't saying. 'I fret about my family,' she claimed. 'I'd like to see *your* lives come out right, at least.'

Gifts given to her for birthdays and anniversaries were often forgetfully returned as gifts to the givers the following year. Mysterious sums of money arrived in the mail for those most in need. She also wandered widely and wildly. In one breakneck year she managed both to go to China and to follow New Zealand's rugby warriors from game to game around the British Isles. The baffling thing about the latter journey was that she had no knowledge of rugby or patience with sport.

One reckless New Zealand author, with rather indifferent result, tried to fit her into a novel. I never dared. In any case she made a point of saying, when I was in earshot, that she didn't think me much of a novelist. She had only to read Tolstoy, which she ritually did once a year, to see that my books were missing a cosmic beat. 'You have a lot to learn,' she never tired of announcing. 'If only you'd stop breeding children, you might sire something as good as *War and Peace*.'

Charity was not always beyond her. One surprising letter to me read: 'Congratulations on winning the [Katherine Mansfield] award for your short story. Found the theme interestingly unhealthy but memorable. Suppose your nervous system is still taking a battering from earning a living for a family by the art of the written word.'

When I volunteered for a protest voyage into France's Pacific nuclear test zone in 1972, I seemed, for once, to have her approval. Quick to the telephone to express her pleasure, she also thought to inform me that people generally acted from more than one motive. I said that was no news. 'Good,' she said.

'Good?' I asked.

'I remember going to Spain,' she explained.

There was a long pause. What was she telling me? I didn't ask. It might have been the moment to ask about Willi and much else in her past. The moment went. Besides, the present was pressing. My father was fighting cancer. It was possible he might die in my absence.

'Don't worry,' she urged. ' He'd be disappointed if you didn't sail. I'll see he's comfortable.'

'Thanks,' I said.

'What for?' she said. 'In that way I'll be with you.'

She couldn't not be. She has never not been.

The following year she had a favour to ask. She missed New Zealand's far north, her years as monarch of tiny Rawene. Everyone knew her; she had been midwife to half the population of Hokianga in her day, and had nursed scores of others back from death's door. Moreover she knew who she was. An historic house in Rawene — once the headquarters of James Clendon, the first U.S. consul in New Zealand — had just been purchased and was being opened to the public. The New Zealand Historic Places Trust offered her a job as caretaker. Delighted, she asked me to drive her north to take up the post. Her progress, as we neared the Hokianga, was regal, with everything but flags waving along our route. Cars stopped and hooted; horses were reined in; groups of well-wishers gathered. There was halt after halt for cakes, scones fresh from the oven and cups of tea. Matron McLennan was returned from exile. It was a matter of pride and prestige to offer her hospitality.

Finally I delivered her to Rawene. We drove past the hospital and down into the township; she gave her old palace a pensive look over her shoulder as we left it behind. 'It needs a coat of paint,' she noted. A minute or two downhill we arrived at the Clendon house. Though neglected and dusty, it was prettily situated, sitting among Norfolk Island pines and bright flower beds, and overlooking the sea. But was she going to survive happily here? I was apprehensive.

'You'll be all right?' I asked as she began to unpack.

'All right?' she challenged. 'What do you mean all right?'

'By yourself,' I explained.

'I know this place like the back of my hand,' she said patiently.

'Ten years ago,' I pointed out.

'What's changed?' she argued.

'Perhaps the back of your hand,' I suggested.

'Never,' she told me.

Unpersuaded, I drove back to Auckland. A day or two later I had a depressed letter: 'Well I'm still alive but that's about all,' she told me. 'Sorry to worry you — I suppose you must hate aged aunts pestering you — but I'm bored.' This was followed by a telegram: PLEASE PLEASE LOVING NEPHEW, it read. PLEASE COME AND RESCUE ME QUICK. YOUR DEAR AUNT.

I replied: COMING QUICKEST.

I drove north fast. She was sitting impatiently on her suitcase in the empty living room of the house. Her face was desolate; her voice small. It hadn't worked. She lacked authority in the town; she lacked a real role. Caretaker of an historic place? Residents of the Hokianga didn't rate history highly. It had cleaned them out of timber, of kauri gum, of industry, of employment; history had done them enough damage. They also thought it strange that she should have returned, not to the hospital on the hill, but to the decrepit Clendon dwelling. Rawene's villagers now democratically treated her as one of themselves, not as the witch of the wild Hokianga. With no children to deliver, no doctors to intimidate, no patients and nurses to scold, she felt transparent, a lonely ghost. She had three times scrubbed the floor of the house; the place was no longer dusty and, with a few sticks of antique furniture, open to the public. The public was slow coming. Sis was fast leaving. We drove back to Auckland with no halts, no farewells. She never went back.

In August 1976, months short of the stroke which silenced her, I chanced on Aunt Sis in an Auckland street. She was then well into her seventies and struggling to keep an anti-nuclear banner aloft in a Hiroshima Day memorial parade. Age hadn't left her less forbidding. Nor had time sweetened her tongue.

'What are you doing?' I asked, though it was plain.

'What are you?' she asked.

'Hurrying to keep an appointment,' I explained.

'With a woman, I daresay.'

'With a friend,' I admitted.

'Get your mind above your belt,' she ordered.

I took the banner obediently. We walked side by side for the last time.

Her departure from this world was in keeping with litigious Shadbolt custom. She left few worldly goods. Her will bestowed the last of her little wealth on nephews and nieces she thought needy, otherwise on those she thought shared her feeling for the fate of the human race. The selective nature of the document kept lawyers contesting her sanity for six years.

By way of rehearsal the family divided sourly over how best to dispose of her body. Mourning made way for an all-in wrestling match. There were those who felt Sis belonged to the larger world; there were others who thought she belonged to her family. There was much to be said for both viewpoints, though I failed to see why Sis shouldn't have some public farewell. Luckily for my equilibrium, I was hiking through Lapland in the week of her death. I received a letter from a cousin informing me of the fracas. 'Come home quick,' she urged. 'You've got the makings of your next novel here.'

The problem there is that novels need a footing in the plausible. The Shadbolts in full feud are not disposed to be; not with a respectable riot in the making. There hadn't been one as fulfilling in years, not since Cousin Donald broke my pipe over his knee, and I punched him into Aunt Evelyn's Ethiopian statuary. On that lively occasion male relatives leapt masterfully into the melee and female relatives screamed. Beer was thrown, tears shed, and it was agreed that family functions were better for being few and far between. I have never been able to understand commentators who claim New Zealanders are passionless; they should look into my neck of the woods.

In the end an unnaturally speechless Aunt Sis was annexed by those of the family who wished a private funeral. Non-Shadbolts were, for the most part, shut out from the ceremony. When Cousin Timothy appealed for a seemly truce he narrowly escaped disembowelment. The funeral finished with a great many of my relatives refusing to speak to a great many other relatives; the remainder, a minority, were in shock.

Uproar took years to subside. When litigation had finished, there was next to nothing left of her money, which satisfied all but the beneficiaries named in her will. As it happened, I was one. In court, a female relative contesting the legacies was questioned by one of the many lawyers involved. 'I note the name Maurice here,' he observed rather irrelevantly. 'Would he, by any chance, be Maurice Shadbolt the author?'

'I believe,' she said frostily, 'that he may describe himself as such.'

'You mean that he is not?'

'I mean merely,' she glared, 'that he may describe himself as such.'

'Come,' the lawyer said. 'He has published a number of books, surely. Does that, or does that not, make him an author?'

'If they are his own work,' she said darkly. She had long maintained that my first wife, playing Collette to my Willy, had written the novels and stories published under my name. It made sense. In the hope of founding a literary dynasty, she had reared four sons on a diet of wholesome literature and fruity elocution. Each in his turn had shown promise. Their poems were published in school magazines and read sonorously at Shadbolt gatherings. One by one, however, they had disappeared into the underbrush of academia, never to be seen again as other than teachers and professors in Toronto, Sydney, Singapore and Manchester. It was unfair that they had failed to function in the world of letters, and that I had; and only to be explained by fraudulence. Though I mysteriously managed to publish the other side of divorce and remarriage she persevered in divulging the shame and disgrace of my authorship to all comers and on occasion attempted to correct any misapprehensions my editors and publishers might have in this respect. I was now, I learned, living off the literary industry of a second wife too. I don't know what she said of my third. On the other hand I knew what Aunt Sis would say: 'That's the end of it. You'll never write *War and Peace* now.'

Sis might just have been impressed by a reviewer in *The Times Literary Supplement* who, a dozen years after her death, discussed a distinctly more modest novel of mine in the same breath as *War and Peace*. On second thought, probably not.

Twelve

Uncle Jack, who made himself felt in the 1940s, was more in the lawless line of Benjamin. They had convictions and confinement in common. The tallest and most rugged of Grandfather Ernest's six sons, Jack was a robust boxer and footballer; he was also possessed of a powerful confidence in himself, and a perilously persuasive tongue.

For reasons of his own, with no nod to patriotism, he was fast away to World War II. When he wasn't fighting Germans he was felling fellow warriors. In the Middle East he battled his way to the light-heavyweight boxing championship of the Allied forces, and succumbed only to a British professional when he contested the heavyweight title too. During the German invasion of Greece, he was mislaid when New Zealand forces withdrew bloodied. On the run, he made a lusty best of things. He found a supply of retsina and a passionate widow in a serene seaside village and decided war had a sunny side. Then German patrols began raising dust on nearby hills. His Greek hosts grew nervous; they might be shot for harbouring a runaway. Nevertheless, they suggested he stay; they could arrange a long-term hideout.

That didn't appeal to Jack. He begged, borrowed or stole a sailing dinghy, loaded it with wine and a modest supply of bread and cheese, and set off for Africa, to get into the war again. His knowledge of seamanship was next to nil; he lost his compass, his composure, and more and more weight. Though he steered for the sun, Africa proved elusive, the war too. There was storm and hangover. There was sun and thirst. With food gone, little water left, he found himself becalmed deliriously somewhere in mid-Mediterranean. A vessel took shape in morning mist; a vessel of war. German or British? It no longer much mattered. More to the bloody point, the thing was passing him by. He roused himself sufficiently to place a feeble shot across its bows. Miraculously, the huge ship hove to. A boat was lowered; Jack was lifted aboard in a stretcher. A British skipper welcomed the fainting fugitive.

'A lost Kiwi?' the skipper said.

'That would be right,' Jack agreed hoarsely.

'I'm what you Australians and New Zealanders call a Pom,' the skipper said.

'I'll tell you a secret,' Jack whispered.

'Yes?' The skipper bent low.

'You are,' Jack confided, 'the best fucking Pom I ever fucking saw.'

He was borne off to a hospital bay, and woke in Alexandria. There he learned, on the late side, that he should have been steering for Crete. Hundreds of New Zealanders defending that island had been slain, maimed or captured by Hitler's paratroops. His Mediterranean cruise had something in its favour after all. In an Alexandrian hospital he was fattened and made fit to fight again. Once or twice he had a sergeant's stripes; mostly he didn't. In the vicinity of Germans, he might be a sergeant. Otherwise he was a disciplinary problem. That didn't make him any less useful a killer. Surviving bayonet charge and artillery barrage, he fought across northern Africa with the New Zealand Division for the next two years. In 1943, with Germans cleared from the desert, and assault on Italy under review, a number of New Zealanders were given home leave. Jack was among those judged to have done their share of slaughter.

Back in New Zealand, like many on leave, he was baffled. The country was carrying on as before. While he and his comrades argued with death in distant desert most New Zealanders were leading easy lives. For them the war was only an occasional inconvenience. Some grumbled about shortages. Others were plainly profiting from the war. Suspiciously many able-bodied young men walked the streets in civilian clothes.

There was more to it. While New Zealand troops battled around the Mediterranean, Japan had entered the war. Its seaborne samurai had raced down the Pacific to imperil Australia and New Zealand. To hold the line Australia had sensibly recalled its forces from the European theatre of war. New Zealand, mindlessly loyal to Britain, and respecting Churchill's belief that the European theatre of war was primary, had not recalled its troops. Its security had fallen into American hands. American troops swarmed everywhere.

To Jack this made no sense. New Zealand was better defended by New Zealanders, not by U.S. marines. New Zealand's fight was in the Pacific. Not in Africa; not in Italy. 'Not on your bloody life,' he said mutinously. He was not alone. Hundreds of heroes on home leave refused to return to the war in Europe. What to do? Could the cream of New Zealand's gallant soldiery now be prosecuted as shirkers and cowards? Ringleaders were arrested but never court martialled. Others were rounded up in shamefaced fashion and also released. Few returned to fight in Italy. Jack was not one of them. He declared his war done and married an old sweetheart. By the war's end they had their first child.

Somewhere in those war years Jack's life reached its high point. Peace, never up to expectations, was all downhill. Jack remained a disciplinary problem, with more than a sergeant's stripes at risk. His first difference with the law came while employed on Auckland's waterfront. Police apprehended him as he pedalled his bicycle off the wharves, at the end of a working day. He had four blocks of pilfered New Zealand export butter tucked in his trouser legs.

Taken to court on a charge of theft, he defended himself Shadbolt style. He disclaimed all knowledge of the blocks of butter; it was a mystery to him how they had come to reside in his trouser legs. Perhaps his wife had asked him to buy a pound of butter on his way home; perhaps in consequence he had absent-mindedly slipped one into his trousers while loading a vessel. Certainly not four. He grilled police witnesses until they became uncertain of what they had seen. 'Four blocks of butter in my trouser legs would have been obvious,' he told them. 'Would I have been so stupid?' A good question. It was a lightweight defence, but not lacking in comedy. The trivial nature of the theft was such that it might, in the normal course, have made a four-line paragraph somewhere inside the evening paper. Instead Uncle Jack's courtroom romp made the front page. A good-humoured magistrate, in view of Jack's war record, let him off with a fine and a warning. No further blocks of butter fell off the back of a ship in Jack's vicinity.

In 1951 New Zealand was shaken by a six month waterfront strike. It was the climax of a long feud between shipowners and waterfront unionists. Shipowners were backed by a newly elected right-wing government, police and troops. Unionists were led by romantic left-wingers who had learned the Marxist alphabet in the hungry 1930s. They failed to read their new situation or to see themselves as isolated in a post-war world filling with prosperity. It was bound to end badly, and did; the government wished to break waterfront unions, and would. The rhetoric of New Zealand's past labour struggles won few friends. There were running brawls and baton charges. Jack was back at war again, using his fists to stunning effect. Meanwhile soldiers worked cargoes. Finally scab unions were formed. No old unionist would be allowed back to work the wharves. Jack was loyal to the last, 151st day of the strike. Then he walked away. From that point he felt he owed nothing to his fellow men. His wartime marriage came apart, after three children, and Jack himself drifted from town to town, city to city.

He wasn't the only one in his family to discover post-war New Zealand difficult. His young brother Tim, after a war as a Fleet Air Arm pilot, running bombing missions across the Baltic Sea, found his job as a rural schoolteacher unchallenging. He returned to flying, this time with jet fighters, and spun his plane into an English hillside; his two sons were left fatherless.

Jack's older brother Arthur, on the other hand, hadn't been to war at all, failing to make the army for medical reasons; his restlessness suggested he was now regretting it. At least he could pick up the pieces. He sailed off to England, leaving his marriage behind, and worked clearing bomb damage. Then he inconspicuously returned home. He reopened an old and abandoned gold mine on the Coromandel peninsula and proved, after a year or two, that it was better left abandoned. Then, like Benjamin and Ernest before him, he took over some bush country — in his case near Auckland — and began clearing it. Living a spartan life in a pioneer slab hut, much like the one in which he had been raised, seemed to satisfy him. He had no large vision for the land, or none he confided to his family. He was happy to sell his felled timber off as firewood in the city, have a night on the town, and head for the hills at daybreak. Axe and saw gave him an honest living.

Jack's means of support, by contrast, were looking more and more murky. He bluffed his way into jobs where expertise was needed — as a foreman on construction sites, say — and decamped before his lack of qualifications promised disaster and exposure. A second marriage seemed to steady him; he adopted a child. A suburban property deal turned sour. In a fit of pique, with no apparent premeditation, he burned his house down. Investigators and police found nothing amiss; he collected the insurance. He was emboldened to repeat the performance a year or two later. This time too investigation disclosed nothing of unlawful nature, though suspicion was strong.

Jack had hit upon a rewarding vocation. Rather than see if he could be three times lucky, he let it be known that he was open to offers of employment; he became a prospering arsonist, with a professional's pride in his craft. When an inner-city landlord or householder thought to dispose of a derelict property to advantage, Jack was called in. There was never a trace of accelerant found in the ashes; Jack could be trusted to do a clean job and insurance companies paid up without large protest. He spent most of a decade refining his technique. But somewhere along the line over-confidence undid him. His word-of-mouth reputation had grown dangerously; he was not inclined to dampen it. Finally he loitered too long near one of his more satisfying conflagrations. His arrest gave him a second chance to test his courtroom talent. The police case proved no match for Jack's witness-box oratory; he wasn't Ernest Shadbolt's son for nothing. He was found not guilty.

That wasn't good enough for Jack; rather than rest on his laurels he sued the Attorney-General of New Zealand for $203,000 as compensation for wrongful arrest. (Where did the $3000 come from? Presumably Jack thought a round figure might make his claim less credible.) He conducted his own case, this time direly. The action was thrown out of court. Frustrated policemen kept a closer watch on Jack. Seeing the writing on the wall as an arsonist, he moved on to the seedier side of Auckland's underworld. Less and less careful of the company he kept, he was picked up for managing a massage parlour of poor reputation. It was a come-down for a soldier of distinction and an incendiarist of flair. This time the prosecution was successful; Jack was given a prison sentence. When my father died, and I needed hands to help carry his coffin, Jack was given leave from jail on a compassionate two-hour pass. He was still a powerful figure; he refused to look humble or apologetic. He couldn't stay on for the family wake; after the funeral service he was driven back to his cell by a warder.

When released, he lived quietly and for the most part within the law. He wasn't to do much with the fifteen years left to him. He was at his best eluding Hitler's legions. The mistake of his life was leaving that Greek village.

Thirteen

*T*oo young for the first, too old for the second, my father Frank managed to miss both world wars. This was providential. He would have got himself killed with no nudge from the Kaiser or help from Hitler. Unlike his young brothers, he was no footballer, no boxer, no warrior. He was a long time recovering from his blissful boyhood on Banks Peninsula. The North Island of the 1920s was tougher territory, and Auckland especially bitter. The city teemed with ex-soldiers, sullen survivors of Turkey's heights and of France's trenches. They had been promised the world when they sailed off to battle for the British Empire. On their return, often minus limbs, sometimes minus wits, they found themselves unwanted and queueing for work. Those unlucky enough to be given land by the government found it too rough to raise more than rabbits; they hiked back into the city to join the jobless.

At some point my youthful father found himself at the head of a queue, and taken on as a quarryman. Marvellous as it seems to me now — he was as vague as any man I have known — he was entrusted with the job of firing explosives, and soon won a ticket attesting to his competence with hazardous substances. This resonant occupation meant he could help support his parents. It also allowed him to flirt weekly with fortune. Like Ernest he had inherited Benjamin's unhappier genes; he was a luckless gambler too. There was little left of his pay packet after he had split it between his parents and Saturday's horses. Benjamin had wanted the Canterbury Derby and the Grand National; my father merely wanted a coup convincing enough to say goodbye to gelignite and return to Banks Peninsula his own man. Setting up such a coup with bookmakers became his frustrating vocation. Work merely provided the wherewithal. He may have had girl friends. If so, they were not allowed to interfere with his long-term mission. From their point of view he might not have seemed a good bet maritally; from his point of view all were a potential encumbrance.

All the same, now twenty-eight years of age, he went to Saturday dances with his young brothers and sisters. Enter my mother, Violet Kearon.

Eighteen years old, Violet had lately left school and was working as a secretary in an Auckland legal office. She lived with her widowed mother and brother in Glen Eden, a suburb neighbouring Green Bay, where Frank resided with his parents. She and her friends cheerfully walked the little-lit roads of patchily rural western Auckland to Saturday dances, sometimes six miles there and back. There was always the chance of making new friends, of meeting promising bachelors. My father, that night in Blockhouse Bay hall, looked by far the least eligible man on the dance floor. He was the untidiest young fellow Violet had seen in her life. His suit was crumpled; his tie askew; his shirt tail hung out. Perhaps he'd had an unusually demoralising day at the races.

'Look at him,' she whispered to her friend Beryl. 'What a fright.'

'You'd better hide,' Beryl warned. 'He's looking at you.'

This was true. Young Frank Shadbolt was travelling with purpose toward Violet. She left her move late. Before she could excuse herself she was on her feet, in a waltz, in his arms. That changed everything. Calamitously untidy Frank might be, but he was a robust and stylish dancer, with a fine ear for rhythm. He was also a charmer. He demonstrated this by taking over the dance hall piano. His years with his melodious Aunt Amelia hadn't been waste. Without a sheet of music before him, he rattled through the hits of the 1920s, and sang them too: *Ramona, If You Were the Only Girl in the World, When I Grow Too Old to Dream*, and not least *When Irish Eyes are Smiling*.

My mother's eyes — half Irish, as it happened — were bright enough by the end of the evening. Plausible Frank was at pains to make her feel she was the only girl in the world. There was no long courtship. They were married within a year. A wedding photograph shows my mother pretty, my father proud. He wears a double breasted suit stiffly buttoned. She wears a silk dress with wide hat. It was the end of 1929. Wall Street had just crashed and world economies were crumbling; there were darknesses loose in the debris.

My mother Violet was pure Celt, as much Welsh as Irish. Since she was nine years old her father had been a name on a headstone a hundred yards up the hill from my grandmother's smallholding on the ferny edge of Auckland. Joseph Kearon had been a seaman, a socialist, something of an adventurer. He was also that freakish figure in the family of man, an Irish atheist. The Kearons, otherwise Protestant, had long been one of the the best known families of seafarers out of Arklow in County Wicklow. Originally inshore fishermen, they had been forced out into the open sea by industrial poisoning of their oyster beds and favoured netting grounds. Their search for work took them aboard large vessels and beyond the horizon. Kearon-owned or Kearon-manned vessels were soon sailing most of the world's seas. Their success as deep-water men allowed them to move from humble dwellings in the often disease-swept fisheries quarter of Arklow to healthier residences on Ferry Bank, overlooking the harbour and a forest of masts. Arklow was the last citadel of sail in the British Isles; the town's mariners had contempt for steam. In the late nineteenth century there were eight or more sailing-ship skippers named Kearon affluently domiciled on Ferry Bank.

In keeping with family custom Joseph had gone to sea in his early teens, sometime in the late 1870s, in a sailing ship skippered by his father, bushy-bearded Captain Kearon. Joseph's was a family always in feud with the sea. Irish politics were puny by contrast; the Kearons had no patience with the hue and cry of turbulent Catholic townsfolk. They identified themselves with the Protestant Ascendancy and buried their dead alongside Anglo-Irish aristocrats; they spelled their name Kearon to distinguish themselves from Papist Kearins or Keirins. They were not a long-lived clan. Kearon remains, after fire or shipwreck, were scattered on most ocean floors. Joseph had a brother swept away by storm south of Cape Horn; another brother lost in a lifeboat when his ship took fire off Valparaiso. Hours at the helm in the world of the mariner, steering by the stars of an indifferent universe, left him in doubt of a benevolent deity. Otherwise he loved the tall ships leaning into the wind and was at home in the world's great ports of call. Good-looking, lively and loveable Joseph had lady friends in most. He sometimes gave the sea away; once in San Francisco. He hiked across the American continent, walking the West when it was still wild. Later in life he talked with authority about such as Wild Bill Hickock and Wyatt Earp before movies made their names familiar. He panned for gold here, worked on railroads there, but finished up back in Arklow at the helm of a Kearon-captained vessel again.

His large vice was literature. His mate's cabin was crammed with books. There were books on art; books on religion, evolution and revolution; there was Winwoode Read and Thomas Paine; there were socialist prophets like Edward Bellamy and Daniel de Leon; there was Shakespeare, Milton, Byron, Shelley and Keats. And there was Gibbon's *Decline and Fall* in five volumes. Above all, there were the works of that patron saint of seafarers, Jack London — a man's man, after Joseph's own heart, and a socialist too. By his books I seem to have known him. His sea-stained library, long to outlive him, would colour the lives of his descendants for half a century.

Meanwhile there was a family disaster. In 1894 his father, Captain Kearon, returned to Arklow, after a long voyage, to find his cherished wife Mary weeks buried in Arklow's Kilbride Cemetery. The captain's grief was not to be borne; he followed her to the grave, by his own hand, inside four months. The inscription tells its own tale:

> *In Loving Memory of*
> *Capt. Joseph Kearon*
> *of Ferry Bank, Arklow,*
> *who departed this life*
> *5th day of February, 1895,*
> *aged 58 years.*
> *Also*
> *his beloved wife*
> *Mary Anne Kearon*
> *who died 25th day of*
> *September 1894, aged*
> *48 years.*
> *Erected by their sorrowing*
> *children.*

Joseph's world had fallen apart. As an atheist and socialist he had little in common with his socially circumspect brothers and sisters anyway; now he had no base in Arklow either.

In the early 1900s Joseph took shore leave in New Zealand. He was then in his robust early forties, a talker and tale-teller. And for most women a blue-eyed beguiler. Was it time to swallow the anchor and settle for life on land? He was persuaded to think so.

Walking the rumbling volcanic heart of the North Island — and waiting upon the giant Waimangu geyser to spit mud and rock five hundred yards skyward — he observed a lovely young woman in her early twenties beside him. She was dark Welsh, slender, and sloe-eyed. Joseph never had difficulty finding an excuse to fall into conversation with a likely lady. He lost no time now; he made the most of the passing minutes before the fierce spectacle began. Her name was Louisa Morris, he learned; she was from Te Awamutu, on the southern frontier of the Waikato, presently visiting an aunt in Rotorua.

The geyser — a legacy of an eruption which had devastated hundreds of square miles of the North Island interior two decades earlier — suddenly roared high. The sky darkened with mud and debris as the earth shook; terrified birds took wing. When the commotion returned to the innards of the earth there was an even more aweing silence.

'A fine sight,' Joseph observed.

'Yes,' Louisa agreed shyly.

'You are finer,' Joseph declared.

That, near enough, was that. Forty years later, a longtime widow on pilgrimage, Louisa led me to the spot where she met Joseph. The Waimangu geyser roared no more. There was a steaming lake fringed with fern and pine; birds now sang unruffled. We stood there in silence.

'It was his eyes,' she explained.

There was a long pause.

'Eyes?' I asked.

'His sweet Irish eyes,' she said.

Her holiday finished, Louisa returned to Te Awamutu with Joseph Kearon in fervent pursuit. The Morris family had arrived in New Zealand sometime in the 1870s and had taken up land confiscated from Maori rebels on the uneasy frontier with the still Maori-held King Country. Te Awamutu's original military settlers, planted there by the colonial government lest tribesmen in the south return to the fray, had walked off in despair of winning a livelihood from dank

Waikato acres, their muddy flocks often lost to flood; they sold out for ten shillings or less an acre to poor Welsh late-comers like the Morrises. The Morrises were not prospering either, as it happened, but they had expectations. Louisa had been born into a large family in 1883; her first memory was of life on a fraught frontier, of the unconquered Maori monarch, King Tawhaio, riding into town with his whooping retinue. On such days Louisa's mother hid her children under the house until Maori din subsided.

Louisa's parents didn't take warmly to the fluent Irish stranger in her wake. Sedately Welsh, staunchly chapel, they saw no future in Joseph's persistent courtship of Louisa. For one thing, he was almost twenty years older than their daughter. For another he had no penny to his name. For a third he had far too much bookish talk for their liking. Louisa could surely do better for herself than an unreliable and Godless Irish seaman. Louisa refused to be swayed: she married sweet-eyed Joseph in 1905. His skills as a seafarer redundant, he took a job as a railway navvy, hacking a route through cruel country for the North Island's main trunk line. Louisa lived in rough railway quarters while Joseph laboured. Their first marital difficulty came when she unpacked his possessions, particularly his books. Most were incomprehensibly literary or political. One volume, however, was dizzyingly personal. It was a photograph album Joseph had compiled over his years on the world's waters. Within were portraits of most of the women he had known; it seemed he had done better than a girl in every port. In some localities there were two or three, and in San Francisco still more. Fearful and lonely Louisa sat and wept. What kind of wild Irish philanderer had she wed? Had her parents been right?

Confronted by his weeping wife, Joseph did the decent thing. He heaved the incriminating album into the fireplace and put a match to it. 'The past is the past,' he told her. He again managed to convince her that he worshipped the ground she walked on. Everything says he did.

Fourteen

Within a year Arklow Joe, as he was known, had saved enough to do better by Louisa. They travelled north and took up two or three cheap acres in a nondescript gully of scrub and clay, at the junction of Woodglen and West Coast roads, just outside Auckland's urban outpost of Glen Eden, then hardly more than a rail stop, a shop or two, and a cemetery filling with the city's dead. Their tiny two-bedroom cottage sat in the bend of a creek, just under the railway north. Arklow Joe cleared scrub, broke clay, and made a small paradise of the unpromising site. There were peach, plum, fig and apple trees growing; cabbages, potatoes and peas flourished in his garden; there was a cow or two grazing, and chickens and pigs. He planted willows to protect home and garden from flood. In short, he made Glen Eden live up to its name. This Irish Adam made it his business to see his Welsh Eve lacked nothing. And his library had a home at last. If he itched for life at sea, missed his salty family in Arklow, it didn't show. Joseph proved to have a countryman's touch; he cured his own bacon, churned his own butter. Not that their modest beachhead in the foothills of Arcadia sustained them. He navvied on roads or railways, when the work was offering; otherwise his head was in a book. Louisa's only rival was Arklow Joe's library. Literacy sat lightly on her family; her own home had been graced only by the gospels. Socialist Joseph, poetry-loving Joseph, could be a troublingly remote stranger. I suspect he might have been a worry to himself too. When I look into his face, in photographs, I see strength of character; I also read melancholy. Was it from the reflective Kearons, rather than the extrovert Shadbolts, that I inherited a gene which, more than enough in my life, has meant depression? I certainly inherited colour-blindness from Arklow Joe, if in a less excessive form than his. 'Look at that pretty pink gorse flower,' he was known to say.

The junction where their cottage sat was a site favoured by lonely men on the swag, itinerants looking to sell their labour to timber-millers and dam-builders in nearby bush country. They pitched their overnight tents under roadside pines before moving on in the morning. Many were Irish, from most of the counties of Ireland, men who knew a good samaritan when they saw one. Those in most need knew Arklow Joe as a man to be relied on for a billy of tea, a handful of eggs, and a round or two of bacon. Moreover, he was good for a yarn. 'Tell us a story, Joe,' they would ask. 'Sing us a song.' Arklow Joe needed no encouragment. Sometimes there was an accordion; often a fiddle. Music billowed about the smoke of their campfires. Arklow Joe was a man among men again. In quieter voice he talked socialism, and Ireland's freedom. Louisa, on the whole, wished he would not. In other respects, however, he left her with no cause for unease. He showed no symptoms of wanderlust, never talked of a return to Ireland.

There were other settlers busy slashing holes in the scrub to the west of Glen Eden. Whatever their political leaning, Joseph was popular with them too. They came to yarn, to get authoritative Irish advice on the growing of potatoes, and borrow his books. Believing that enlightenment must bring a better world, he always had dozens of books on loan to neighbours: Arklow Joe's was the district's first library.

Many of the settlers between Glen Eden and the Waitakere foothills were from the Yugoslav province of Dalmatia, then resident in the Austro-Hungarian empire. First known as 'Austrians', later as 'Dallies' or Dalmatians, they or their fathers had mutinously fled Europe to escape military service. Bands of them had first worked digging kauri gum in bare, bleak and remote regions to the north of Auckland. In the nineteenth century kauri gum had been found useful as a base for hard-drying varnishes. By the turn of the century this petrified product of long-fallen forest was one of New Zealand's principal exports, rivalling even gold in value. Gum was a godsend for the refugees from the Emperor Franz Josef's domain. A man needed only a spear, a spade, and strong arms to gather it. With a little capital accumulated, diggers moved to the city or its outskirts. Those who shifted into the city often became fishermen. Those lingering inland founded orchards and vineyards which prosper to this day.

At first their presence was suspect, particularly in World War I when they were seen as potential spies and traitors, cousins of the Kaiser, by patriots in need of a nose to punch. But they had one reliable friend in the district. Arklow Joe was a fellow spirit, a free-thinking Irishman who talked the brotherhood of man; and an anti-monarchist to boot. Many of his Dalmatian friends had socialist notions of a Marxist colour; some would later help found the New Zealand Communist Party. Would Arklow Joe have joined them had he lived longer? Possibly not. He was more romantic than revolutionary; Shelley's verse said more to him than any Marxist manifesto; Jack London more than Lenin.

Yet he thought little of a twenty-mile weekend walk, into the heart of Auckland and home again, to hear radical and anarchist orators on the waterfront. Legendary socialists and strike leaders like Tom Mann and Ben Tillet, on their way from Sydney to San Francisco or vice versa, often called into Auckland to mount a stepladder and announce mankind's new dawn near. Joseph liked the robust speakers from the I.W.W. (the International Workers of the World, better known as the Wobblies), men who knew the world much as he once had, from the decks of pitching ships, as rouseabouts and railway gangers on the North American continent. He was less taken by their revolutionary programme of sabotage and arson. His socialism took gentler form. He was a reader and soon a seller of *The Maoriland Worker*, which weekly called capitalism to account as a breeder of poverty and war. Later there were meetings, also requiring long tramps, at which the founding of a New Zealand Labour Party was earnestly canvassed. Joseph was all for it, and to his death a loyal member. Twice in his last years he perplexed his children and dismayed his wife by leaping from his armchair with a roar of delight. The first was when news of the Irish Easter uprising reached him in 1915. The second was when Russia's Czar was toppled in 1917.

Meanwhile there was his marriage, his Louisa. She gave birth to their first child, another Joseph, in 1907. My mother Violet followed in 1911. To the end of their own lives they remembered a loving if often absent-minded father. He always had a story, even when sharpening his cut-throat razor on a leather strap and lathering up for a shave. Carried away by the climax of one tale, he managed to slice off half his moustache; his children were even more awed. He presented his moustached profile, and then the unmoustached.

'Which is the more handsome?' he asked. 'With or without?'

They voted it off. Without drawing breath he whisked away the remnant moustache and started a new story. There were Irish lullabies to soothe them to sleep; rebel songs to rouse them. Arklow Joe was an original, a father worth remembering, a friend to the world. They were never to meet his like in this life. Nor were they to have him long.

Fifteen

At the end of World War I the great influenza epidemic, having mustered strength elsewhere, struck New Zealand with extraordinary virulence. Ten thousand died in a population of hardly more than a million. Louisa lost three brothers in a week. Waikumete cemetery, up the road from the Kearon cottage, was as busy a place as any in New Zealand. Gravediggers couldn't cope. When young Joseph and younger Violet walked to school they saw coffins stacked high on the platform of Glen Eden railway station; there were scores awaiting burial, and scores more every day, even with mass graves dug. Arklow Joe correctly deduced that this was an unhealthy state of affairs, and pushed kerosene up their noses before they walked to school. Was it a seafarer's precaution against cholera in unwholesome ports? It seemed to work. Classmates succumbed, teachers dropped, but the Kearon children survived. Arklow Joe himself seemed to show symptoms; he shook them off. Death was waiting for him elsewhere, though he missed his first appointment. In 1919 he fell between the wheels of a slow-moving train and had the presence of mind to flatten himself between the rails while wagons rumbled overhead. He survived badly battered and constitutionally depleted, walking on a stick. Labouring was now out of the question; even digging his potato patch was impossible. The year after he was in hospital again with a fever. While joking with a neighbouring invalid, he made the mistake of laughing too long; his heart stopped. He was fifty-five years old. Neighbours, especially his Dalmatian friends, turned out in scores to farewell him; there had been no man more loved in the district than yarn-spinning Arklow Joe. Nor one whose loss was more mourned. Even his death was in character. He had gone with a laugh.

Louisa was thirty-seven years old, with a thirteen-year-old son and eight-year-old daughter to support. Her wider family, the Morrises, now penniless in Auckland, could be no help. World War I and the influenza epidemic had left the Morrises a family of widows. Letters to Arklow, telling of Joseph's death in New Zealand, brought no offers of help. Louisa was on her own. She had another handicap. She was beginning to grow deaf. But at least she had the land her husband had made fruitful. To augment her small widow's pension she began working as a charwoman for Auckland's wealthy, and would for the next quarter century. Though his father once had larger plans for him, son Joseph was taken out of school, at the age of fourteen, and put to work in a footwear factory. The three survived the difficult 1920s, sometimes on bread and dripping. Elsewhere it might have been the jazz age; it was never much noticed on my grandmother's tiny landholding. My mother was left in school longer, to learn shorthand and typing, become an office girl, and — at the age of eighteen years — marry Frank Shadbolt. It was a day or two after Christmas 1929. The 1930s began days later.

My Uncle Joe, son of Arklow Joe, was better prepared than most. His father might have been dead ten years; his father's library lived. Without much formal education, Joe found an alternative to the footwear factory on the bookshelves in his mother's cottage. First he read for entertainment; then for elucidation. The library asked most of the questions that might be asked of this world; it even suggested answers. As the decade soured Joe turned to his father's library more and more, especially after he was passed a Social Credit tract by a workmate. Trying to make sense of this prescription for the world's ill, Joe grabbed up volumes likely to shed light. Among them were books on socialism. Soon he was eavesdropping on street-corner orators, especially on those of Marxist colour. The New Zealand Communist Party was tiny, but making an impression out of proportion to its number as unemployment grew in the cities. Communists were battling evictions, leading demonstrations against wage cuts and job cuts, and fighting for free speech. As the world grew murkier such orators made more and more sense. Most to the point, they spoke of a working man's bastion in the making in the Soviet Union. Such a society, they said, was within reach in New Zealand too. Very soon Joe was possessed of a Party card.

About the time my uncle pledged himself to revolution my father's quarry closed. No one needed his knack with explosives. He and my mother, unable to pay rent, moved into the Glen Eden cottage with Louisa and young Joe. Costs were low; the orchard and vegetable garden Grandfather Joseph had established was there to sustain them. My mother soon proved to be pregnant. Then there was a car accident, in a vehicle driven by an uncle. Their child, a daughter, was stillborn. It seemed that they might not have another.

With time on his hands, my father took an interest in the propaganda pamphlets his brother-in-law was distributing and selling. Before long he was a recruit to young Joe's cause. My fluent father did more than pick up a Party card. He also took a seat on the executive of the communist-backed Unemployed Workers' Movement, soon doing more than a little orating himself. Soup kitchens multiplied; demonstrations grew. And on April 14, 1932, anger roared through the centre of Auckland. Swinging police batons welded fifteen thousand peacefully protesting unemployed into a venomous mob. Young Joe was among them, and my father. The commercial heart of the city was stormed. After an ugly hour or two there were few shop windows in central Auckland unshattered; it was a looters' picnic. Finally naval ratings were called out with fixed bayonets. Rioters moved aside, to let menace pass, and then went back to smashing and looting. Close to midnight my wild-eyed father, having lost his brother-in-law in the battle, arrived home in Glen Eden. 'The city's gone mad,' he reported to my mother. As evidence he produced a handful of wristwatches from a back pocket.

'Where did they come from?' she asked fearfully.

'They were lying in the street,' he explained.

'You're not a thief,' she told him.

'No,' he agreed.

'So bury them,' she said.

He fetched a spade. My father's pathetic handful of loot was buried beneath a plum tree by the light of a kerosene lamp. Shaky and breathless, Joe turned up in the middle of this midnight ceremony. He had seen the riot begin. The charismatic leader of the city's unemployed, Jim Edwards, had been appealing for calm when the first police batons fell. Edwards was still calling for order when batoned down himself. The crowd reacted with spirit. Workmen stripped palings from picket fences and fought back. Joe was passed a paling with the suggestion he defend himself; defend himself he did when he found batons swinging on three sides. He escaped with bruises and cuts. Neither my father nor my uncle were ever to forget the vengeful howl of the crowd as it filled the city. Decades later it was still shading the inner lives of those who heard it. It also heralded the nearest thing to revolution New Zealand had known.

'Does it matter who began it?' my mother asked.

She was nervous. She was pregnant again, determined not to lose another child. Next day she had more reason for fear. Armed men were patrolling city streets. Police were rounding up unemployed leaders. Jim Edwards had gone into hiding. My father seemed a candidate for handcuffs too. Days passed, then weeks. Perhaps police cells were full. The knock on the door never came.

Elsewhere in the city the fugitive Jim Edwards was finally arrested and brought to trial as ringleader of the riot. Young Joe Kearon made a courtroom appearance as witness to events. He testified that Edwards had been pleading for peace even when the batons were drawn. But there was a posse of policemen to testify otherwise. Edwards was sent to prison with two other officials of the unemployed movement. Without leaders, and with the penalties for protest plain, the unemployed began to back a more conventional panacea: reform rather than revolution, by way of the Parliamentary Labour Party. 'Something disappeared with the riots that never returned,' said one witness to events. 'The prison sentences had an effect.'

Duplicated in other New Zealand cities, if less dramatically, the riot panicked politicians. Measures were taken to ameliorate the condition of the more desperate unemployed. To ensure no repeat, street demonstrations were banned. Right of assembly in the open air was restricted. There was a curfew placed on political meetings. It was another two years before such measures were challenged by street speakers — some of whom were imprisoned too — and three years before they were lifted. Muffled and isolated, communists meanwhile became an inoffensive sect, riven with faction fights, quarrelling more with each other than capitalism. My baffled father began playing safe too. He and Violet were now parents; I had been born seven weeks after the Auckland riot.

Sixteen

After such riches my times seem tame. How compete with Benjamin, Ernest and Arklow Joe, with transported convicts, robust bush lawyers, weathered mariners, and their awesomely steadfast womenfolk? Or — in the next generation — with heroic Sis, turbulent Jack, revolutionary Frank and rioter Joe? Yet time and delinquent memory may already be distilling today's commonplaces into tomorrow's fireside tales. This is to remind time of its business. Memory needs no nudge.

I recall water. I could feel it, taste it, see through it. It showered away in silver drops when I tried to grab up a small fistful. I could stir it in slow circles with my finger and leave no mark. More intriguing, it held pictures; I could find sky, tree and my face there when it ceased to quiver. What I saw was of this world and also not. The real world did not flutter away at a touch. I could stub my toe and skin my knees on the real world; it could make me cry.

The water brimmed from a clear spring among filmy fern, a few yards from a decrepit cottage in a gold-mining township. The year was 1934. I was two years old, or less. The cottage was ours. The spring was our water supply. My mother filled a bucket from the spring to cook and wash. We lived a dozen yards from a railway line; the floorboards trembled terrifyingly as trains roared out into the world with the gold my father and his fellow miners freed from clammy caverns under our feet.

How had we got there? My footloose Uncle Arthur, on the lookout for work, had miraculously happened on employment in the Waihi goldfields to the south of Auckland. Through the depression the district was a lone niche of prosperity in New Zealand. Jubilant Arthur, after winning favour with a foreman, thought he could get my father taken on too. 'Come down and join me,' he urged his brother. He didn't need to ask twice. My parents were on the next train, or near enough. My father was giddied by his weekly pay packet; my mother marvelled at the things money could buy.

After a few months we moved from the collapsing cottage to a farmhouse which promised more peace. It sat high on a plateau behind Waikino township. We shared the place with Uncle Arthur, his wife Biddy, and daughter Yvonne. Yvonne and I could wander safely. There were cows in the fields; there were trees on the hills. And I had a pet pig. It wasn't all pastoral. Up valley there was the thunder of the Waikino battery, crushing and stripping the ore from quartz twenty-four hours a day. It was a tolerable sound. It meant employment. It meant workmen with money. My father laboured near, at a mine called the Golden Dawn; he walked to work. One day I managed to meet him as he finished his day underground. I took his grimy hand and trotted beside him to the Waikino pub. He sat me on the bar among his workmates and bought me a raspberry concoction. 'Starting your boy off early, Frank?' these men joked as I sipped my drink. I wondered at their filthy faces. Their mothers, I thought, would have something to say when they got home.

Then conversation became opaquely political. Twenty years earlier, in 1912, the Waihi goldfields had staged one of New Zealand's most savage contests between capital and labour, between British mine-owners and native New Zealand trade unionists. Nationalism didn't enter into the equation then. Newspapers and drum-beating politicians saw the strikers as treasonous, betraying the British Empire. There had been gunfire, and a union leader slain, others clubbed close to death. The strike ended calamitously for the unionists. Many were hounded from town by baton-swinging constables. Others, among them future leaders of the New Zealand Labour Party, were imprisoned. Scab labour was brought in to work the mines. These right-minded citizens often had convictions for violence and robbery. They zealously entered the fray, with the police for once on their side. Strikers' homes were razed and looted. In the district the names of those scabs were still known and cursed. They and their descendants were shunned for decades. British mine-owners, by their nature, continued to make militants of men.

My father may or may not have still held a Party card. He still knew the Party line. He passed out propaganda sheets. This made brother

Arthur nervous. 'Don't you know which side your bread is buttered?' he asked. 'Do you want to go back on the dole?' Arthur further pointed out that if my father drew attention to himself his belligerent role in the unemployed movement might be recalled. His job would be in jeopardy. With mixed feelings, my father kept his head down. He was quiet at union meetings. He took no leading role in disputes between management and men. But in the boisterous Waikino pub, a place loud with politics, he was an unfettered militant among many.

The year of my baptismal pub visit was 1935; New Zealand was about to elect its first Labour government. The lukewarm socialism of that government wouldn't satisfy my father, nor many like him. Wanting something more in the nature of a Soviet Five Year Plan, they welcomed the result of the election with reservations. Yet they soon had to concede that there was change for the better. Defying conventional economists, the onetime working men of that government drafted dramatic social change. Credit was made available for large public works and new housing, new schools; there were thousands of jobs made. Children were fed, and deprived families had a reliable roof over their heads. If it wasn't socialism, it was at least an end to misery. Orthodox economics said it was all perilously spendthrift. Newspapers warned of creeping Bolshevism. Nevertheless Labour's reformist programme worked. New Zealand was the first Western nation to leave the depression behind. I didn't notice. The world was.

Parents made up most of that world. They loomed high on all sides when I sought to put my existence in hazard. Somewhere beyond were my uncle and aunt, and my female cousin. There were birthday parties and trips to town. There were noisy adult occasions with beer. Uncle Arthur, the only Shadbolt brother under six feet tall, was a stocky, jolly, laughing man with facial scars honourably earned in the boxing ring as a hard-punching welter-weight; he made my father laugh and forget politics. My mother was more fearful. She couldn't believe their luck. She wasn't happy when my father used his pocket money to place a bet with the local bookmaker. He might believe in social revolution; he was still a Shadbolt.

The largest event in my life was a mysterious steamer trip to Auckland, with sheep and cows drifting past on each side of the Waihou River. We went to stay with Grandmother Kearon and Uncle Joe in Glen Eden. Grandmother Kearon spoiled me with cream buns. Uncle Joe took me for rides on the bar of his bike. That was good.

Less good was that my mother was inexplicably whisked off to hospital. She promised a surprise and was as good as her word. Beside her in hospital, between one day and the next, was a baby with a spotty face. 'Your brother,' she informed me. Was that what her trip to hospital was all about? It was a pointlessly complicated way to have a baby. It made more sense to stay home and have the postman deliver it.

Disgruntled, I travelled home with my mother to our home on the Waihi goldfield. A disappointment all round, my brother howled too much for his own good. It also struck me that I was unnecessarily neglected. My unattractive brother continued to be filled with his own importance. I suggested that we sell him off and have a more reasonable baby delivered. This proposition was not taken kindly. My brother, sensing my desire to give him a dishonourable discharge, howled all the more.

Other family dramas were more routine. A peeping tom yielded the largest: a shadowy face at the window of marital bedrooms. Aunt Biddy saw the prowler first. Uncle Arthur said it was her imagination. Sighting the face one night, my mother gave a scream. My fearless father jumped naked from the bath tub, hurtled to the window, threw it open, and leapt. There was another and more terrifying scream, and it wasn't the intruder. My father had garotted himself on the clothes line, doing all but disastrous damage to his genitals too. He was saved from strangulation and emasculation by collapse of the line. My mother found him stridently blaspheming among the Monday wash. On the positive side, the peeping tom, shaken by my father's unholy lamentation, made no repeat appearance.

I had a playmate, the Waikino publican's son. His name was Stanley. Stanley had several advantages. He was a boy, unlike my cousin Yvonne, and didn't mind getting muddy. He didn't howl, unlike my malfunctioning baby brother. He had a useful supply of lemonade from his father's pub, sometimes sausage rolls from his mother's oven. He was considerably older than me, a sweet-natured and faintly feminine boy with a winning smile. Possibly he was uncomfortable with boys his own age. He was also responsible. He could be trusted to keep me off my mother's hands while she met my noisy brother's demands. Stanley and I walked the fields and looked at cows and horses. He hooked ugly eels from the creek with a bent pin on a string. We found tiny eggs in a fallen bird's nest. We sat on the back of my pet pig, now perilously plump, and persuaded it to carry us a few paces.

Stanley was murdered. He was bashed to death on lonely roadside, along with a young woman employed at his father's pub. Gentle Stanley had gone walking with her, as he often did, on a mild evening. The killer in wait was a spurned suitor of the young woman. She was his target. Stanley's death was incidental to vengeance. He had to be killed too, as a witness to her murder. There were newspaper photographs with X marking the spot where Stanley's body had been found. He was my first friend to die. Fearing the affair might warp my view of life, my parents hid newspapers and tried not to talk about it in front of me. They seemed to think I was better off remembering my pet pig before it became pork.

The world was, mostly.

The colonial goose was laying fewer golden eggs for British shareholders. The grottoes of the Golden Dawn mine no longer gleamed, and we moved five miles from the township of Waikino to the town of Waihi. My father had a job in the large Martha mine, the oldest and most enriching in the British Empire. It sat on the Martha hill, its cathedral-like pumphouse stark above the wooden banks and pubs of the rather Wild West main street of the town. We had a large old house built in the heyday of the goldfields. We must still have been modestly in money. One day my father came home with a box which, when he finished fiddling with switches, talked and played music. We stood before it, marvelling at the magic of it all. Saturdays began to fill with racetrack commentaries. For weeks afterward I crept stealthily up on the thing, hoping to catch sight of little people singing and riding horses inside. They were never at home.

My father met with a difficulty in the form of a visit from old Party comrades. My father was having no problem with the Labour government. The comrades were. 'They'll sell out the working class,' they informed my father.

He failed to see what this had to do with him, personally.

'We'd like you to take a more active role in matters,' they said.

'Meaning what?' he asked.

'The working class has to be radicalised for the struggle to come,' they announced. 'You haven't been making yourself felt in the union.'

'I have a wife and two children,' he explained.

They pointed out that the Soviet Union, the world's first workers' state, was imperilled by reactionary forces.

'You're asking me to save the Soviet Union?' he said with wonder.

'Think about it,' they said with confidence. 'We know you won't let the Party down.'

My father did his best not to. He also lost his job. Perhaps workmates made some protest; perhaps they didn't. There was certainly no message of sympathy from Joseph Stalin thanking Frank Shadbolt for his solo attempt to save the Soviet Union. We were fugitives again, back in Auckland, at Glen Eden, in Grandmother Kearon's house. My father started looking for work in a location less imperilled by reactionary forces.

I began to have some notion of what his world was about. There was an adult gathering at the Glen Eden house. It may have been a meeting of the unemployed in the district; it could have been a Communist Party cottage meeting; it might have been a Left Book Club discussion group. Looking for attention, perhaps, I wandered off into Uncle Joe's bedroom, fumbled behind his wardrobe, and found the .22 rifle he used to shoot rabbits. I hoisted it on to my shoulder and marched back to the living room. It was smoky, warm, and filled with people. They sat on the couch, on all the chairs. Two or three men sat with legs swinging on the dining table.

The problem was that no one noticed my arrival. My father was having a fierce argument with a comrade and everyone was looking his way. I was obliged to level the rifle, first at my father, then at others around. That produced a pleasing hush. People seemed about to speak, but nervously thought better.

'Good God, Frank,' a man said. 'Has the revolution started?'

'Time for the barricades,' said another.

Laughter defused it. My uncle rescued his rifle and returned it to his bedroom — to the top of the wardrobe this time, well out of juvenile reach. My mother hustled me outside, to play in my grandmother's orchard.

'Rifles hurt,' she informed me.

'What is the revolution?' I asked.

'You'll find out,' she promised.

'Soon?'

'Who knows?'

'What are barricades?'

'Something made of bricks and sticks for people to hide behind,' she said.

'From the rifles?'

'So they won't get hurt.'

'Do people get hurt in revolutions?'

'Sometimes,' she sighed.

'Are we going to have one?'

My questions seemed to disturb her. 'Go out and play,' she ordered.

I went into the orchard and began building a barricade so I wouldn't be hurt. Wives, lovers and female friends might argue that it was the first of many.

My brother Peter was now two years old, a marginally more tolerable companion. I could introduce him to such as I knew of the world and its ways, which wasn't much. To remedy this I was sent to school. My mother presented me to the infant mistress, and departed. I listened tolerantly to this teacher for an hour or two before diagnosing proceedings as childish. When her back was turned I collected my school bag, stalked home, and reported in to my mother.

'I've finished with school,' I informed her.

'Finished?' my mother said with dismay.

'So what happens next?' I asked.

'This,' she announced. There was a stinging slap on my rear as she ushered me out the gate; she pointed me unprofitably back to school again. By the day's end I understood that attendance was necessary on a routine basis. What happened next was a dozen years of the same. I never found it possible to pardon anyone concerned.

Seventeen

*H*aving accepted one school as a necessary evil, I learned there was another in wait; the family was on the move again. Somewhere in the centre of the North Island, in the King Country, was a town in need of a shot-firing quarryman. The job involved rupturing rock and levelling hills to keep a limeworks in business and the country's pastures green. It sounded right for my father, especially its obscure situation; it seemed the place for an anonymous start. My father took a quick trip, laid claim to the job, found a dwelling, and reported back with enthusiasm. Overnight we were ready for the journey south. Uncle Johnny's Model T Ford stood steaming at the Glen Eden door; family possessions, mostly crockery and pots and pans, were bundled aboard. My brother and I, then my mother and father, were squeezed in too. Shaking violently, Uncle Johnny's vehicle barely heaved up the first hill we met; there were more than a hundred miles still to travel.

Uncle Johnny was a man with shrill, hiccuping laugh. Younger, he had been a promising boxer. In the worst of the depression he had made pocket money by selling himself as a punch-bag to professional fighters. His ears had been flattened, his nose broken. And he had been crashed to the canvas too many times for the health of his head. He was no longer a promising boxer. He was an itinerant house painter. The times were now kinder to him, with houses everywhere in need of fresh paint, and unpainted new ones beginning to rise. The batterings he had taken in the ring explained his high-pitched laugh. There was no woe in the man even if his wit had been scattered. And he was generous; he was delighted to help his brother make a fresh start. No hundred miles was harder won. His vehicle was given to hysterics, with gusts of blinding fog from the engine and evil emissions from the exhaust. There were punctures and more enigmatic breakdowns.

Half the journey was comprised of us standing on the roadside while Uncle Johnny and helpful fellow motorists meditated on the moody engine. Once it was just that petrol was lacking. Mostly it was water. Mile by mile we laboured into the heart of the North Island, lurching in and out of ruts and potholes, crockery clinking, pots and pans crashing, suitcases bouncing on the roof, a reasonable facsimile of John Steinbeck's beleaguered Joad family in *The Grapes of Wrath*. My father wasn't a rebel of the dimension of Tom Joad, but he could pass at a pinch. (Or so I thought when I read *The Grapes of Wrath*, four or five years later; the westward journey of the Joads was too familiar for comfort.)

Then we were driving into a town called Te Kuiti. The name means 'the narrowing in', which was a summary of my parents' situation. Their lives were imperceptibly contracting as we travelled. Faintly Swiss in character, Te Kuiti sat under high hills, in a grassy valley. Aside from the fiercely carved Maori meeting house at the south end of the main street there was little to distinguish it from any other New Zealand rural town. It was three decades past its frontier beginnings and looked less. Teams of oxen in the knee-deep mud of the main street might have gone. But there were still hitching rails, horse troughs, ramshackle shops with boardwalk frontages, blacksmiths and booze dens in back streets. Grey founding fathers, the pioneers of the place, still walked the streets sturdily on market days. Maori horsemen, the descendants of undefeated rebels, cantered noisily through the town.

In the second half of the nineteenth century Te Kuiti had been home to the Maori King and his followers; whites were unwelcome. Then it was a lonely trading post. The railway arrived, not without hiccups. The first surveyors in the region had been captured and held hostage. An uneasy truce was arranged until money changed hands, outlaws were pardoned, and Maori consent to the railway won. Locomotives stormed smokily through the town and ended the region's isolation. Men arrived with large rolls of banknotes. Tribesmen decided to sell their land rather than dwell on it defiant and destitute. With land sales came speculators, merchants, timber millers, bush fires, pastoral farming and patches of industry. One side of the long main street was dedicated to the railway that ended the district's seclusion. There were lawns and flower beds. It wasn't an ugly town. Nor could it be called fetching. A wandering river, a onetime Maori canoe route to the populous Waikato, gave its centre some individuality. A canoe or two might have given it more. Horses had put them out of fashion.

The last of our journey took us to the shabby southern outskirts of town, close to the limestone quarry which was to employ my father. The dwelling my father had found was something between a shed and a shack. It had two bedrooms, a living room, a water tank and an outdoor privy. The floor creaked and one wall had a sinister lean. The rusty roof didn't look heartening either. There were unkempt fields around, lone willows and skinny cows.

'This?' my mother asked with dismay.

'This,' my father said. 'It hardly costs us a penny.'

My terse mother could believe it. Before harsher words were spoken Uncle Johnny unloaded our belongings and disappeared tactfully in the direction of Auckland. My mother gave the dwelling a second look and sighed. She supposed she had seen worse. We had a home. My father had a job. And I had a school, a mile walk through town. Sometimes I made my way there through thick frost; sometimes through saturating rain. Sunny days allowed me to loiter and look into shop windows, and especially at the blacksmith shoeing horses. There were private hotels and boarding houses with ferny pot plants in their windows and lonely men peering out. There were diversions closer to home. Booms from the quarry told me my father was renewing his acquaintance with explosives. My mother flinched every time she heard a roar. She feared that sooner or later my father would do himself damage. Given his unworldly temperament, it was a reasonable fear. Meanwhile she did the family wash at the riverside, as neighbouring Maori women did. Afterwards she strung the clothes over scrubby vegetation to dry. She was a reminder to her neighbours that poverty wasn't exclusive to brown skins.

There were others with less. In a field nearby was a shed even closer to collapse than our dwelling. Early one evening there was a fire lit outside. My mother worried about robbery, or worse. My father ambled over to see who the newcomer might be. He was some time returning. 'It's all right,' he reported. 'Just an old swaggie.'

'A swaggie?' my mother said.

'Looking for work,' my father said. 'He'll be on his way south in the morning.'

'To where?'

My father shrugged. 'A sheep farm. A timber mill. Who knows?'

My mother was relieved. 'Poor man,' she said finally. 'Doesn't he have a home in the world?'

'He's not complaining.'

My mother asked, 'Does he have everything he needs?' She might have been remembering her Glen Eden girlhood, Arklow Joe's kindness to strangers, itinerant workmen with swags on their backs and blackened billy-cans ready to swing over a fire.

'He's living rough,' my father said.

'What about food?'

'A little wouldn't go amiss,' my father agreed.

My mother produced a couple of hard-boiled eggs, some scraps of cold mutton and a potato or two. I went with my father to deliver this sustenance. We found the swagman smoking a pipe beside his fire. He was old; there was a half century of New Zealand history in his weathered face and leathery hands.

'The wife sent this,' my father said, passing over the food.

'Bless her,' the old man said, distinctly moved.

'It's not much,' my father said apologetically.

'It's all I need,' the old swagman argued.

In the morning he was gone, his campfire cold. Nothing else marked his passage. It was like water closing after I had passed my finger through.

'The last of his line,' my father informed me. 'You won't see many like him any more.'

That was one picture I could keep.

Some summer evenings I walked with my mother. My brother was in bed, and my father listening to the radio. She liked the riverside at dusk with sunset in the sky. Did I know then that my mother had been a furtive writer of verse? Possibly not. But her feeling for place was plain, and for the printed word. Arklow Joe's library had been her legacy too. Her brother had found belief in social justice there; she had discovered literature. My father had reservations. 'What does poetry *do?*' he asked.

'It makes the world worthwhile,' she told him.

So she shared her bounty with me. The stretch of river we walked was shallow, used as ford by trucks and horses. Pale stones glimmered under the fast current; willows and large fern overhung the water. Upstream we might see a Maori woman beating clothes on rocks at the river's edge. Downstream there could be a trout fisherman casting a fly. There was a whitened log, with skeletal branches, riding out into the river. On the evening I recall best my mother and I clambered along this log, bent down and cupped our hands, gathering up and drinking the sweet water which tumbled from forest and gorge and tasted of those places.

I was suddenly stunned by it all: by sunset sky, willow and water, and my mother's grip on my hand. I said to myself, 'This is beautiful.'

I seemed only just to have noticed what the word meant.

I also told myself fervently, 'I must remember this.'

I diligently practised remembering that riverside scene through my seventh, eighth and ninth years. Then I had no need to try. I had found memory. I had begun to see that nothing need die. I had certainly started to fill a small storehouse of private mythology. I may even have been composing my first fiction. The decor has been durable.

Eighteen

We moved into the town. The year was 1938. Our new house, some jerry-builder's apprentice work, was not a large improvement on our last. Finding he had raised the front wall without door or window, he grudgingly banged in an off-centre pane of glass as a concession to human love of light. It looked like a child's drawing of a house, and wasn't much bigger. It was Maori-owned, and there was confusion at first about the identity of our landlord. In the first week no less than three men styling themselves such turned up to claim rent, until finally a fierce, pipe-smoking and elderly woman, with a moko, or chin tattoo, camped on our back step to warn counterfeit proprietors away. She all but frightened us away. When this drama ended the advantages of the dwelling could be seen. It was sunny and quiet, far from my father's noisy quarry, nestled under sheep-grazed hills. It was hardly a hundred yards from the town centre, and a shorter walk to school, mostly along riverside.

Next door our neighours were two spinster sisters and their canary. The young men they might have married were bones in the gullies of Gallipoli or in the soil of the Somme; the town's male population had literally been gutted by World War I, leaving the place with a wealth of spinsters and widows. They ran shops and boarding houses, worked as dressmakers, and taught school. Often they were sweet; sometimes they were bitter. Our greying neighbours were sweet. They belonged to the Salvation Army and dressed in uniform for Sunday services. Sometimes the Salvation Army band played hymns outside their home. The rest of the week their pampered canary called the tune.

At school I had one of the bitter ones. Her name was Miss Graham. She was still fighting World War I. There was a romantic lithograph of the Gallipoli landing beside the blackboard and we were frequently invited to look at it long and hard. As she pursued seven-year-olds vengefully around the classroom, lashing at our bare legs with her cane, she screamed that we would never be worthy of the men who gave their lives at Gallipoli. Later, when I learned that her fiance had been killed there, I found it less difficult to forgive her. Her scars were worse than those she left on us; her anguish, unlike ours, was lifelong.

Yet it was a history lesson of sorts, and my first. I have Miss Graham to thank for my fascination with the infamous Gallipoli campaign in which, so it is said, New Zealanders for the first time found a powerful sense of their own identity. In that respect I was her most receptive pupil. With lingering memory of her cane on my calves, I would twice in later life hike over that useless and unlovely limb of Turkey where my fellow countrymen fell victim less to shot and shell than to the posturing of the elegantly lunatic louts of Britain's high command. Twice in my life, as my tears dried, I would look across the Aegean to Troy and wonder what Homer might have made of my distant tribesmen intruding on his territory; how *he* might have chronicled that blind, brutal and inglorious campaign. Out of such wonder I would try to persuade Gallipoli to give up its New Zealand dead — first in a play called *Once on Chunuk Bair*, then in *Voices of Gallipoli*, an anthology of tales told by weary warriors who seemed, at the end of their lives, to need a storyteller's ear. Miss Graham could have done with one too.

On the other side our neighbours were Maori, the Waikai family. Bill Waikai was the town taxi driver. He was a large, loud and laughing man. The Waikai backyard was filled with cars in disrepair and empty beer bottles, evidence of prosperity. My parents were never to own a car, and beer was for birthdays and Christmas. We were among the least affluent families in a neighbourhood of poor whites and moneyed Maori. If this does not accord with the authorised picture of New Zealand race relations, so much the worse for the authors of the picture. By our modest measure families like the Waikais were wildly wealthy; they were still living off the largesse that came with land sales early in the century. They were generous to relatives, friends, and neighbours. Amiable Bill didn't charge for a ride to the railway station or the town hospital if he saw fit, especially in emergencies. They often judged us as deserving. Bill sometimes dropped in with wild pork from a hunting trip. He also liked talking racehorses with my father; sometimes they shared a small bet.

More of my future was in the making. The Waikais took us to feasts or funerals at the carved Maori meeting house which rose theatrically at the south end of town. It had been sculpted, toward the end of the nineteenth century, at the behest of Te Kooti, the most murderous of Maori rebels. At first a devout Christian, Te Kooti spurned the enfeebling New Testament and embraced the Jehovah of Abraham, Isaac and Jacob; he made the books of Exodus, Joshua and Deuteronomy a plan of campaign against white colonists and their brown collaborators. (*Cursed be the fruit of thy body, and the fruit of thy land, and the flocks of thy sheep. Thy carcass shall be meat unto all the fowls of the air, and unto beasts of the earth.*)

After massacres and magical escapes, this South Sea Israelite found sanctuary with the tribesmen of Te Kuiti, with whom he was left to fester until a colonial pardon came. Here, walking the same ground, I heard tales of Te Kooti by the time I was ten. We played Te Kooti wars — a version of hide and seek with wooden rifles — in the limestone caves behind the town. Hemi Wi, playing rebel, would snipe me from behind a rock. I, playing colonist, would fall with a powerful groan. Then it was his turn to tumble to my shot. Four decades later, Te Kooti would return to haunt me less playfully, to ride lethally and enigmatically through a narrative called *Season of the Jew*. In his story corpses never rose to fight again. Meanwhile I gazed without comprehension at the large and mysterious meeting house and angry ancestral figures his carvers had bestowed upon the tribesmen of Te Kuiti, in gratitude for sanctuary given. With a ripple of wonder I also looked at living figures about me, at white faces and brown. I had a sense of much unspoken; of silences in the land.

The world sometimes wasn't.

Nineteen

We were to be a decade in Te Kuiti, from my sixth year to my sixteenth. Through those years there were sorties back to Auckland, to stay with Grandmother Kearon and visit other relatives. At Grandmother Kearon's my brother and I fell greedily on Arklow Joe's library: our most damaging boyhood fight was to be over a volume of Byron's verse. Otherwise we fed ourselves undiscriminatingly in this wild garden of words. I had the notion of making my favourite books my own by copying them out in juvenile scribble. The exercise was useful. I discovered that such as Rider Haggard and Edgar Rice Burroughs — and sometimes, so help me, Jack London — could be improved on.

My Shadbolt grandparents' house at Green Bay was loud and bewildering. I seemed to have something like a score of burly uncles, though they numbered only five. Perhaps I was counting the equally muscular friends they brought home to rowdy Sunday dinners. Food was roast beef and Yorkshire pudding in a huge pile. Family feuds were many, and mostly settled with boxing gloves on the back lawn. Sometimes, more amicably, an oval ball surfaced and a rugby scrum went down for the finer points of the game to be considered. Unattended grandchildren were liable to be trodden underfoot. Above the commotion my grandfather might be booming on about his latest ordeal with the law. Little was left unsaid in the Shadbolt household.

That was drastically different from Grandmother Kearon's Welsh family, the Morris clan, or such as had survived combat in France and contagion post-war. They were little, apologetic people who lived in the inner city. Grandmother Kearon made visits to show off her grandsons. These were occasions of agonising inertia. Once my brother and I had been admired, we were left to sit in comfortless chairs, in gloomy parlours, and look at our feet. Windows were sunless and curtained with lace. Undernourished pot plants peered out from corners. There were purely decorative pianos which served as a shelf on which to stand family photographs. There was never ice cream on hand, though there was always tea and lumpy fruit cake. By comparison with the boisterous Shadbolt tribe the Morris family was monumentally lacklustre. Yet I now see they had much in common. Behind both families was a history of lost chances, lost land, and dimmed hope. Their forebears had travelled twelve thousand miles — the Shadbolts in shackles, the Morrises in steerage — to begin again in a land which promised affluence and freedom. They were also-rans, the residue of the nineteenth century's pioneer heroics. The unhumbled Shadbolts made enough din not to notice. The self-effacing Morrises went to church.

The two families had something else in common. They had secrets. My grandmother's cousin Bess Morris, a once popular and lively girl, married into a family called the Gunns. Now widowed, she lived where she had always lived, with two sons in the working class, inner-city suburb of Newton. When Grandmother Kearon took us visiting the first call was always on Bess Gunn. Hers was an enigmatic place. I couldn't read between the lines. On the other hand, some of the lines were alarming. One day, as we were leaving, I heard my grandmother say cheerfully to Bess, 'Now don't you go giving anyone poison again.'

Poison? Dear God. Even if it was Aunt Bess's custom to administer arsenic to all and sundry, it seemed a remarkably tactless thing to say in front of children. But Bess, to the best of my recollection, just laughed oddly. Was I privy to a bizarre family joke? Had Bess once inadvertently dispatched the family cat with a plate of rat killer?

There was another clue to aberrance in the atmosphere: Bess's two sons were a puzzling contrast. The oldest, Harold, was a tearaway on a motor cycle, a daredevil gang leader always in the company of other young men on fast wheels. The young son, sweet-natured Roy, took to his bed at the age of sixteen, for no apparent reason, and never got up again; he made dolls. Indeed he made a tidy business out of it. If I ever asked dreamy Roy why he remained in bed making dolls, I don't recall his answer. No one else seemed to think Roy remarkable.

It was years before I winkled the tale out of my grandmother.

When Bess married into the Gunn family, she acquired not only her short-lived husband Alex, but also a brother-in-law named Dennis Gunn. Dennis was a small time hoodlum, the despair of his family. In the year 1920, with pickings poor, he acquired a pistol and bailed up the Ponsonby postmaster after hours. The postmaster must have refused to hand over his cash-boxes. Anyway Dennis Gunn shot the man. His haul amounted to just under £68. He left his fingerprints on the cash-boxes, and on the pistol he threw into a nearby gully. That was one mistake. His other was having evaded military service in World War I, which meant his fingerprints were on police file. A score of suspects was reduced to one; Dennis Gunn was arrested and tried. For the first time in New Zealand history a man was sentenced to hang on the strength of fingerprint evidence alone. It was Dennis Gunn's one and unenviable distinction.

His brother Alex and sister-in-law Bess had perjured themselves to give Dennis an alibi. A brother was a brother, after all. At the last minute they tried to forestall due process with a more desperate remedy. On the eve of Dennis's execution Bess attempted to slip Dennis a phial of poison, perhaps cyanide. The handover was clumsily managed; the phial fell to the floor and was recovered by warders. Alex and Bess were rushed from the prison, and Dennis died according to the law's schedule at Mount Eden Prison next morning.

Dennis Gunn left no children. It was left to Bess's boys to live in the shadow of their executed uncle and their mother's bold attempt to do the hangman out of a job. At school they were bullied and beaten. Harold reacted by becoming the hot-shot of the neighbourhood. No one was going to make him suffer. He was to, however. A motor-cycle accident at high speed all but took his life and left his legs of little use. Roy, as reported, just took to bed and made dolls. Perhaps his response was the wiser. Neither of them was to walk far into adult life. Society, with some justification, had broken Dennis Gunn's neck. Did it have to cripple his kin too?

I last saw them at Aunt Bess's funeral. Bess had been a funeral specialist for years. No matter how remote her connection with grieving relatives, Bess would arrive an hour early to lend condolences and view the face in the coffin. She was lost in admiration of the corpses. They were all beautiful and peaceful; there was never a dud. Her own funeral was on the modest side, with a sprinkling of friends and neighbours and relatives. She wanted a grave with a good view, and this came to pass. Well placed for the Day of Judgement, she had a panorama of hundreds of headstones in the middle distance with all Auckland beyond, capped by the dramatic volcanic cone of Rangitoto. There would have been one disappointment. Fine as the real estate was, no stone was ever raised to mark her residence.

Harold was there in a wheelchair, a wasted man in dark and baggy suit which might have been in fashion forty years earlier. Feeble Roy rose from his bed for the occasion, also rather clumsily clad, and managed to make it to the graveside limping slowly on two sticks; he teetered a little, and for a time seemed likely to topple into the grave. Did he still make dolls? It was hardly the time to ask.

There is a parable about capital punishment here.

Benjamin Shadbolt, ex-convict and
squire of Duvauchelle, *c*1875.
Canterbury Museum

Elizabeth Shadbolt, née
Perham, Benjamin's loyal
widow, *c*1890.
Canterbury Museum

Amelia Shadbolt, devoted daughter of Benjamin and lifelong spinster. Also foster parent and perhaps actual mother of Frank.
Canterbury Museum

Ernest Shadbolt, boxer, farmer, litigant, and Ada Shaw on their wedding day, 1898.

Ada Shadbolt, patient pioneer, wife
of Ernest, and mother of ten.

Ernest and Ada Shadbolt and most
of their children on one of their
ill-starred farms, c1920.
Renee (Sis) is tall to the rear.

Violet Kearon, secretary, c1928 before marriage to Frank Shadbolt.

Quarryman Frank Shadbolt and Violet Kearon on their wedding day, 1929.

Frank and Violet Shadbolt in middle age, c1960.

Renee (Sis) Shadbolt, nurse,
Spanish war heroine, *c*1953.

Soldier, boxer and incendiarist Jack
Shadbolt (right), his first wife, and
brother Arthur, 1953.

Louisa Morris, unmarried, *c*1904.

Louisa Morris's Welsh pioneer parents, *c*1900.

'Arklow Joe', seafarer, socialist, lover of literature, father of Young Joe and Violet, c1910.

Young Joe Kearon, communist, soldier, c1940.

'Arklow Joe' Kearon and Louisa Morris on their wedding day, 1905.

Maurice Shadbolt, apprentice writer, Red Square, Moscow, 1957.

Maurice Shadbolt, candidate ancestor, with first child, Sean, 1962.

Twenty

Our Te Kuiti dwelling held no unhappy secrets. Aunt Sis, back from Spain, brought the civil war into our living room. There was nothing so dramatic in our vicinity. Karl Marx's class struggle was imperceptible. Te Kuiti was typically and rurally conservative, though there were Party members and sympathisers among passing itinerants, schoolteachers, railwaymen, and timbermen working in sawdust-scented clearings beyond the town. They found my parents hospitable. The Party-backed Left Book Club, modelled on Victor Gollancz's English version, had a base in our household. Anything up to twenty people might take over our kitchen and living room for discussion nights and lectures. A wounded member of the International Brigade came to stay, and warned of fascism on a global march. Such as Hitler, Mussolini and Franco had to be halted before the world was aflame. My father was impressed. Much to my mother's relief, he had renounced his calling as a quarry shot-firer to work less perilously as a post and telegraph linesman. That job took him over the hills from Te Kuiti, into quiet wilderness, the world of lonely townships and lonelier farmers.

He used his radio to eavesdrop on the larger world. Through static he heard news of Joseph Stalin's accommodation with Hitler. War followed soon after. It was much as the man from the International Brigade had predicted, with the difference that the Soviet Union was mysteriously trafficking with fascism. My baffled father, despite his domestic responsibilities, his wife and two children, thought to end his mixed feelings by volunteering for the army. Before he could present himself at a recruiting office, however, he was tripped by the Party line. The war, it seemed, had to be opposed. It was an imperialist conflict. Party men had no role in the affair. On the contrary, for the sake of the Soviet Union, they had to fight it to their last breath.

'And let Hitler win?' my father asked in disbelief.

It made no sense. Finally and sorrowfully he allowed that there might be wiser heads than his thinking on the matter. Contrary to appearances, the Party might know best. That produced a problem. As government employees he and his workmates were asked to help win the war by contributing to a patriotic fund. My father, in difficulty, refused to contribute. 'What's up?' he was asked.

'I can't,' he said with no conviction.

'Why not, Frank?'

'I'm against the war.'

He was also out of work. Perhaps he was judged a security risk, unfit to keep the country's lines of communication open. Learning that his old job at the quarry was vacant again, he returned to loosening up limestone landscape with gelignite. It was not a happy year or two; they were soon unhappier still. In the patriotic fervour of the time dissidents and pacifists were hounded. Our household was identifiable as a centre of sedition. My father had been seen saving a couple of visiting Christian pacifists who preached against the war in the main street. A public spirited mob, after kicking and punching the pair about, wanted to throw them in the river. My father managed to get the bruised men clear and persuade them out of town. Menace lapped in our direction, but never arrived. By way of precaution, my father kept a couple of sticks of gelignite handy on a high shelf. What did he have in mind? Exploding it in the path of an advancing lynch mob? Blowing us up, in the manner of an antipodean Masada, before rape and pillage began? I never knew and suspect he didn't either. Sometimes packages of Party leaflets arrived from Auckland. Though he was finding it difficult to believe a word these leaflets said, my father pushed them into town letterboxes. He sometimes took me with him on one of his dusk walks. I would leaflet one side of a street, and he the other. He wasn't happy with what he was doing, or with himself. He wanted the war won, and Hitler beaten. So why?

'It's not for me to make sense of the world,' he told my mother, or no one in particular.

He had lost a safe job, and returned to a risky one, for the sake of a policy he thought absurd. He didn't use words like loyalty or duty, though they might have explained. Perhaps he was asking the world to make sense of him. It soon had something to say.

To impress me with the quarryman's craft he took me to his place of work for the first time; my mother made up a small parcel of sandwiches for my lunch. The day promised to have more bangs than a cowboy movie. I was not disappointed. After holes were drilled my father planted charges along a cliff face, lit fuses, and walked calmly to cover. I blocked my ears like the men around me. There was detonation after detonation. Small rocks spat skyward and large boulders grumbled, crashed and split. This was repeated several times. There was soon no novelty. Near lunchtime, having eaten my sandwiches, I was bored and looking elsewhere for entertainment. I was around a corner, investigating frogs in a creek, when my father found himself in difficulty with a premature charge. Half a hillside was in murderous motion; there was the thunder of rolling rock. As din diminished, and dust rose, I heard men's voices.

'Christ,' one was saying. 'Frank's under that.'

As I began running, another called, 'Get his kid out of it.'

I was grabbed and hauled off in another direction, making much protest.

There was more yelling, and more, and men running. I demanded my father.

'He'll be all right, son,' someone said. 'We'll get him out.'

The voice did not have conviction. Nor did others coming and going. No one was willing to tell me my father was dead.

Finally there was a voice with authority, perhaps a foreman.

'It looks like Frank might be all right,' he said, taking my hand. 'He's asking if you're all right too.'

Dug out of the debris, and hoisted into the cab of a truck, my father was raced off to hospital. He had been dumped and bruised when he lost his footing in the avalanche. His workmates said he had no right to be alive. A ton or two of boulder had rolled over his leg without breaking bone; another had scraped away much of his forehead. Blood teemed down his face and dripped from his clothes. Nevertheless he was doing his best to smile.

I was sped home to tell my mother of my luckless day at work with Dad. Bill Waikai drove us both to the hospital. My father was already in bed and bandaged.

'That's it,' my mother said. 'No more gelignite.'

'No,' my father agreed.

After a month or two invalid, limping on a stick, he took a job as a railway navvy, shovelling away slips of earth on the main trunk line. There was less money in the household. But my mother knew my father likely to be alive at day's end.

I had my own difficulties. Some schoolmates, once friendly, turned sour. They had heard of my anti-war father. A show of virtue seemed in order. This meant beating me up. Sometimes I found myself fighting solo against six or more assailants. To be fair, they seldom launched themselves at me more than one at a time; they took turns. 'Your father's a fifth columnist,' they announced as they struck at me with fists and feet. 'Your father's a traitor.' Not a Shadbolt for nothing, I sometimes got a respectable punch in. More often I got home muddy with a black eye or blood nose.

'What is it?' my mother asked. 'What's going on?'

I decided not to say. My parents had enough problems.

For survival, I developed a so far unsuspected resource. It was storytelling. Before an attack was pressed I would fall quiet.

'There's something you don't know,' I would announce.

'Like what?' a prospective belligerent would ask.

'I can't tell you,' I said, but course did.

At first the stories were rather desperate improvisations, making free with town gossip and rumour; they also credited our teachers with intense sexual lives.

In short, then, I would halt proceedings with a tale. (I hadn't then heard of Scheherazade and her heroic 1001 nights.) Later, when the occasion for them had gone, the stories became ever more elaborate, and largely cliff-hanging in character, sometimes shamelessly borrowed from such as Rider Haggard. They suited rainy days best, under dripping trees. I timed climaxes to the return of the sun.

My parents' problems grew no fewer. There was a new visitor to the house, an attractive young woman named Doris. Lean, nervy, long-haired and chain-smoking, she was a teacher in a nearby country township and a Party member. She could quote Marx and Lenin with impressive efficiency. At Left Book Club meetings Doris saw it as her duty to bring my father back into line. She had problems with other members too, as well she might. Among them were a tattooed Norwegian ex-seaman and anarchist, a Trotzkyite Maori, a Fabian beekeeper, and a one-legged Jewish second hand dealer and Social

Crediter. Doris had much to say at these meetings; my father said less than might have been expected. The explanation came in due course. One meeting ended badly. My mother came upon my father kissing militant Doris goodnight at our gate. She also heard him utter the word darling. Darling?

Upheaval was instant, our household in turmoil. Darling must soon have fled the scene of the kiss. My brother and I, in our pyjamas, were roused by the commotion. We stood barefoot and bewildered on the cold kitchen floor. We wept as adult voices grew louder. Our father was pleading a misunderstanding. Our mother wasn't believing a word. I judged matters to be serious. For my father was saying, 'You aren't taking my boys away?'

'To Auckland,' she announced. 'Tomorrow.'

She gripped my brother with one hand, me with her other.

More may have been said before I took a part in proceedings. I saw a way of keeping them together; I could refuse to leave. I detached myself from my mother, and took two or three slow paces toward my father. Then I grabbed his hand.

'I'm not going,' I said. 'I'm staying with him.'

Declaring for Dad was a dangerous strategy. He was helpless in the kitchen, incapable of frying an egg without flame roaring to the roof. I would starve. I was sick with fright. I saw no way, however, of uncoupling my hand from his.

My father wasn't slow to see his advantage. 'You see?' he said. 'You see what you're doing to us?'

'Me?' my mother said. 'Me?'

'You,' my father said with new confidence.

I was a weapon in an adult war.

'He doesn't understand what it's all about,' my mother claimed.

This was true. I merely saw unhappiness in the making.

'A kiss,' my father said. 'What's a goodnight kiss between friends?'

'You called her darling too,' my mother pointed out.

My brother, also understanding that something grave was up, began to wail immoderately. That ended it. Soon neighbours would be roused.

My brother and I were bundled back to bed. Unhappiness rumbled on elsewhere in the house for the rest of the night.

Next day we were on the train to Auckland. My threat to live with my father seemed to have weakened; or wasn't taken seriously.

It failed to survive daylight.

On the other hand, I am not sure my mother forgave me.

Without my father, we found shelter in Grandmother Kearon's Glen Eden house again. My mother took a job in a factory producing boots for fighting men. I was back at Glen Eden school; my brother was there for the first time. Uncle Joe, conscripted for the army without protest, was in khaki and seen only on weekend leave. Germany's invasion of the Soviet Union had ended Joe's dilemma. He had also been unhappy with the bizarre Party notion that Hitler should be left unbeaten for the good of the world's working class. Like my father, he was still sentimentally of the far left. But they appear to have lost their Party cards between depression and war.

Months passed. My anguished father communicated frequently. It is reasonable to suppose that among his many promises was a pledge to swear off escorting doctrinaire females to the front gate. He had returned to working as a post and telegraph linesman, his past political beliefs irrelevant with the Soviet Union in the war. The war now had no more vehement civilian supporter. He wanted us back. He had found a new and attractive riverside house. Then came a telegram. Our disaster-prone parent had fallen from a pole he was wiring. He was in hospital with broken ribs, a punctured lung, and concussion.

My mother may have put in another day stitching boots, and my brother and I a day or two more at our new school, but there is reason to think not. We were on a train south.

Much changed for the better. First there was our new home. For once my father had chosen well. It sat a dozen yards from the riverside and its fringing trees. It was gripped by a fruitful grape vine. It was sunny. It was the first passably conventional house my brother and I had inhabited. Walls didn't lean; floors didn't shake; windows were where they should be. Our parents also grew more commonplace in character. There were no Left Book Club meetings, no tattooed Norwegian seamen, Trotskyite Maoris, Fabian beekeepers or one-legged Social Crediters. Above all there were no chain-smoking country schoolteachers. The virtue of our new location, however, lay in the fact that there was no shouting; our parents seemed to be much as other parents again, perhaps even in love. But we also knew larger things to be afoot. More and more relatives were in khaki, either at war or soon to be. Uncle Joe, the most loved, came to stay for the last of his final leave in the first week of December 1941. He was expecting to be sent to North Africa, where the New Zealand Division was defending the Suez Canal. December 8 was his final day of leave. He was packed and ready; I went to his room to farewell him. At that moment my father switched on the radio to catch a news bulletin. A commentator was reeling off an account of a surprise Japanese air attack, a day earlier, on a place called Pearl Harbour. United States vessels were sinking; loss of life had been large. I was slow seeing the significance of this. My father and Joe looked at each other quizzically.

'It's all on now,' my father concluded.

'I won't see the desert,' Joe judged.

He never did. A week or two later he was sailing into the tropical Pacific. At school we drilled for Japanese air raids to come. My mother joined the St. John's ambulance, learning to bandage casualties. My father was in the Home Guard, drilling with a broomstick, later with a rifle, while limping veterans of the Gallipoli campaign bellowed commands. New Zealand defence chiefs obsessively believed that the Japanese would roar ashore on the stormy western side of the North Island rather than on the hospitable east; that Hirohito's hellish battalions would lift out of house-high surf and scale sheer cliffs. Te Kuiti's defence works were based on that baffling assumption. Large logs were perched on precipitous corners of roads out to the coast. The idea was that these would be rolled down upon the invaders. Contingency planning also provided for the Te Kuiti airfield, useful for Tiger Moths at best, to be defended bitterly, lest it be commandeered as a base for Nippon's bombers. Gorse and long grass were to be fired should retreat prove necessary. In anticipation of further disaster men were trained for protracted guerrilla warfare. On a weekend exercise two platoons were sent out to familiarise themselves with the region's forest. It took most of a week to find them again. This suggested that the forest might war with the Japanese more efficiently than Te Kuiti's fighting force. In another exercise, which took the form of a mock battle, a number of jaded men were seen heading off to the local cemetery soon after blank bullets had been discharged. Asked for an explanation, they explained they were dead.

My brother and I, not to be left out, joined the Boy Scouts. This soon seemed ridiculous. Japan wasn't to be rolled back with reef knots. I organised an alternative defence force, styled it the Home Guard Assistance Corps, and appointed myself Major General. Modesty prevented me taking more senior command. Friends were given lesser rank, mostly of lieutenant. Those especially favoured were permitted to be captains and colonels. Rank was indicated by our armbands. Privates were few and probationary. Nurses were recruited too, if not in number. We wrote to the Prime Minister asking for two dozen .303 rifles, Bren guns, and a tank or two. The Prime Minister failed to acknowledge our patriotic plea. And the Home Guard Assistance Corps was not invited to assist in defence of the realm.

In a frustrated attempt to prove our martial worth, armed only with catapults and acorns, we made a kamikaze attack on a platoon of genuine Home Guardsmen dug in on the riverbank in wait for inscrutable orientals to pour down upon Te Kuiti. There were yelps on the few occasions our missiles found a target. Unfriendly adults then put our column to flight. We then fell to feuding among ourselves, digressing only to flush red-faced lovers from the long grass on the riverside. In disgust, I resigned my command and discharged my force from further duty.

This may have been premature. Te Kuiti's morning of panic followed soon after. A coastal farmer parted his curtains and reeled back from the spectacle beyond his window. In the dawn light there were warships large and small, even the least of them mighty, and aircraft carriers too. Just one conclusion was possible. The farmer raced to his telephone and rang the Te Kuiti exchange. 'The Japanese are here,' he announced. Then he fetched his shotgun from the wall to hold off Asia's hordes.

The news was soon out in the street. The Home Guard was alerted. People began packing for flight. It was Te Kuiti's bad luck, it seemed, to be the first New Zealand community in Japan's invasion path. Those who thought the town had no future had their fears confirmed.

Then the town policeman was pedalling his bicycle through the town and advising shopkeepers to keep their doors open and telling other civilians not to flee. He had a message from Wellington assuring him that the farmer had not seen what he thought he had seen. He wasn't allowed to say what the farmer *had* seen. That was secret.

Soon, however, more was clear. Wartime censorship meant there was no way of lowly Te Kuiti knowing that an American fleet was quietly passing up the coast to engage Japan in the Coral Sea. The town Home Guard would now never be needed. Out on the coast the lonely farmer watched the last vessel sink below the horizon. Not to be a hero after all, he emptied both barrels of his shotgun in salute. Then, with a sigh, he hung his weapon on the wall again.

Twenty-one

*S*ometime in the last decade, at a literary function, an elderly woman swooped on me. Her eyes were shiny with emotion, her face all grievance.

'You should be ashamed,' she said.

Of what? Her face wasn't familiar. Guilt settled on me all the same. What had I done?

'I've followed your life with interest,' she explained. 'I've bought all your books. The least you could have done was to write and thank me. Even a short note would have been sufficient. It's as if I never existed.'

I was even more unnerved.

'I'm sorry,' I began.

'So you should be,' she said.

'But I don't seem to know you,' I went on.

'Who wheeled you in a push chair when you were small? Who gave you your first books to read? Who did you tell your first stories to? Who encouraged you to write? Who dried your tears when girls broke your heart?'

People about were beginning to stare.

'You?' I asked feebly.

'Don't tell me you can't remember Isobel Gordon. You used to call me Auntie when you walked hand in hand with me. Don't tell me you've forgotten.'

I struggled. Isobel Gordon? *Auntie* Isobel? For the life of me, literally for the life of me, no bell rang.

She went on. As she emptied her cache of recollection the detail began drowning me. It had a perilously authentic colour. Skilful transitions and fluent asides argued a lovingly polished tale. Relatives, friends and mere acquaintances must have heard it often. They must have been appalled by my heartless neglect of Auntie

Isobel Gordon, my nurse and mentor. But there was something majestically amiss in her account of my childhood and adolescence. At no point had we lived within a hundred miles of each other. I felt obliged to point this out, listing times and places where her story didn't square with such as I knew of my life. The information didn't slow her long. 'You're in a muddle,' she announced briskly.

'Memory is difficult,' I had to agree.

'Mine is most clear,' she insisted. 'You were a lovely little boy with a marvellous imagination. You just had to write. All you needed was love and encouragement.'

'You have to be talking about someone else,' I protested.

'Who?' she said, more and more aggrieved.

'Another Shadbolt,' I proposed meekly.

'It's an uncommon name,' she pointed out. 'Have you heard of another author called Shadbolt?'

'No,' I had to admit.

'Are you trying to tell me I'm mistaken?' she challenged.

At that point I wasn't up to telling her anything. Since she refused to fall apart I began to. Did I have an existence about which I had not been informed? A life in which I walked hand in hand with Auntie Isobel Gordon and told her stories? It seemed more credible by the minute. Eavesdroppers on our conversation were fascinated, and had reason to be.

The encounter ended badly.

'I admire you as a novelist,' she said. 'Your ingratitude makes it impossible for me to admire you as a human being.'

'What can I say?' I protested.

There was nothing I could.

'Just one letter,' she said. 'Just one note of thanks, to say you remember me. It would have made all the difference to me. *All* the difference.'

Her distress growing, tears apparent, she sailed off through the crowd and into the night; she had made her point. Equilibrium lost, I likewise left the function early. Should I have taken guilt aboard and apologised for my doppelganger's callous behaviour? I could have played along tolerantly with her fiction. I have with worse.

So whose story am I in?

And who were those girls who broke my heart ?

Our rented houses had grown larger. Suddenly we owned one. On high ground, among fruit trees, it had a splendid view across the Te Kuiti valley; there was pasture around, grazed by cows we could call our own. The bulky and reddish one, which kicked like a horse when I milked her, was named Bluey. Her gentler and more loveable companion was near blind and called Helen Keller.

As an authority on the Soviet Union, our gallant new ally, my father now had surprising status in the town; he played poker in the Cosmopolitan Club with local businessmen.

'What do you think about Stalingrad, Frank?' they asked.

'The Russians will hold,' my father predicted with confidence.

The Russians obliged. He soon had a reputation as a prophet too. On the other hand, the cards still didn't fall his way.

Encouraged by our new neighbour, Mabel Wilson, my mother sometimes wrote letters to *The King Country Chronicle* on the compatibility of Soviet socialism and the Christian ethic. People stopped her in the street to say they found her letters enlightening.

The house had been found for us by the Wilson family. Mabel was an intimidating left-winger active in the Labour Party, the Rationalist Association, the Left Book Club, and the Society for Closer Relations with the U.S.S.R. (In later years she would add racial equality and homosexual law reform to that list.) She had taken a compassionate interest in my parents. A short, brisk and busty woman, with a flash of gold in her teeth, reading glasses on an elegantly embroidered ribbon round her neck, Mabel was an emancipated woman in early suffragette mould. A schoolteacher, a lover of literature and music, she was married to a tolerant post office employee named Norman. Norman Wilson seemed not to mind, or to notice, that his wife often took aboard a lover with a cause. Quiet Norman had been a war hero. The Victoria Cross aside, he must have won all the decorations worth winning on the Western Front. He never talked of it, or of the friends he had left buried in Ypres or on the Somme; his medals were interred in a shoe box at the foot of his wardrobe. He hadn't yet decided what to do with them; he never attended Anzac Day memorial parades. He was also a part-time bookmaker. From my father's point of view the Wilsons were perfect neighbours. He could talk politics with Mabel, horses with Norman. My brother and I had new friends too. The Wilsons had three girls, Meredith, Florence and Jennifer. Mabel was making it her business to see that they were as emancipated as their mother. She hoped for all three to be doctors; Meredith was already away at medical school. Mrs Wilson took a generous interest in my education too.

'What are you reading?' she asked me.

I told her I found *For Whom the Bell Tolls* a good read. Also *Of Mice and Men*, though the death of Lennie was sad.

'Don't you think Hemingway a little advanced?'

'*Of Mice and Men* is by Steinbeck,' I pointed out.

'Just the same,' she said.

She sent me back to Dickens and *David Copperfield*, to Mark Twain and *Huckleberry Finn*. 'You can't run before you walk,' she informed me. I was fourteen before she thought me enlightened enough to take on Olive Schreiner's *Story of a South African Farm*.

For a time she was more than a neighbour and family friend; she was also my teacher. In that year there was an election. Classmate Billy Prince lifted some school chalk and we walked through Te Kuiti writing *Vote Labour* perishably on telegraph poles and fences. A National Party official cornered us, demanded our names, and reported us to school; he requested stern measures. Our beefy school headmaster Mr Howes did his best to oblige; he wasn't known as Bully Howes in his profession for nothing. There was a short inquisition.

'And you chalked *Vote Labour* through the town?' he said.

'Yes,' we agreed.

'Nothing else?'

Billy looked at me. I looked at Billy. We both looked at the floor.

It was one way of admitting we hadn't chalked *Vote National*. We had the sense that things might have gone easier if we said we had; that he was inviting us to lie. With confessions won, however, Mr Howes unfolded his thick leather strap. 'Hold out your hands,' he ordered us in turn. Then the leather began crashing. Billy screamed. I also did my best not to. Mr Howes judged six blows each sufficient. Nursing our numb hands, with tears spurting, we made our way back to our classroom. Mrs Wilson, who detested corporal punishment, and Bully Howes even more, made no effort to shield her contempt for proceedings in the headmaster's office. She steered Billy gently toward his desk. As I resumed mine in as much disarray, she whispered in my ear, 'Consider yourself a martyr to the cause.'

It didn't take the pain away. I didn't have the makings of a martyr. My spineless second thoughts said that an occasional *Vote National* mightn't have hurt us.

As for Bully Howes, I met him diminished and grey-haired in an Auckland bus queue more than a decade later. He polished his glasses and, altogether out of character, peered at me nervously.

'It's young Shadbolt, isn't it?' he asked.

It was, I agreed.

'Haven't I read a short story by you somewhere?' he asked.

'Possibly,' I said.

'I suppose you're writing others.'

I supposed I was, I allowed.

'Many?' he asked.

A number, I admitted.

There was a long pause.

'I imagine,' he said finally, 'you might, one of these days, write about that strapping I gave you.'

Nothing was less on my mind. It was, however, on his. It may even have lost him some sleep.

'I had to, you know,' he informed me.

I said I supposed he did.

'So be fair,' he asked.

I hope I have been.

The town remained a child of the railway that fathered it. There was never a day without the noise of shunting engines, never a night without steam rising from the brightly-lit railway yards. There was always the lingering reverberation of freight and passenger trains hurtling out of the dark island and into the dark again. Some times of day were more important than others. The Auckland-Wellington express passed through at 7.15 p.m., the Auckland-Wellington limited at 11 p.m.; the Wellington-Auckland express at 3 a.m., the Wellington-Auckland limited at 7 a.m. It was a town of train-watchers. On Friday and Saturday nights, before the movies (the State mostly with mediocre Hollywood musicals, the Empress with grainy westerns) townsfolk watched the Wellington-bound express pause for fifteen minutes at the railway platform and passengers rush the refreshment room for sustenance — meat pies and fruit cake and tea in thick china mugs. The spectacle, though, was city folk. It was the time of day when Te Kuiti viewed the outside world, if only as faces at passing windows. After the movies they went to watch the limited pass. No night at the movies was complete without watching

134

the trains before and after. Those journeying faces, peering into misty Te Kuiti as the trains pulled away, had a mystery which local faces never had.

Even in peace Te Kuiti wasn't colourful; in war it was still less festive. The winter show was a lone, lively and week-long oasis in a dour season. It allowed farm wives to show off their cakes and preserves, their husbands their livestock, children their schoolwork, and farmers and townspeople to mix. More exotically, there were sideshows and showfolk. Their outlandishly bright trucks, tents and caravans spoke of a more spirited world. There was, for example, a spellbinding magician called Ranee. *The Mistress of Mystery,* said the legend above her tent. She was a lean and beautiful Indian woman, with a provocative smile, in filmy sari. Her turbaned husband — or might he have been brother or lover? — served as her barker. He promised feats of a breathtaking kind within Ranee's tent; he claimed that Ranee, in her time, had bewitched presidents, prime ministers and monarchs. It was now our privilege, for a mere shilling (sixpence for children), to let Ranee perplex us. A sample of Ranee's prowess was offered. A volunteer came forward from the crowd; Ranee then made an egg disappear and reappear in and around the volunteer's anatomy. When laughter ebbed, the volunteer was rewarded with admission to the show.

The first time I paid. Silky-voiced Ranee, as promised, did extraordinary things with doves, rabbits, silver rings, billiard balls, coins, razor blades and playing cards; nothing in her supple hands was solid for long. Reality could be revised, and the rules of the human world suspended, with an incantation or wave of wand.

I fell in love with Ranee in fewer than five minutes. I couldn't not. So long as the winter show lasted, I was a fervent volunteer for her pre-performance show; I laid more eggs than our fowls in a month. It was not just for the sake of the free show to follow (Ranee was soon using me as an audience volunteer within too). I was trying to make myself indispensable; I wanted to run away with Ranee in a coloured caravan. What we were to do about her loud-mouthed husband I hadn't yet determined. He soon began to object to her frequent use of me inside and outside her tent.

'They will think him a paid accomplice,' he protested.

'Him?' she said, and laughed.

'There are other boys,' he pointed out.

'But this one is best,' Ranee said.

Her smile was even more auspicious. Just when I thought we were near an adulterous understanding the winter show ended. Between dusk and dawn Ranee's caravan disappeared. Scraps of paper and a faint confetti of popcorn drifted over the waste ground where it had been parked. Te Kuiti was a morose country town again. If my heart didn't break, there must at least have been a hairline fracture. Perhaps her husband had divined my intention and raced her to safety. Perhaps she was a faithless flirt after all. Yet as the opening day of the next show neared, I sometimes found myself breathless. Familiar showfolk began moving into town. Ranee never arrived. Was she off winning the hearts of prime ministers, presidents and monarchs again?

I set about making myself a magician.

Twenty-two

War was still an earnest affair. Convoys of large American trucks drummed along the main street. Sometimes they parked for a coffee break, their drivers passing out chewing gum and chocolate to children, and doing deals on Lucky Strike cigarettes with adults. These tall, drawling men were saving us from the Japanese. The cost was soon visible too. Trainloads of bandaged wounded, survivors of war in the tropics, passed through on their way to hospitals. Wan faces — with eyes that had seen such lethal locations as Guadacanal and Tarawa — looked out as carriage after carriage of casualties rolled through. As much to the point, popular young men of the town were beginning to return limping and pale from North Africa and Italy. Others had been left under rough crosses on battlefields. There was a new generation of widows, spinsters and fatherless children in the making.

I had a walk-on role in these global proceedings. *Butter for Britain!* the slogan on a patriotic poster urged. *Win the War!* I dutifully milked Bluey and Helen Keller night and morning, separated out the cream, and carried it off to the dairy factory on the way to school. There it became butter and cheese for beleaguered Britons. In a land awash with dairy produce, New Zealanders loyally denied themselves more than a small ration of butter and cheese for the duration. Consumption of cream was illegal. We pilfered a little of our own only for Christmas strawberries.

Otherwise, on the Shadbolt farmlet, I fed fowls and raked hay. Filling the barn with hay was especially satisfying. I still find it difficult to imagine a tolerable childhood without a haybarn. It made a hideout from prying parents, a place to sulk or read, a gang den for furtive plotting and esoteric rites; and an arena for boxing matches. At the edge of adolescence it was also a useful site for sexual experiment. Mabel Wilson had urged my mother to send away for a manual devoted to the facts of reproduction. The notion was that my brother and I would be better enlightened. The plain brown parcel arrived with other mail on a Saturday morning. My mother snatched it up and raced away. My interest was quickened. That night, after lights out, I crept down the passage to eavesdrop on my parents as they talked before the kitchen fire.

'Look at this, Frank,' my mother was saying.

'Hmm,' my father said non-committally. He sounded interested all the same.

'And at this,' she said.

There was a long silence.

'Did you know that?' she asked.

'No,' he claimed.

'My God,' she said finally.

My father cleared his throat. 'What do you think, then?' he ventured.

'They wouldn't know what to make of it,' my mother announced.

It wasn't difficult to connect their conversation with the parcel in the post. My problem was locating the book when my parents were out. In the end I found it almost beyond reach, back in its wrapper, above the radio. I read excerpts to my brother; we found it disappointing. My parents seemed to have forgotten that one of our annual duties was taking our melancholy cows to a neighbour's bull for servicing.

My mother finally decided that a simplified form of sex education served her sons best. 'Keep away from girls,' she said.

Girls?

'They get you in trouble,' she warned.

That was nothing short of a challenge. I turned to sophisticated Jennifer Wilson for a more comprehensive tutorial. We disrobed in the barn and, when physical examinations were complete, lay silent in the hay. I failed to find anything more manly to do than offer Jennifer some potent American cigarettes pilfered from an uncle just back from battling Japanese in Pacific jungle. We smoked wickedly and went home.

It was an indifferent debut. Jennifer, on the other hand, went on to become a wealthy gynaecologist.

With only a little more expertise, I gave myself with ferocity to the substitute national pastime, learning to scrum, tackle, kick and pass a rugby ball. In fantasy I was already wearing the black New Zealand jersey with the silver fern. I was turning out at Twickenham, Murrayfield, Lansdowne Road and Cardiff Arms Park to battle with New Zealand's rugby rivals. So too I daresay was the skinny youngster who brought me down in a cruel tackle once. When I protested that I didn't have the ball, and was therefore no target for a tackler, he rubbed his knuckles in my face. I had the theory; he had the practice. I next saw him as a hard-breathing mountain of muscle in a soiled black New Zealand jersey with silver fern, more or less as mutual fantasy proposed. Only one thing flawed the picture. He was distraught in a dressing room, after a losing game against Australia, covered with mud, blood and national shame. He had spent much of the game trying to demolish the face of an Australian relative of mine and getting his own made anew. He had yet to win the rare distinction, in an international game, of being ordered off the field by the referee. He would.

'You won't remember me,' I suggested.

'You're the writer,' he said.

I agreed I was.

'You writing about this, then?' he asked with suspicion.

I thought not. He relaxed.

'A bugger of a game,' he confessed.

I couldn't bring myself to tell him different.

Less robust, I was a long time learning that though I loved the game, I preferred others to play it. I was more comfortable coaching. There was a feeble swan song in a veterans' game at the age of forty. For eighty footsore minutes I tottered geriatrically out on the wing. It seemed the safest place to be. Time and again I instructed the nervy centre inside me not on any account to pass the ball in my direction. There was a scrum seconds from the end of the game. We won it and the ball travelled from hand to hand along the back line. Then my panicky neighbour had it. In terror, as tacklers closed in, he flung it toward me. Old instinct prevailed. I ran into it and crashed over the opposition goal line, scoring for the last time in my commonplace footballing career. Hubris left me bedridden for a week.

In lieu of a luminous sporting future, perhaps, I took up conjuring with more dedication. Like Ranee, the Mistress of Mystery, I could tell stories with playing cards, coins, billiard balls and matchsticks. Before adolescence was out I was a professional of sorts, a boy wizard in top hat and silk scarf, making a modest income. I even swore an awesome oath upon a phosphorescent skull, in a darkened room, among members of an ostensibly ancient brotherhood of sorcerers. My most impressive stage feat followed soon after. On the Halloween anniversary of Houdini's birth the brotherhood entertained orphanage children. One of our less sober performers had a gruesome guillotine. First he sliced a cabbage and carrot to prove the blade lethal. Then he invited someone in the audience to place a neck under it. A pretty little orphan braved herself to volunteer. Her head was clamped down. But the garrulous deceptionist on the stage failed to trip the trick-switch which would ensure the blade fell harmlessly. The child was seconds from decapitation. Observing peril from my place in the wings, I charged across the stage, skidded, fell, whispered a warning to my colleague, and won applause for my comic diversion. The girl lived, though not to tell the real tale; she sweetly thought I was part of the performance too.

There was a bitter post mortem. The almost murderous performer argued that he would have remembered the trick-switch had it not been for my unwarranted intervention; the girl would have come to no harm. Others congratulated me on presence of mind. Celebration of Houdini's birthday did not call for human sacrifice.

By then I was closing with my twentieth year and relinquishing my wand anyway. I had learned that reality resided only in the eye of the beholder. I knew that cunning and craft could go a long way. But language had begun to look more miraculous than anything in a magician's apparatus. Language allowed no trick-switches; heads did roll.

As war lengthened family life grew more conventional in character. My eleventh and twelfth birthdays were behind me, and soon my thirteenth. There were frosty winters and hot summers. There was the river and home-crafted canoes. The region was rich in limestone caves requiring investigation. In subterranean silences the faintest drip of water rang eerily. Some were rumoured to be ancient burial places heaped with old Maori bones. I began bypassing likely caves when I learned of the fatal consequence of violating tapu — trespassing on that which is sacred — from Maori friends. Your hair went white overnight; your teeth fell out; you went mad and were dead in a week. Ghosts were plentiful too, especially near riverside campfires at dusk, though such apparitions tended to turn into wild goats on closer inspection. A Te Kuiti childhood was never short on rumour, terror, and death in sorry form.

A land whispered around me. A land still often unknown, more ample than maps of the world showed, and mine. I was comfortable with its silences; I knew them in myself. Sometimes, in the cab of my father's post and telegraph truck, I journeyed out into cool recesses of the New Zealand interior. My father's task was largely to link reclusive farmers to their fellow men. Such farmers ran their sheep and cattle on hillsides littered with charred stumps and streaky with erosion. They were wizened and weathered and made strangers welcome with powerful home brew. Often as not they were short on wives, thus lacking children too. That was not their intention when they came to farm. They meant, after warring with wilderness, to marry and multiply. Wilderness won. Bachelors wedded to half-tamed hill country, they no longer knew why they were there. The roads from farm to farm were rough, winding, and overhung by dense and dripping trees. Nothing friendly rose along the roadside; there were forested heights and valleys faint in mist. And here and there human beings dying of loneliness.

The war ended. The last of Te Kuiti's sons arrived back. Home was no longer as they remembered it on the battlefields of North Africa, Italy and the Solomon Islands. Women were their largest disappointment. One veteran found his wife in adultery and threw himself under a train. Another in similar circumstances shot himself. A third, younger, found his girl friend fickle. He loaded his rifle and emptied it into her head as she kissed her new lover goodnight. It was about midnight when he presented himself at a policeman's house.

'You'd better lock me up,' he said.

'You?' said the good-natured police sergeant in his dressing gown. 'What for?'

'Murder,' the young man explained.

'Don't play silly buggers with me,' said the yawning sergeant. 'Do you know what the time is?'

'Don't I look like a murderer?' the young man pleaded.

'Do yourself a favour,' the sergeant suggested. 'Go home and get a night's sleep.'

'Not until you've locked me up. I'm good at murder now. I could kill someone else.'

'So where's the body?'

'Up the road,' the young man said. And seemed to be serious.

The police sergeant instructed his wife to make a cup of tea for their surprise visitor. The quiet young man sat on a kitchen couch and looked at his hands, turning them over and over, lifting his head only to ask, 'Don't I look like a murderer? Don't I?' Meanwhile the sergeant hiked up the road. The young man was right; he was very good at murder, having practised it for two or three years. What the sergeant found blighted his career; he resigned from the force soon after.

Others back from the war just reached for the bottle. When it was emptied they looked for a head on which to break it.

The town, like most in New Zealand, had grown for utilitarian reasons. It began as a wooden encampment, a base to buy Maori acres and woo them into lucrative shape. Utilitarians still prevailed.

There was a stock and station agent named Masters. Mr Masters had lately acquired some derelict acres outside the town. His son Michael, a classmate of mine, was due a birthday party. Mr Masters lacked labour to put his acres in order. He instructed Michael to invite as many boys as he wished to his birthday party, especially those of a sturdy kind. A swarm of us turned up bright-faced, bearing our birthday gifts, on the day named. There were no games, no party hats, trifles or jellies. We found ourselves packed on the rear of a truck and being driven out of town to Mr Masters' land. There we were handed spades, slashers, posts and fencing wire. We were expected to clear Mr Masters' weeds and fix his fences.

'Make a good job of it,' he ordered.

Most guests accepted this extraordinary form of festivity without question and began slaving away in the summer sun. Having my own notion of what a birthday party should be, I thought it a mean cheat. By the time I had dug my fourth post hole, my sense of injustice was burning bright. There wasn't even a glass of lemonade on offer. I retrieved my gift for Michael from the cab of Mr Masters' truck and marched four miles home.

My mother found me slumped moody in the kitchen. 'You're home from the party early,' she said.

'Buggers,' I told her.

'I beg your pardon?' I had never sworn in front of her before.

'The world's full of them,' I informed her.

Town scandal was seldom other than sexual. There was the Anglican vicar who vanished after indecencies committed on Bible Class boys. There was the glassy-eyed Baptist preacher who mowed through the women in his congregation like a harvester and was finally put to flight by uncharitable husbands. And there were the town beauties who disappeared, between one day and the next, to have babies far from the town. Months later they returned unabashed; and more often than not went off to give birth to another.

Brutality too was commonplace, tolerated by those whose ostensible task it was to civilise the town. The first day of the secondary school year was designed as a nightmare for newcomers. In the lunch break senior pupils formed two lines. New boys were then obliged to run the initiation gauntlet twice over. They were kicked and punched back and forward, reeling from fist and boot to boot and fist. Bullies became more so, stripping their belts and using them to leave long weals on bare legs. Small and sickly boys were not exempt from thuggery. I used some tricky footwork to duck the worst of the proceedings. Tactful male staff of the school made no appearance in the playground. Possibly they shut the staffroom windows to keep out cries of anguish. After the lunch break they marvellously managed not to notice the bruises and skinned knees, the black eyes and bleeding noses. Three or four years after I survived this rural rite there was a near fatality, and an inquiry; teachers pleaded ignorance of the first-day ceremony. Meanwhile it was a licenced breeding ground for sadists. Years later I saw the same unlovely faces calling for the blood of anti-apartheid demonstrators who succeeded in halting a rugby game in which a South African team figured. Not to my surprise, my onetime tackler, with the nasty knuckles, was conspicuous among them.

My restless parents finally judged the social climate unhealthy. They saw no future in Te Kuiti. Their sons might soon become local louts. My father had several times tried to get posted elsewhere, and failed. 'We're like insects in a bowl,' my mother complained. 'We climb a little way out and slide back again.'

Then at last, in 1947, a job came. My father was to be a post and telegraph line foreman in Auckland. We left for the city. On a frosty King Country morning Bill Waikai drove us to the station to catch the 3 a.m. express to Auckland. There were handshakes and farewells before we climbed into a stuffily warm carriage filled with snoring sleepers. We peered out as the lights of the town trickled away. We were suddenly faces in the window ourselves. Then the last light was gone. I was fifteen years old, and my brother twelve. Ahead was dawn and the city.

Twenty-three

So far as it had a personality, Auckland in the late 1940s still had the character of a country town. It was a century past its genesis as a collection of tents and reed shanties on a scrubby shore. The population was hardly more than a quarter million. Farms and orchards persisted within five miles of the port. Between were battalions of wooden bungalows camped along haphazard tram routes: they were no longer villages and not quite suburbs. Such centre as the place possessed was a canyon of colonial buildings called Queen Street. In narrow lanes flanking the street were pioneer buildings — pubs, cottages, mills — from the city's beginnings. Queen Street had risen over reclaimed land and a reeking tidal creek. Memory says that in mid-century it was mostly deserted. It cannot be true. A quarter of a million people cannot all have been in hiding. Metaphorically it might have been. The place was distinctly empty of vision, its hushed inhabitants waiting on a city to happen. Four decades on, with the last of the colonial past levelled by entrepeneurs and wreckers, the glassy towers of the global village tawdry on all sides, it is still waiting. Other New Zealand cities make sense; Auckland never managed to.

My new school, Avondale College, began as a hospital to house American casualties in the course of war in the Pacific. It was in the third year of its existence. Though it had capable teachers, and a headmaster of sensitivity, it failed to make much impression on me in the two or three years I was familiar with the place. For some reason I loathed every hour of my schooldays; I failed to make much of them, or to crack the code of the system. I slumped from somewhere near the top of my classes to somewhere dangerously close to the bottom.

Something essential was missing. It took me years to identify the

lack, and by then it was too late. What was missing was the land in
which I lived. My forebears were absent; they had no history. A
century of sweat and sorrow had gone with no acknowledgement.
There was seldom a paragraph in a history textbook of New Zealand
concern; there was never a line of New Zealand verse in the literature
we studied. When I met up with verse by the New Zealand poet
Eileen Duggan, obscurely shelved in the school library, I read it with
an illicit thrill; I had a sense of forbidden fruit. She used Maori words
and spoke lyrically of places close to home. What was going on here?
We were imbued with all of the world other than that of it which
mattered most. Scholars now call this species of cultural servitude
the colonial or post-colonial condition, something which links
societies as disparate as the West Indies and South Africa, Australia
and Malaya, Canada and Kenya. In the 1940s, though, we failed to
identify it as an affliction. It was. Our world was.

1948 was a heady year. I managed no more than two months of
school. It began with a polio epidemic which closed New Zealand
schools for a third of the year; we had correspondence lessons until it
was thought safe for young people to crowd institutions again. Our
first rented Auckland house was set in apple orchard, not far from
Arklow Joe's lost domain; the forested Waitakere Ranges reared at
our back door. My brother and I finished our correspondence lessons
fast and filled our days fishing, hiking, and reading. We bicycled
from one end of the Waitakeres to the other. We found ruins in the
forest, huts where gumdiggers and sawyers had camped; and once an
abandoned sawmill which, but for a little rust, still looked
serviceable. There were graves too, of failed pioneers. Their
fenceposts were rotting away in the earth, as they namelessly were.
Again, as in the King Country, I had a sense of unsung lives lost in the
land: old hopes, old despairs. Summer looked likely to last forever.
Our father missed Te Kuiti cronies, but soon settled down in the city.
Our mother had grown strangely introspective; it was some time
before we knew why.

    School resumed as the year began cooling. The rugby season
began belatedly too. Soon after, in a muddy clash, I was wrestled to
the ground in a tackle. A gruelling ruck formed over my prone form.
A boot crashed emasculatingly into my crutch. A medical
examination, mainly concerning my genital arrangements, became
necessary.

My scrotum in hand, the doctor was thoughtful. 'You've only got one,' he told me.

'One?' I asked.

'Testicle,' he explained. 'See?'

I wasn't up to counting.

He began groping further, rather painfully. 'Have you always been like this,' he asked, 'or is it new?'

I wasn't informative on that score either. I had a sense of shame. Was I a freak?

'Never mind,' he said. 'It's nothing a hospital can't fix.'

'A hospital?' I asked faintly.

'And a surgeon,' he said.

That sounded inauspicious.

Then I was holidaying in a hospital bed. The surgeon split my scrotum, hunted the missing half of my manhood out from low in my abdomen, and hitched both testicle and scrotum to my upper leg; there they were to reside for two or three months, until acquainted with each other. 'Nothing to it,' the surgeon said.

That was his view of the matter. Walking was painful when I was judged fit to return to school. Rugby was out of the question. Worse was concealing the nature of my malady from classmates. I wasn't taken with the idea of being called 'One Ball' or 'Oddball' for the rest of my schooldays. I therefore did nothing to dampen the rumour that I had just been cured of venereal disease. I was seen with awe by intimates. There were sympathetic smiles from girls I had thought frosty.

What I did have, however, was soon on show. It was called maturity. My voice broke in weeks; a beard began to bristle; I grew an inch or two in height; I woke moist from my first racy dream. I also sat the School Certificate examination without undue grief or preparation and went back to hospital to have my scrotum and testicle freed from my leg. My mother, the same week, was rushed to hospital. She gave birth to a daughter. I was unveiled too. I was, in all but name, a man.

My last year at school had less personal drama. My mathematics master confessed his despair and excused me from his classes. 'You'd be better off in the school library,' he informed me. I took his word for it and went off to read Rabelais. Quotations from same confirmed my reputation as a sexual desperado. I may not have been better off; I was better informed.

There was also a bruising brush with geography. Sixth form pupils were instructed to interest themselves in local industry. Industry was light in the western suburbs of Auckland, and mostly with a rural base. A son of New Zealand's leading winemaking family, the Corbans, was one of my form mates. I selected the Corban vineyard as my project. There was something of a stampede as most males in the sixth form decided to make it their choice too. We travelled out to the vineyard on a spring morning, contemplated the processes of winemaking, and discovered the Corban wine cellar. Among its many pleasures was creme de menthe. After an hour of sampling we were exhilaratingly light in the legs. We arrived back at school hours overdue and fighting drunk. One classmate collapsed on the front steps. Others raced vomiting to latrines. The rest of us were just rowdy. There was a sobering inquest.

'I believe this was your notion, Shadbolt,' the headmaster said.

'In the beginning, sir,' I admitted.

'So you admit you were the ringleader?'

'I admit it was my project first, sir.'

'Then you must understand that I have to think long and hard about your future here,' he explained.

'Yes, sir.' I saw disgrace compounding.

Expulsion was in order, but I had one or two dozen companions in guilt. How expel a third of the sixth form? We weren't; there was safety in numbers. And the New Zealand wine industry was ruled off limits for geography projects.

It has to be significant that I retain next to no school friends. Sometimes I sight a once familiar face in the street; a teenager peering from a web of middle-age wrinkles. We find no more in common than ill-assorted survivors of a disaster, a plane crash or shipwreck. We pass words; we pass on. It mystifies me that though I must have mixed with at least half a thousand contemporaries in my school years almost none have have left themselves interestingly on the record: just one fellow novelist (Maurice Gee) and one remarkable Olympic champion (Murray Halberg). Otherwise none of my school friends evolved into politicians, television personalities, distinguished academics or scientists of note; I never see their names in a newspaper, unless obscurely among death notices. None have been seen as worth an obituary. Born in the depression, reared in war, ours was a submissive generation. Made conscious by our parents of the perils of instability, we had our wings clipped before we could fly.

Security was a national religion. We were destined for dependable jobs and inoffensive opinions. We were also, in some sense, cripples.

There was one classmate who had more to say for himself than most. He was black-haired, gangly, earnest, and Jewish. His name was Carl Freeman. There was no mistaking the nature of his rhetoric. He was also a child of the 1930s. His Marxist parents, however, were still active; his mother had been a communist candidate for Parliament. I sometimes sided with him in classroom debate; he saw a useful sympathiser. In my last school year he asked me along to a youth club. 'It's mostly people like us,' he told me.

I saw what he meant. Though the organisation had a neutral enough name — the Young People's Club — it was far from nonpartisan. It had liberal wartime beginnings, as a place where young of most persuasions could exchange views on the world. Since then ideologues had drummed out those with unreliable views, meaning those which differed from those of the New Zealand Communist Party. The clubroom, in an attic near the Auckland waterfront, was now richly clothed in revolutionary posters and Marxist aphorisms. It was becoming a recruiting base for the Communist Party.

I was not to know. It might have made no difference anyway. I had nothing against Lenin, though I had inherited a suspicion of Stalin. It was more to the point that there were unattached and lively-eyed girls in the club. Also most club members were literate. They read poetry. They talked novels. They were thoughtful about movies. They produced plays. It didn't matter that their taste was ideologically coloured. I didn't know such a fraternity existed. It was a rousing climate for a teenager fresh from a rural town, one who had never talked more than rugby to contemporaries.

Outside the clubroom, the cold war was frosting the world. New Zealand's Labour government of 1935 was now in its dotage, its fourteenth and last year of office. The notions of national independence which fathered the party, four decades earlier, were frayed or forgotten. In their place were the platitudes of grey authoritarians. To prove itself a useful ally of the United States, in the panic of the first post-war decade, the government proposed military training for eighteen-year-olds. Politicians who had preferred prison to conscription in World War I now wanted to push their grandsons into uniform. First there was the formality of a referendum —

formality because dissidents, among them disillusioned veterans of two world wars, were denied access to the radio. The letterboxes of the land filled with government propaganda. Unfashionably principled members of the Labour Party resigned. The result of the referendum was already determined. The marvel was that somewhere between a quarter and a third of the population would vote against conscription.

The Young People's Club, allied with trade unions and church groups, organised protest meetings and street demonstrations. I alarmed my parents by joining in a march. They thought I should keep my head down, stay out of trouble and find a safe job as a schoolteacher. I pointed out that they had never kept their heads down in the depression. 'That was different,' they informed me. 'We had to fight. You don't. You have your own life to live.'

I was to live theirs before I lived my own.

Twenty-four

*I*n September 1949 Grandfather Ernest Shadbolt fought his last court case. He managed to turn a son's minor traffic ticket into a marathon hearing. Expensively for his son, he also lost. Home in poor humour, listening to race results on the radio, he took a turn. He rolled quietly from his armchair to the floor. The radio was silenced. An aunt and my grandmother revived him with brandy. He sat upright and pointed at the radio. 'Who,' he shouted, 'switched off that bloody machine?' The radio was resuscitated too and he returned to listing his losers.

In early October he milked his last cow. Five minutes later, sitting to breakfast, his head fell into his cereal. It didn't rise. Neither a full card of winners nor a barrel of brandy could have revived him this time. I knew something awesome was in the making when I arrived home from school that day. My father was on his knees and sobbing. In his hand was the evening newspaper obituary. MAN WHO FOUGHT INJUSTICE DIES, said the heading. I had never heard the grief of son for father before. It was a terrifying sound; I was soon echoing it. Had the tribal Shadbolts grieved so, back on Banks Peninsula, when patriarch Benjamin expired and the nineteenth century perished prematurely with him? Anyway another patriarch was gone, another adventure.

Six muscular sons carried Grandfather Shadbolt's coffin into the red-brick Anglican church along the road from his house. Grandmother Ada declined to be present. 'I don't believe in goodbyes,' she disclosed. She sat the ceremony out at home and calmly welcomed us back when it finished. There wasn't a tear. In the course of the rowdy wake, she sat beside me. It seemed she had been observing me while I watched uncles and aunts laughing and tearful.

'You must be eighteen,' she said.

'Seventeen,' I informed her.

'And I believe you're going to be a writer.'

It was news to me. 'I don't think so,' I said cautiously.

'Then what?'

'A lawyer, perhaps,' I told her.

'A lawyer?' she said. Memory tells me she shuddered.

'I've been reading a book about Clarence Darrow,' I explained.

She didn't think that a good and sufficient excuse. 'It's time the Shadbolts put law behind them,' she announced. 'It's time for a writer.'

'Why me?'

'You listen,' she said. 'You watch.'

'That doesn't make a writer,' I argued.

'It helps,' she suggested.

'Anyway I wouldn't know where to begin,' I told her.

She bent low, her face close to my ear. 'With the Shadbolts,' she whispered.

'Us?'

'We need a writer,' she said mysteriously.

'For what?'

'To make sense of all this.'

She glided away to another grandchild.

What was she telling me? At home, nonetheless, I wrote in my diary, in red ink: *Write about the Shadbolts!* It would be forty years before I felt I had an even chance of surviving family fray.

Anyway an aunt had already determined that any future chronicler of the Shadbolts would have a formidable task. With Ernest's corpse still cooling on the kitchen floor, she busied herself burning his papers — his manuscripts, petitions to Parliament, correspondence, and dog-eared law books. I have a suspicion that some surviving clue to forefather Benjamin's identity might have been extinguished too. I was left to stitch together the rags and tatters of family legend in a longish saga called *The Lovelock Version*, my fictional and fantastic version of Ernest's 'Shadbolts By Land and Sea'. And then, with more respect for the record, here.

A month later I finished school. Miraculously, my sullen indolence considered, I had been credited with university entrance. Benjamin couldn't have rejoiced more in his ticket-of-leave. I gathered my books, said goodbyes, and found a job in a wool store. My hope was to build a bank balance before beginning university. On the first day of my adult life the Labour government of 1935, to no one's surprise, was voted out. There was another and less compassionate New Zealand in the making. The welfare state was to be trimmed. Trade unions were promised a tough existence. Criminals were promised capital punishment. The underprivileged were promised nothing. And there was war talk in the air.

'Keep your head down,' my parents warned me.

For most of the summer, helping sort and bale New Zealand fleeces for far countries, I had to anyway. In February I enrolled for university; in March lectures began. About that time some national worthy was denouncing New Zealand universities as sanctuaries of subversion, meaning that independent thought was insidiously encouraged. Auckland University had perhaps four thousand students. Among them was one member of the Communist Party. His face was familiar to me from the Young People's Club. His name was Don Wolf. It was my fate to find the lone representative of the international communist conspiracy sitting next to me in English and history lectures, whispering a Marxist commentary in my ear as the year unfurled. I read Christopher Caudwell's *Studies in a Dying Culture*. Caudwell was a brilliant young English Marxist who died bravely in Spain. He posthumously persuaded me that I was witness to the death throes of bourgeois society. All that I learned, all that I was learning, could be of no value in the wiser world to come. But I baulked at the atheism. I failed to see why it should be a precondition of socialist belief. It seemed to me even then that life might be something more than a fortuitous arrangment of chemicals; human beings too. Besides, I didn't see anything unwholesome about the Christian ethic. 'You're an idealist,' Don diagnosed. 'Still, we have room for them in our movement.'

After lectures, I sometimes walked with Don down to the Young People's Club. The girls were still there. There were weekend tramps and camps and revolutionary songs around log fires in bush huts. I fell in and out of love, more than once with the daughter of a left-wing lecturer. Her name was Wendy. Wendy had large shiny eyes, long plaited hair, and promised to part with her maidenhead when I was capped a lawyer. In frustration I began to rendezvous with bohemia. Another of Don Wolf's ports of call was Queen Street's one late-night coffee bar. At six the pubs closed. By seven the grill shops were emptying of customers. At eight the cinemas began their programmes. The coffee bar was then a lone island of light and warmth the chilly length of Queen Street. Inside were the disaffected, the disenchanted, and the merely lonely.

Presiding over this antipodean clone of cafe society was a tall, lanky and wry refugee from Nazi Germany who worked as a landscape gardener. Let us call him Hans. He claimed impeccable political credentials, and had persuaded most of Auckland's social dissidents that he was all he seemed. He had even bewitched New Zealand's most celebrated writer of the 1940s, Frank Sargeson, in part by supplying him with continental pornography of the homo-erotic kind Sargeson required. Hans also had a complex relationship with New Zealand's security intelligence service, possibly trading names for favours. While laughing with the left, he had also been the anonymous author of scabrous right-wing and anti-semitic publications. He often recruited inhabitants of the coffee bar to work as muddy labourers.

Among them were unpublished novelists biding their time as newspaper proofreaders, impoverished painters producing portraits for tobacco money, corduroy-trousered actors in search of a theatre, and architects desperate for clients. And there was a Marxist or two, like Don Wolf, taking a break from the theory of surplus value. One was George Hyde, a tall, fierce-eyed and dashingly blond Englishman, an art student expelled from the academy for an indiscreet series of paintings based on Adam's escapades with Eve; he now quoted loftily from Stalin on the remaking of mankind. There was Frank Malley, an editor of a Party-line news sheet, to which I contributed paragraphs, optimistically titled *Youth Forward!* Frank was comfortable company. He didn't quote Stalin; he preferred Walt Whitman. For what it is worth, George was to become a leading layman in the Anglican Church, Frank an accomplished potter.

Don was dismissive of coffee bar company; he didn't want me beguiled. 'Petit bourgeois intellectuals,' he informed me. 'They just imagine they're at odds with society.'

'Aren't they?' I asked. I had, after all, noted their threadbare condition.

'They're all talk,' he announced. He claimed he went there for the coffee; I suspected it was for news of parties.

'Interesting talk,' I argued.

'You worry me,' he said.

He worried me more.

Early in the year Don and I commandeered the university Labour
Club, coloured it red, and renamed it the Socialist Club. In mid-year
the new government, having fallen brutally upon power, began to
hack away at the welfare state. First to go were food subsidies which
had cushioned New Zealanders in depression and war. Trade unions
called a one-day strike; ten thousand unionists marched up Queen
Street. In palm-shaded Myers Park, in weak winter sunlight, they
gathered to hear speakers. I was one, speaking on behalf of the New
Zealand student socialists. At the foot of the stepladder, after my
incendiary contribution to the national debate, I met a battered and
kindly-faced man, scruffily dressed, with a stub of cigarette in his
mouth. He wanted to know how to spell my name; he was writing a
report for a trade union journal. He informed me that his name was
Ron Mason. It meant nothing. A minute or two later, a student
friend sidled up to me. 'Do you know who you were talking to?' he
asked.

I didn't.

'R.A.K. Mason,' he informed me with awe. 'New Zealand's
greatest poet.'

'Him?' I couldn't believe it.

'Him.'

A poet? A great one? The man didn't conform to my
prescription. It was to be some time before I read him, longer before
I knew anything of his story. A perceptive classical student, with a
fine if bleak lyrical gift, he had been the harbinger of a genuinely
native New Zealand literary tradition in the 1920s. Though then and
later read and admired outside New Zealand, conspicuously by
Dylan Thomas, his work had not been welcome in his own country;
legend says he ditched one printing of his poems in Auckland
harbour. In the 1930s he became one of the few New Zealand writers
to join the Communist Party. His comrades didn't win much pleasure
from his delicately chipped lines. Possibly he couldn't himself, any
longer. His lyrical gift foundered on the shoals of ideology. Younger,
and prophetically, he had argued that 'Poetry usually dies in agony if
it gets so much as a whiff of politics.' He was three decades nursing
that agony.

Within a week or two I met Mason again. 'Look at this,' he said with a shy tremble. He pressed a crinkled piece of paper on me, a poem. The Korean war had begun; General Douglas MacArthur, commander of Western forces in Korea, had just been reported as saying that enemy corpses, frying on a burning tank, made a good sight for his old eyes.

Mason was moved to express himself in verse; for the first time, and perhaps the last, the poet and the political man met. The bitter poem was called 'Sonnet to MacArthur's Eyes'. I wasn't to know that it was literally Mason's last gasp as a poet; I might have seen the moment as more significant. On the other hand I had met my first authentic writer. Not one I could take seriously; and never as a model. I was never to hear him say anything out of the ordinary in two decades. I sometimes saw him sad-eyed on street corners, stub of cigarette on his lower lip, a bottle or two parcelled under his arm.

At least I'd been warned.

One rainy midwinter night I walked out on a philosophy lecture and hiked up Queen Street. Newspaper posters told of military catastrophe in Korea. In an office in a Karangahape Road arcade I asked to join the Communist Party.

'I can't say I'm surprised,' said the bulky Auckland secretary, a man named McLeod. A Calvinist of a communist, a onetime soldier and sometime psychiatric nurse, he liked to look enigmatic; he also enjoyed the authoritative sound of his own voice. With hindsight, I can imagine him conducting an efficient Soviet purge, or herding rebellious peasants off to Siberia.

'Oh?' I said, puzzled.

'We've been expecting you to put in an appearance,' he disclosed.

'Me?'

'We're urgently in need of new young comrades,' he explained. 'How old are you?'

'Eighteen,' I said.

He took up his pen, as though to record this particular, and put it down again.

'You've thought about this?'

'I have,' I claimed.

'And you're sure about it?' he asked. 'Do you have to?'

'I'm not sure what you mean.'

'You might be more use if you weren't a dues-paying member.'

'I see,' I said, though I didn't.

'You could be,' he explained, 'a Party member in all but name. You could attend branch meetings and take part in policy discussions. But you wouldn't be known as one. If challenged you could deny membership. You could find that helpful at university and elsewhere. We might too. Having someone who isn't known as a communist can be an advantage.'

'If you say so,' I said with some frustration.

I was never to learn whether I was or I wasn't. For practical purposes, on the other hand, the number of communist students at Auckland University had doubled. There were now two.

My relaxed approach to higher education alarmed my mother. 'You'll finish up working on the roads with a pick and shovel,' she warned.

The worst of fates. So must thousands of New Zealand mothers, with depression memories, have admonished their sons.

Then, seemingly apropos of nothing, she asked, 'Isn't it time to think of teachers' college?'

At the least I mounted the steps leading up to the office of the Auckland Education Board. I was to be interviewed as a teacher trainee. I could see myself reflected in glass doors. I was wearing a tie and had a satchel in hand. A teacher trainee? The picture was not persuasive. I vanished. Minutes later I was in a coffee bar listening to a red-bearded vagrant pick flaws in the existentialism of Jean-Paul Sartre. We fought distant ideological disputes, seldom our own.

My savings were depleted; my engagements as a conjurer few. I took work which clashed with lectures and tutorials. Higher education failed to interfere even less with life. There were Party meetings, coffee bar conversations, tramping weekends, and female friends. By the end of the year I was an active trade unionist, an immoderately articulate member of the Amalgamated Society of Railway Servants. And a failed student. And a striker on a picket line. The strike lasted a fortnight, and finished with no ill feeling. A meaner one was coming.

Twenty-five

There was a message from Party secretary McLeod. He wanted to see me.

'You're on the railways,' he said.

'For the summer,' I agreed.

'Can you remain in place there?' he asked.

'What for?'

'You'll see,' he promised.

He gave me the names of Party men in the railyards. 'Make yourself known to them,' he suggested. 'A new face is useful.'

'Mine?' I said with wonder.

'As good as any,' he said enigmatically.

Civil liberties disappeared from New Zealand. One summer day they were there. The next they were not. To silence striking watersiders the government took emergency powers in disuse since the depression. These precluded any member of the public giving aid or comfort to a striking watersider, on pain of a prison sentence; to offer a striker a sandwich was unlawful. Newspapers were censored, public meetings banned. Expressions of sympathy for strikers, or sentiments which might be construed as such, could also win a prison term. Freedom of speech was gone.

Don Wolf and I organised a university gathering to protest. We enlisted an impressive range of speakers: professors, lecturers, lawyers, clergymen. Then we had a message asking that we present ourselves urgently to Comrade McLeod. We were expecting congratulations on our initiative.

McLeod, though, was furious.

'What the hell do you two think you're up to?' he demanded.

We rather thought it was obvious.

'And who told you to?' McLeod roared.

It was, we argued, a natural reaction in current circumstances. Aside from free speech, there was the issue of academic freedom.

'You didn't refer it to me,' McLeod said.

That was true.

'It has never been approved by the Auckland district committee of the Party.'

That was also true. We were just a couple of students doing our best.

'You will cancel this meeting,' McLeod ordered.

We couldn't believe it. 'Cancel?' Don said faintly. It would make fools of us both.

'It could be seen as provocative,' McLeod explained.

The shameful truth was that we hoped the meeting might be.

'And we are not,' McLeod finished, 'going to give the government any excuse to crack down on the Party. You, comrades, are guilty of adventurist behaviour. Consider yourself reprimanded by the district committee.'

To the bewilderment of many, we cancelled the meeting.

There was comedy here, though I was slow to see it. The waterfront unions were said to be commanded by communists. They might have been less ruinously heroic if they had been. They were largely led by suicidal syndicalists bewitched by the sound of their own oratory. Communists sensitively dived for cover when trouble began. Persuaded that the revolution was at hand, with counter-revolution hard behind, they left beleaguered watersiders on the barricades and began meeting in obscure parks and in bush clearings outside the city. Otherwise they communicated in invisible ink. That was unnecessary. They already were.

Commotion reached the railways. Soldiers moved on to the waterfront to load and unload cargo. The question was whether railwaymen would handle the tainted goods. It went to a union vote. With fellow comrades I argued the need to back the watersiders; otherwise, we claimed, the trade union movement was imperilled. The vote went narrowly against us. Failure to win railway union backing left the watersiders even more on their own. Goods began arrriving from the waterfront the next day. Rather than handle it, I joined other militants walking off the job.

Comrade McLeod was again out of sorts. 'That,' he informed me, 'is no way for a good communist to behave.' A good communist, he explained, would stay on the job and fight to have the vote reversed. To walk out on whim was individualistic. No matter that others had. They were men who knew no better. I did, or should. Mine was not the behaviour of a disciplined Party man. It was that of an anarchist.

I didn't seek a second opinion. With my career as an undercover cadre in ruin — an adventurist, individualist and anarchist — I made a late return to university. I had begun to think journalism a likelier vocational bet than law. The ladder was shorter, the rungs fewer. And Wendy of the shiny eyes and plaited hair might be persuaded to surrender herself rather sooner. I walked up Queen Street and into the headquarters of reaction, *The New Zealand Herald*, to ask for a job. The *Herald* had been founded in the 1860s with a call for the blood of insurgent Maori tribesmen; now it was howling for trade union hides. Its evening rival was no improvement: it was urging that the police be armed and empowered to shoot strikers on sight. It was Hobson's choice. On the promise of eventual promotion to the *Herald* newsroom, I took employment as a proof-reader. The reading room was a hushed and lifeless place, a series of hutches occupied by ageing men who had joined the *Herald* with promise of promotion to the newsroom and found themselves settling for less. They wore Harris tweed jackets with leather-patched elbows, and sometimes a faintly sporty pork-pie hat. They talked of unwritten books, chances missed, wives, children and mortgages. They corrected the columns of the *Herald* with a scornful air.

My gentle mentor in the maze was a retired British army colonel named Robert H. Neill. Elderly, grizzled and dwarfish, Robert H. Neill gave as little attention as he could to the solecisms of the *Herald*. Unlike his frustrated colleagues, he didn't lament his lowly standing in the fourth estate; he turned his proof-reader's hutch into a branch office of Grub Street. Most of his time at the *Herald* was spent profitably plagiarising the *Encyclopedia Britannica* for free-lance articles compiled in stylish script. He wrote gripping first hand accounts of events he had never glimpsed. He wrote authoritative travel pieces on lands he had never seen. There was no corner of the twentieth century or quarter of the globe left uncoloured by the busy pen of Robert H. Neill; he had been everywhere, done everything, and there was no one to say different. He was fluent enough to get away with an eyewitness report of Adam's difficulties in Eden. It was a poor week when he sold fewer than four articles. Though they posed as robustly factual, most were undiluted fantasy. I had met my first professional storyteller. I now suspect he may have been fictional too.

'I think you want to write, ' he said.

'Perhaps,' I said.

'Would you like me to tell you how?'

'Please,' I asked.

'There are four rules,' he explained.

'Four?'

'All of them golden,' he said. 'First you don't talk about it. Second, you park your bum on your seat. Third, you place paper on your desk. Fourth, you pick up your pen.'

'Then?' I asked.

'*Then?*' he said. '*Then?* Well, what do you think?'

I was silent. He looked at me with compassion.

'You write,' he said.

He was less confusing company than Comrade McLeod.

Our windows were open to the last of summer. They were also open to the sounds of fray on the streets. Watersiders' demonstrations were being aborted by police batons. If I leaned far enough from the window, four or five storeys above Queen Street, I could see fists at work, fallen men, and strikers led away in police hammerlocks. The last test of strength between capital and labour in New Zealand was proceeding to script.

Mr Cunningham, the grey and weary head proof-reader, had seen it before. He remembered the depression, the riots, and the *Herald* presses protected by sandbags and armed men. He had been an aspirant journalist then; he had afterwards been relegated to the reading room, where he remained a modest servant of the *Herald* for the rest of his working years. He supposed that if events on the street grew uglier the *Herald* might be imperilled again. Otherwise his personal view of matters was a mystery. I found it difficult to keep mine to myself.

'Something of a red, aren't you, young Shadbolt,' Mr Cunningham observed.

'Sometimes,' I confessed cautiously; my job might be at risk.

'Good,' he sighed obscurely, handing me a bundle of fresh proofs. 'Don't let anyone — anyone — tell you what you should think.'

It was heartfelt advice. Two or three years later, long after I left the reading room, the telephone on Mr Cunningham's desk rang. The caller identified himself as a member of New Zealand's security intelligence service. 'Can you confirm that a Maurice Shadbolt once worked under you?' he asked.

'Indeed I can,' Mr Cunningham said with surprise.

'Did he, in your hearing, utter sentiments of a subversive or inflammatory nature?'

'Subversive?' Mr Cunningham said. 'Inflammatory?'

'That is correct, sir,' the caller said.

'And why is it necessary for you to know?'

'He has applied for a government job,' the caller explained.

The vigilant investigator got short shrift. 'With respect,' Mr Cunningham asked, 'weren't you ever young?'

With coffee bar bohemia two minutes up the street, and the university a ten minute walk, I set up shop as a viper in the *Herald* nest. Police inspectors, and sometimes sergeants, were instructing New Zealand journalists on how they might least informatively report the strike. New Zealand newspaper proprietors not only acquiesced in this procedure. They did their best to improve on police emendations to their stories; there was seldom a clause in *Herald* columns which could conceivably hearten strikers. Journalists who mutinously thought freedom of the press an issue were menaced with dismissal notices. Yet genuine news sometimes leaked out. Several naval ratings who refused on principle to work the wharves had been locked in a latrine block; they were denied food and obliged to drink water from lavatory cisterns. A sub-editor managed to bypass the censors with this report; he was sacked and warned never to look for work on another New Zealand newspaper.

My role was humbler. Seeing heavily edited or censored copy shelved in the reading room, I found the temptation too great; I spirited it off, sauced with newsroom rumour, to a group of watersiders and sympathisers who met, more and more bleakly, in a pub called The Thistle. Their watering hole neighboured Auckland's sole left-wing bookshop, where the bulky best-sellers of Marx, Engels and Lenin were still dustily on show. The prophets of socialism were no comfort to the melancholy drinkers in The Thistle. Possibly the intelligence I gathered wasn't either. Some of it found its way into conspiratorially produced strikers' bulletins and pamphlets

— seldom cyclostyled in one house twice, never distributed by the same vehicles; the police were on the prowl for illicit propagandists. Though I didn't see much of this clandestine drama, my imagination would later make the most of it in the novel *Strangers and Journeys*. The experience was akin to being associated with a resistance movement in an occupied country. Police ferocity confirmed it.

Among my acquaintances in The Thistle was a house painter named Jimmy Reid. A harmless, humorous and gently spoken man, he had been a safecracker of talent. After one of his less successful ventures, he found himself in prison reading a frayed copy of Robert Tressell's *Ragged Trousered Philanthropists*. That socialist classic changed Jimmy's life. He put crime behind him and became, like the hero of that novel, a left-wing house painter. Often alongside Jimmy in The Thistle was a gangling, freckled, red-haired, and rather introspective striker named Bluey Lovelady. Bluey joined a makeshift strikers' march on a Friday evening. As police began ending the march Bluey sighted Jimmy observing events from nearby pavement; Jimmy was a mere bystander. But suddenly police were attacking Jimmy and bundling him off in a police car. Bluey did the honourable thing. With another striker he went to police headquarters with the notion of bailing innocent Jimmy out. A hostile constable at the heavily guarded entrance told them to return in five minutes. A second inquiry produced a dozen policemen drawing batons. Bluey and his friend were beaten and kicked. They fled into a neighbouring park, though soon overtaken. They were comprehensively kicked around again, batoned with system, and finally abandoned bloody on the grass. This was the prescription of the then Mayor of Auckland: he proposed that police use their skills to 'let strikers go around bruised and bleeding for a bit'. In pain himself, Bluey raced his savaged companion to hospital; he never got Jimmy bailed that night.

Bluey couldn't believe it had happened. In the end he preferred not to. He failed to make peace with the experience or see the end of the strike. Weeks later he killed himself.

On the sunny first day of winter there was another attempt at a strikers' street march, this one to inform fellow citizens of a public meeting to protest the emergency regulations. So long as the strike itself was not discussed, such a meeting was legal. The march, perhaps of a thousand threadbare workmen and their wives, was meant to be peaceful.

With foreknowledge of the event, I notified Mr Cunningham that I needed to see my dentist. By the time I reached upper Queen Street the march was over. Two or three hundred police had halted the march and given strikers five minutes to disperse. On instruction from their leaders, most turned away; they were still leaving quietly, with two minutes gone, when the first baton charge was launched. The second was even more stunning. I found bleeding men and bruised women still sitting dazed on the footpath, others being helped to hospital, in pale winter sunlight.

There were journalists present, none of more ingenuity than the man from the *Herald* and his police supervisor. He recorded that 'a column of marching strikers and sympathisers carrying banners attempted to break through a police cordon and in the ensuing melee the police drew and used batons in reply to attacks with sticks and bottles.'

Sticks? Bottles? *Attacks*? My untutored eye saw only a few torn banners, weeping people, and patches of blood. Most men had their scalps split by baton blows to the back of their heads, confirming they had been struck while in retreat. To be fair, women hadn't been batoned. They had merely been battered by police fists.

So much for journalism. Or so I supposed. Truth has its season, if seldom in winter. Forty years later, in the week I write this, the *Herald* is celebrating those who survived the batons that day; their reviled leaders have become figures of folklore. Those who ordered batons drawn, those who swung them, are forgotten.

'How is the tooth?' Mr Cunningham asked when I returned to duty.

'Nagging,' I said.

I gave in my notice. Few saw me come; none saw me go. I took work with an ailing publisher in a back street, proof-reading business directories. The money was better. So were my spirits.

I was still a student of no merit. When a scab union was formed to work the Auckland waterfront, there was talk of students being recruited. Socialist Club members leafleted lecture rooms with Jack London's polemic *The Scab*. The commotion was considerable. The police were called in to investigate. Comrade McLeod notwithstanding, we also pushed a proposal that the student body express its disapproval of the emergency regulations. This had a rowdy result. Posters appeared. *Shun Shadbolt and his Mobsters*, one of the more memorable urged. Several hundred students voted thunderously to support suppression of civil liberties. The prevailing view was that capital punishment was too good for those who thought otherwise. Our band may have been a dozen strong at best. Among them was a lanky young freshman with a cadaverous face named Kevin Jowsey. (As a published poet he was soon to rename himself Kevin Ireland.) His father was a striking watersider. In lectures, when insurrection was less pressing, he passed me his poems. I began passing him mine.

The strike finished in bitter midwinter. There was no mistaking defeat. Blacklisted by employers, watersiders began looking elsewhere for employment. Having done my duty by the revolution, I found more comfort in coffee-tippling bohemia than with beer-drinkers in The Thistle; more interest in competing with Kevin's verse than in finishing lacklustre essays. Don Wolf showed his concern. 'Stalin says a communist student is a good student,' he informed me. Comrade McLeod also had words. For some reason he deduced I might, after all, have possibilities as a trade unionist.

'Have you thought,' he asked, 'of taking work on the waterfront?'

I was shocked. 'In a scab union?'

'That is correct, comrade,' he said rather stiffly.

I told him that in honesty I hadn't. What was he saying?

'Whatever our personal feelings we have to accept what is,' he told me.

'A scab union?'

'Times change,' he argued.

They were in reverse too wildly for me.

'It's important to the Party that we get men back into place on the waterfront,' he explained. 'You, comrade, could get into the union. Your name isn't on a blacklist. Your face isn't known.'

'It would be as a scab,' I pointed out.

'That is as it may be, comrade,' he said. 'The fact is that one day that union will be at odds with employers, and militant again. You might help hurry that day along.'

There were some things I wasn't up to. Impersonating a strike-breaker was one. Comrade McLeod gave up on me.

Twenty-six

Proof-reading business directories appeared to have no future either. This was confirmed when I failed to detect that a virtuous Auckland draper had been listed as a raper in Bodoni bold. The draper protested his innocence. Costly reprinting was required. As din and dismay settled I took an outdoor job as a builder's labourer.

My employers were five students turned builder after an unsuccessful strike against lecturers at architectural school. These rebels wanted New Zealand architecture to embrace a new and native idiom. Until worthier projects came their way, the five made do with remodelling warehouses and refreshing commercial properties. They were never short on vision, though they were on specifics. Menial tasks were left to unskilled hirelings from bohemia. Politically disillusioned Frank Malley, on the move to mysticism, and courting a woman of wealth, worked as a bricklayer. Others mixed concrete or hammered up scaffolding. The level of conversation was high at lunchtime, or when rain drove us to drink. Unusually for Auckland building sites, if not necessarily to the advantage of the work in hand, the virtues or otherwise of T.S. Eliot's *Four Quartets* and James Joyce's *Ulysses* were debated. I laboured on a factory extension, with the one bona fide builder's labourer in the firm's employ. His name was Arthur. The unorthodoxies of his employers didn't dismay Arthur; their visionary indifference to detail did. Arthur and I excavated the sloping site to instruction. It meant cutting back a considerable bank and levelling off the ground. Leaning on his shovel, Arthur tipped back his hat, rolled a cigarette and looked the site over through seasoned eyes. 'It's going to go,' he announced.

'Go, Arthur?' I said warily.

'We haven't cut back far enough,' he said. 'That whole bloody bank is going to come down with a hiss and a bang.'

He repeated this prediction to our employers. They patronisingly informed Arthur that they were not employing him as collaborator, but as a labourer. 'Start mixing the concrete,' they ordered.

Arthur shrugged. We mixed the concrete. Now and then he shook his head in sorrow.

'Sooner or later it's going to go,' he whispered.

It was sooner rather than later. On a weekend of downpour the unstable bank launched itself downhill — if not with a hiss, certainly with a bang. It carried the unfinished extension before it, demolishing much of the original factory too. This fiasco heralded the collapse of the firm. Recriminations were loud. Arthur was quiet. The five were denied a chance to go back to the drawing board. The road to revolution was paved with the practical, even in architecture. Like the rest of us, they were out on the street again, looking for careers in a more commonplace idiom.

By this time there was reason to suppose I might write. I was no use for anything else. The mystery is that I ever thought I might be.

First omens were not favourable. Kevin and I took our poems to the Young People's Club. It was a cultural evening. We, reading our poems, were to provide part of the programme. Though they now and then nodded dutifully in the direction of political matters, our verses were formidably sexual. There was restlessness in the Marxist ranks, a pursing of puritan lips. When we finished reading, applause was polite rather than warm. A tall, lean pipe-smoker with aspirations as a proletarian playwright finally pointed the finger. 'Of what value is writing like this to the working class?' he demanded.

A fair question. And of what value Shakespeare's sonnets?

A rugged carpenter then rose to his feet. 'Nowhere in your poems,' he pointed out, 'is the leading role of the Communist Party acknowledged.'

That, to tell the truth, had escaped us.

Then the dread word was spoken. 'There is enough decadence in the capitalist world,' said dashing George Hyde, 'without encouraging it within these walls.'

He may have quoted Marx. Anyway it signalled even more spirited denunciation. There was one comfort. As Kevin and I sped for the door Wendy of the shiny eyes put her hand on my arm. 'The girls loved it,' she reported.

This intelligence didn't detain us; we were never wooed back again. Fuelled with black Dalmatian wine, we gave even more uninhibited readings beside hilltop campfires in the forested Waitakere ranges. We had no audience but the Milky Way; the stars raised no objection to our reactionary rhymes.

Poets notoriously take mistresses. I lost once reliable Wendy, the likeliest candidate, to a tall and handsome art student. A red-haired and willowy psychiatric nurse named Jasmine, some years my senior, finally auditioned for the part. Her reading of the role, in Frank Malley's spare room, left little to be desired. I found my way home, on a late night ferry, in exquisite shock. The world rang with goodwill; life was a lyric. Kevin, overnight banished to the outer limits of my existence, took a dimmer view. Man had to rise above lust, he poignantly announced; man, in the long run, was more than a perambulating penis. What he meant, I failed to see, was that I should share affectionate Jasmine; it was not comradely to be exclusive. Nevertheless Kevin's tidings took their toll; my confidence in myself as a Casanova waned. Fortunately for my composure Jasmine found an affluent farmer to marry. I became rather innocently involved with a girl a year my junior. That didn't satisfy Kevin either. He saw me as a satyr. I couldn't win. His verse took on an even more tragic colour.

At the beginning of 1952 I wrote a short story about the bloody strikers' street march I all but witnessed. This would surely satisfy the comrades. Nothing could be more working class. With a view to publishing it in a Party journal, a cultural activist looked it over with a frown.

'I see you use the word scab here,' he said.

'It means what it says,' I argued.

'Nevertheless,' he said, 'it is no longer appropriate.'

I couldn't believe it.

'What better word is there for a man who takes another's job?' I protested.

'Comrade,' he said , as if to someone subnormal, 'such a word, in present circumstances, can only serve to divide the working class.'

'It was all right six months ago,' I pointed out.

'Perhaps,' he said reluctantly.

'So what's different?' I said.

'It is time to look to the future. Your story doesn't. It incorrectly looks to the past.'

'Incorrectly?' I queried.

'Incorrectly,' he confirmed.

He explained that Party policy was now to bring strike breakers into the militant fold. My story therefore served no useful purpose. 'Sadly,' he said.

No one could say I hadn't tried.

I wrote another. There was a left-wing youth congress in Australia, largely a front for the far left. Linked with it was a literary competition, to be judged by an Australian novelist. I had nothing eligible. At the last moment I set aside a Saturday, bought a bottle of cheap sherry and a packet of cigarettes, and wrote a story in four hours, and revised it in one. A girl friend typed it for me on the Sunday, and I mailed it on the Monday. It was about a young soldier abandoned and dying on an anonymous battlefield and possibly incorrect from all quarters of the political compass. I recall little else, other than rising giddily from my desk, sherry and story finished, and making my way clumsily across a smoky room to collapse on my bed. No one had troubled to explain that writers, even if drinkers, mostly avoided alcohol while writing. It was a near dipsomaniacal beginning; of its connection with anything else I am less sure. But the story took a prize, and was published obscurely.

I was in Sydney to pick up the prize. There were other New Zealanders present. Some, though it wasn't apparent then, were also to write. There was a young journalist named Noel Hilliard, with a vast knowledge of 1930s American realists, who would find his own voice, eight years later, in his first, pathfinding novel *Maori Girl*. There was a bulky Maori boilermaker named Hone Tuwhare who would prove that he could weld verse efficiently too. In Sydney our literary idiosyncrasies were muffled for the good of the cause — which was, for the most part, indistinguishable from that of Stalin's Soviet Union. It was a time of proliferating communist fronts; it was also a time of internecine slaughter in the communist world, with such as Czechoslovakia's Slansky, Bulgaria's Kostov, and Hungary's Rajk being silenced by firing squad or hangman. Few of us would feel the experience worth a personal history. *The God That Failed* had already been published; at best we were diminutive footnotes. It had all been done, all been said: we were aspirant players in an heroic drama drastically rewritten as a horror story. We were also, as I phrased it in the title of a scandalously incorrect story years later, knocking on yesterday's door.

It failed to open. Still in Sydney, I learned that my short story had won me a month in Romania. Romania? It had a magical sound. I waited for the air tickets, the plane that would wing me off to that sturdy citadel of socialism. Puzzlingly, the tickets never appeared. New Zealand communists had pointed out to their East European fellows that I was politically unsound. This was legitimate judgement. It was another twenty years before I found myself in Romania for a doleful week. A day would have been enough. Fortune was absent-mindedly kind to me at the age of nineteen.

But this is then. I was back in New Zealand for my twentieth birthday.

What can I say of my parents? They must have been baffled, though they had more or less accepted that I was entitled to muddle away my life. They often baffled me more. Upheavals known as 'shifting Saturdays' had punctuated my childhood, moves from one house to the next. The radio, relaying racetrack commentaries, was always last out of the old house and first in the new. My father refused to be detained long by such worldly business as carrying furniture. Such Saturdays were growing no fewer. They were still at it, now with thirteen marital dwellings behind them; they would eventually tally close to forty, virtually one for every year of their married life. Some dwellings lasted less than two months. This restlessness was more than merely eccentric. Their swings between elation and despair suggests a manic-depressive cycle. (My father being manic, my mother depressive.)

Before a move was made there was optimism: a many-coloured future was about to begin. Soon there was obscure melancholy. The kitchen was too small, or neighbours unfriendly, or the roof needed repair. My mother was moody, my father dour. Then they were house-hunting again. Was it the dynamic of their marriage? Did their visionary quest for some flawless dwelling keep them together? They were never to find it other than under a patch of mown turf in Auckland's Waikumete cemetery. As it turns out, the grave they share is hardly a hundred yards from the house in which they began their marriage in 1929. What is fate trying to say?

One thing is distinct. Through their residential ructions my father retained a secondary agenda. It was still to return to the scene of boyhood idyll on Banks Peninsula. His hope was that my mother might agree from exhaustion. In early 1952 he won her consent to a South Island holiday. It was now thirty years since he saw Shadbolt territory. He mourned changes, though they were few. Akaroa harbour glowed much as he remembered, perhaps even more. Fish still leapt. The hills still shone with cocksfoot pasture. My four-year-old sister was christened before Aunt Amelia's memorial altar in the little Shadbolt church at Duvauchelle. My father drank tea with onetime schoolmates. Finally he compiled an ecstatic piece on his experience for *The Akaroa Mail*. He was especially lyrical when he wrote of Benjamin Shadbolt's old bailiwick: 'Where once the home and garden was filled with the warmth and activity of a young family being raised to manhood and womanhood and being fitted to take their place in the pioneering of a young and lovely country, now there remains a great silence and stillness and smell of decay. It seemed to me as if the old house stood hugging to itself its great horde of memories, jealously guarding them and waiting in an aloof manner for the hand of the wrecker.'

More ominously, he promised that the visit would not be his last: 'I can think of no lovelier place to retire,' he announced.

My mother remained dubious. Two or three years later she succumbed to the proposition. First they would move to Christchurch and there see out the last of my father's working life. Then they would find a cottage beside Akaroa harbour. The plan had pitfalls. The first was Christchurch. The winter was gloomy, with frosty wind off the Southern Alps. In search of comfort they moved house again and again, four times in ten months, rather more than average. Then they terminated their search for an earthly domicile in the South Island and moved back to the North. Some light went out in my father. I found him less and less at home. He was a lacklustre stranger in someone else's life. His chance had come; he had fumbled it.

That is my version anyway. Cousin Kelvin has another. This affectionate observer recalls my father as a bon vivant who refused to be detained by misfortune or diminished by disaster; he remembers a rogue's twinkle in my father's eye until the last. And he insists that my father was by far the most loveable of Ernest Shadbolt's feckless sons. Loveable? Gregarious anyway. In a roomful of strangers he would know the personal history of everyone present in something less than half an hour; they would certainly know his. But my cousin seems to be talking about someone else, a stranger. With a lurch of stomach I realise that I mostly saw my father through my mother's eyes; and as a man more at home with the prescriptions of *The Turf Guide* and *Best Bets* than those of *Das Kapital*. Yet there was still fire in his belly. Radio talkback hosts were to find him a formidably persistent caller in the 1960s and early 1970s, the Vietnam years. One such host, remarkably for radio, called for a minute's silence when he died in 1973. At his funeral service I read Dylan Thomas's 'To My Father'. His words had forked no lightning; he had grieved the sun upon its way.

My brother and I looked elsewhere for male models. We didn't know we were. We simply did. Our models were in character. Peter's was one of the more boisterous Shadbolt uncles, a rugby league player of distinction, a boxer and fisherman. Mine was my mother's bachelor brother, Joe Kearon. He was a gentle, literate and introspective man who gardened and dug graves in Waikumete Cemetery or laboured on West Auckland roads. He had seen out depression. He had survived war. Now half-hermit in his spartan cottage under the Waitakere Ranges, he watched sunsets, smoked his pipe, and tried to make things add up. Still a crusty Stalinist, and ostensibly atheist, he nonetheless had the King James version of the Bible at hand to score a textual point when we argued. Shakespeare was likewise within reach when discussion became heated. Then and later he was tolerant of my ideological lapses. Before I was out of my teens he was far more my father than my father; his tiny house more my home than any my footloose parents owned or rented. His was a place to take problems, woes and confidences. He knew, as my parents didn't, of my connection with the Communist Party. My parents were spared that knowledge, though they had suspicions. ('Keep your head down.' 'Live your own life.') Joe saw no reason to be excited by my confession. 'If you must, you will,' he said, and probably located a line of Shakespeare — or Matthew, Mark or Luke — making much the same point. He would read my first stories in impressive silence. 'Well,' he said afterwards, 'what do you think you're up to here?'

Explanations seldom satisfied him. There was a persistent problem. I was trying to write, he said, the way people spoke. That, he thought, was a grievous mistake. It was not his notion of literature. The language of Shakespeare and Milton was. And what were these obscenities my characters used? No matter that he used them himself. Typed on a page, they made him pessimistic about my literary future.

I met more incomprehension as my doubts about the wisdom of Joseph Stalin, the worth of the Soviet Union, and mankind's socialist dawn, began to multiply. I learned that I could take him only some of the journey, a doctrinal inch or two at a time. The same was true of my parents. As a lapsing Marxist I tried not to leave them too far behind. I could never suggest that the years they had given to the Communist Party were waste. I could never suggest that their energies, and those of thousands like them, had been used to promote, support and disguise tyranny. They hoped, years later, that I would return with uplifting news from the Soviet Union. I disappointed them. I failed my filial duty — to both fathers, as it happened. Joe held out against the bad news longer. 'Socialism might come right, one day,' he sighed, and lit his pipe. 'There has to be a better world than this.'

I didn't say not. I couldn't say not. I never said not. Who would?

When I write of my parents, and their generation, I find myself suffocated by sorrow. Why is this? They asked no tears of their children.

Twenty-seven

Back from Australia, I lengthened my curriculum vitae by stacking lamb carcasses and butter-boxes in frosty cool stores, manhandling bales of wool in dusty warehouses, and loading out lavatory pans from a builders' yard for the needs of the nation. I also began drifting away from the authorised left. I didn't observe this happening, or especially seek it. My companions were more and more of the coffee bar kind — 'the lumpen intelligentsia,' as Don Wolf, always quick to coin a cliche, dismissed them. Yet they made more enlivening company than the Marxist sort. They lived theatrically. Some were to become conspicuous, respectable or notorious. There were others who would finish less colourfully in prisons and mental hospitals; or who would, out of grievance with the world or themselves, take their own lives. Most, including many of precocious distinction, have bafflingly vanished. Who will know, now, that they ever lived, suffered and sang? In novel, novella and story I later tried to ensure that a whisper of these antipodean lives, stifled by time and place, remained on the record. My generation inherited a land no longer a colony and not yet a nation. We were no longer Europeans and not yet New Zealanders. Expatriation, one response, was often as muffling as New Zealand suburbia. Aside from makeshift bohemia there was no middle ground. Not long ago I met a fellow survivor of that time, unsighted for decades. He shook my hand fervently and thanked me for making sense of his life.

'Me?' I said with alarm.

'You,' he insisted. My novel *Strangers and Journeys*, he claimed, had given him a mythology to live by; he was now at peace with his dishevelled past. If I didn't know it before, I knew it then: literature is more than language; a novel more than a text.

The unmapped foothills of bohemia are as hazardous as the region's rumoured sea coasts. Sour grapes grow wild among groves of sweet lemon, and green-eyed serpents glide underfoot. Though grateful for shade and shelter, I was never more than a tourist, with a visa for elsewhere; I didn't raft far up its rivers into the hinterland. In New Zealand the 1950s are now seen as romantic, a time of national innocence. The charm eluded me then, and eludes me still; I recall no more than austere streets and people who didn't know why they were there.

My twentieth birthday was sobering. Not for the last time I saw my life as implausible. In search of verisimilitude I travelled down country and took a job on a New Plymouth newspaper as a cadet reporter. In New Plymouth, though ostensibly in training, I was writing lead stories in under three days. The newspaper's policy was to toss new recruits in at the deep end. Those who failed to drown didn't need training anyway.

'Good,' the chief reporter grunted, and passed my copy as written. Sub-editors gave me no attention either. It was a lonely and mysterious life. No doubt its meaning would be disclosed in due course.

It was. It turned out that I was being groomed for exile in the newspaper's branch office in Hawera, the New Zealand version of Siberia. Few journalists consigned there lasted long; three months was average and six deemed heroic. A year could be terminal. There were nervous breakdowns, marital collapses, and even more bizarre extremes of behaviour. Some kamikaze correspondents vanished without trace, though one was briefly sighted sprinting out of town entirely naked. My situation was roughly that of a raw recruit assigned to hold the line in World War I after the seasoned veterans of Lord Kitchener's army had been levelled on the Somme.

A flat plains town of five thousand people which owed its existence to butterfat and cheese, Hawera's largest distinction was not of human making: it was the dormant and dramatic volcanic cone of Mount Taranaki, patched with snow, wreathed with rain forest, rising to the town's rear. The community's one other peculiarity was less evident. It had been a republic. In the Anglo-Maori conflicts of the nineteenth century Hawera's settlers grew dissatisfied with the pace at which the government was grabbing Maori land. They declared themselves an independent state. Their flag flew for a insurrectionary fortnight.

Outside the town there were still vestiges of battles both tribal and colonial — crumbling trench lines, earth bulwarks and spent bullets. Here and there were memorials to the militiamen who succumbed to the terrible Maori chief Titokowaru; a pacifist who, when finally forced to fight, left the British Empire in graceless retreat. Otherwise history was light on the ground: the scene of the most ferocious slaughter was now an eerily silent park, with picnic tables and swings for children. At such sites, with only my own footsteps audible, I listened for something, possibly for homicidal cries of the past, and picked up at least one message. Appearances to the contrary, my land had a history of no mean kind, sometimes heroic and often tragic, and as fascinating as that of any frontier society. (Indeed the New Zealand wars make the American west seem insipid.) Anyway that history wasn't bland and never boring — which New Zealand was judged to be by fly-by-night journalists and more than a few of its own men of letters. Such intelligence eluded me when I walked the ground where Titokowaru deployed his rebel tribesmen, where his Yankee aide Kimball Bent watched with awe as colonial militiamen were gusted away by Maori guns. But it would be forty years before I found myself able to frame his war in a novel called *Monday's Warriors*, and gave tricky Titokowaru and bemused Kimball Bent a chance to show that there had been no mistake the first time round.

I was soon in sole charge of the Hawera office. Not only was I the repository of town gossip and scandals; I could devise news and interview my typewriter and no one would much notice the difference. It was a reasonable rehearsal for the writing of fiction. More authentically I interviewed visiting celebrities, attended fires, accidents and scenes of the crime, mixed with detectives and lawyers in court, reviewed plays and light opera, and chronicled rugby clashes and tennis triumphs. An amiably alcoholic correspondent for the rival Taranaki newspaper early befriended me. His name was Geoffrey. His hat was professionally tilted back on his head and his right hand usually gripped an emptying glass. He had been six years surviving small towns and provincial newspapers and knew the corners to cut. He wooed policemen, publicans, mayors and fire chiefs so that he didn't have to chase news; it came to him as he sat on a stool in the back bar of the White Hart hotel. He disdained the burdensome business of putting words on paper. A telephone nearby was all he needed; he dictated stories to his office, cliche after cliche clicking into place, between one beer and the next. He was at home in Hawera's effervescent sub-culture of betting and booze. *Sub-culture?* It wasn't so sub. Bar room yarn-spinners had more to say about the community than the local repertory's production of T.S. Eliot's *The Cocktail Party*, about which I wrote an urbane and informed review. Half the population, it seemed to me, was identifiably alcoholic. The other half was feigning sobriety.

It would never have occurred to me that Hawera had a rendezvous with literature. A hundred yards from my office, however, a balding habitue of the White Hart, and every other pub in a ten mile radius, was beginning to get it all riotously down on paper. The name of this comic genius was Ronald Hugh Morrieson. He had some distinction as a pool player and wrestling coach, and more as a jazz musician. When he began publishing his bawdy novels, it was assumed elsewhere that they were pure fantasy, the work of some fevered, sex-driven and drunken provincial. On the contrary. He was writing of everyday Hawera. To the end of his short life town librarians refused to display his novels. Even after death his was not a name to be uttered in polite company. When his posthumous novel *Predicament* appeared (with a preface by me, as it happened) the public librarian refused a launching in her institution. Booksellers weren't enthusiastic either. T.S. Eliot was okay, the Homer of Hawera not.

My life was turning into a Morrieson novel. Crafty Geoffrey showed me how we might share news, thus halving our work, without detection from our respective head offices. In practice this meant I did roughly twice my quota, typing his stories too while he slept reverberantly nearby. Life wasn't without drama. Geoffrey overturned a car in which we were pursuing police, who in turn were chasing a pair of joy-riding prison escapers; the fearless newsmen had to hitch-hike homeward with bruises and no story. There was further humiliation. When we returned to collect our car it had gone. The backtracking fugitives had collared it, bounced it on to its wheels again and careered off at speed.

Geoffrey's imaginative driving was also a handicap the night we set out in search of flying saucers. The province of Taranaki, and particularly Hawera, was at that time under siege by extra-terrestrials. There were nightly reports of unidentified flying objects, cigar-shaped or saucer-shaped, hovering about the mountain.

Sometimes they were solo, evidently reconnoitring the region; sometimes they flew in menacing formation. They were said to be frightening dairy herds dry. The consensus view was that Taranaki was about to be colonised. At all events an interview with a Martian or Venusian would be the story of a lifetime, and not one likely to walk into the back bar of the White Hart. Legwork was needed if we were to get it ahead of the world's newsmen.

'Right,' Geoffrey decided. 'Over the top.'

We toured the town outskirts, checking our flanks, and launched into the no-man's land of rural Taranaki with the car windows wound down. Soon we were travelling audaciously into the district where most reports placed the spacecraft. The mountain rose darkly to our right. There were stars beyond thin drifts of cloud, and now and then the lit windows of farmhouses. These were best not approached. Nervous farmers were said to have shotguns loaded and ready for the green invaders. Save for our own vehicle the roads were empty. Now and then river mist lapped over our wheels. Indications were that the population of Taranaki was hovering indoors, braced for fight or flight. Geoffrey, an hour without a drink, began showing strain. He stopped the car.

'I don't like it,' he said.

I didn't either, but no matter.

'Get out and take a look,' he suggested less than heroically.

I cautiously did. There was a chill wind on my cheek as I scanned the sky. The silence was impressive. All the cosmos seemed to press around. The world was surely in wait for something. If not the second coming, then what? I shivered.

'Anything?' Geoffrey asked hoarsely.

'Nothing,' I reported.

'Then,' he said in pure panic, 'let's get the hell out of here.'

He revved the engine and reversed wildly to point the car home. I jumped aside. 'Look out,' I said, too late.

The back wheels were spinning deep in a ditch. Geoffrey, still trying to control the vehicle, sat some feet above my head. He wrestled with the steering wheel in disbelief. His headlights lit the sky, becoming more radiant as the rear wheels dug deeper and the car rose to the perpendicular. I gave him a leg down.

'I might have known this would end badly,' he mourned, slumping on grassy road verge and rolling a cigarette.

Our unextinguished headlights continued to catch passing

patches of cloud.

'What now?'

'Who knows?' he shrugged.

'The lights?' I asked.

'Bugger them,' he said with indifference.

'They'll flatten the battery,' I protested.

'They might show someone we're here,' he argued.

'Like who?'

'Someone,' he said without conviction.

'Aliens?' I suggested.

'Shut up,' he said.

'Why are you whispering?' I asked.

'Who said I was whispering?' Then, 'You hear anything?'

'No,' I decided.

It promised to be a long night. There was no farmhouse near.

'And we just wait?'

'Until someone comes,' he agreed.

Someone terrestrial at last did. Two carloads of farmers, on their way home after downing beer and throwing darts in their favoured after-hours pub, took less than a minute to right our car. They also jump-started the battery into life. The feeble headlights began glowing with new vigour.

'I wouldn't hang around here after dark,' one son of the soil advised us. 'Haven't you heard of the aliens?'

'Aliens?' we asked. 'What aliens?'

We sped back to the trenches.

Next day my office telephone rang several times. I had communications from members of the public anxious to report further activity in the sky south of the mountain. Their observations had a remarkable consistency. They involved mysterious lights flashing from the earth to spacecraft circling overhead. Did this mean, they asked, that aliens had landed and were signalling for reinforcements?

That was one UFO story I didn't write. Geoffrey, however, had fewer qualms. He not only ran a report on the new phenomenon in the Taranaki skies; he even rang his office to say he could personally confirm the existence of the mysterious lights.

We shared a less cosmic story when fire roared through the grandstand at the Hawera race course. Firemen laid most of a mile of hose, all the way back to town; it produced an unhelpful trickle. They then pronounced the building doomed. Failing to notice, we made our way into the heart of the conflagration. Overhead explosions of sparks and falls of flaming timber said we had ventured beyond the call of duty. Geoffrey took a calm swig from his hip-flask and brushed sparks from his shoulder. 'Dead journalists never make news,' he judged astutely. We made our way singed from the inferno to the awe of an audience of firemen.

Still faintly aglow, I raced to my typewriter to chronicle the hottest event in Hawera since Titokowaru heaped the legendary Major von Tempsky and several lesser militiamen on a funeral pyre. My report was terse and, I thought, admirably to the point. Taking my cue from Hemingway, I let nouns fend pungently for themselves. As it happened, I also composed Geoffrey's account of the blaze. As I began to flag my prose became blowsier, freer with adjectives than facts. I wasn't sparing with adverbs either. Back in New Plymouth the story under Geoffrey's name was judged most atmospheric and superior to mine. 'What the hell happened to you?' asked my chief reporter. 'Did you sleep through it?'

To supplement my thin pay packet I began acting as unofficial correspondent for the weekly tabloid *Truth*. Coarse courtroom dramas and local body scandals were welcome there as they weren't in the seemly *Taranaki Daily News*.

Twenty miles south of Hawera the small meatworks town of Patea was bizarrely terrorised by a pair of octogenarian doctors. They had a grip on all medical services, and the local hospital. Patea people in distress travelled a hundred miles for medical treatment rather than hand themselves over to the incompetent couple. In their care, people had died of neglect and the wrong drugs. One half-blind doctor needed three pairs of spectacles, of different prescriptions, to see him through a surgery. Routine removal of an inflamed appendix meant an incision of a size usually associated with major abdominal repair. The untrustworthy physicians were shielded by influential friends and relatives administering the hospital. With accidents frequent at the meatworks, further fatalities were expected. A fretful trade union official at the works told me he had just sent his pregnant wife south so that their child could be born intact. Reporters were tipped out of a hospital board meeting when letters of complaint were read. Chafing outside the meeting, I managed to get my hands on the letters and quoted from them in an account of my ousting. Agitation ensued. In the United States Senator Joseph McCarthy was then at his zenith. Upright burghers of Patea also thought witch-hunting had much to commend it. They complained to my editor that there was a left-wing journalist subverting their realm. I was called up to New Plymouth and an inquisition.

The editor beckoned me solemnly into his office. He had been circumspect in my presence since I made the mistake of informing him that I was an aspirant novelist. The last of my kind employed by the *News* had fled to Fleet Street and published a novel which pictured New Plymouth unbecomingly and left much local heartburn. Especially unflattering was a cameo portrait of my editor in younger years. Outrage had been considerable, and a libel suit rumoured. Literary use had been made of his world weary expression, his cynical expletives, and his habit of spitting long distance into a wastepaper basket. He no longer practised the last in public view, and saved cynical expletives for intimates. World weariness was, however, powerfully in evidence that afternoon. After gazing coldly in my direction for a time, as was his custom with subordinates, he lowered his eyes and sighed.

'Would you describe yourself as left-wing?' he asked.

'Reporting community problems isn't left-wing,' I protested.

'It can be,' he said ominously 'Do you see yourself as a muckraker then? A crusading journalist?'

His expression was shrewd.

'We all begin with ambitions,' he added paternally.

I was quiet.

'Don't you realise that you are upsetting people?' he persisted.

'A journalist sometimes must,' I argued.

'We rake no muck on the *News*,' he told me tersely. 'Leave Patea alone.'

If the *News* wasn't interested in muck, *Truth* indeed was. I smuggled out a story which persuaded politicians to have medical matters in Patea investigated.

There were more frivolous *Truth* stories. One, in its entirety, read:

A charge of stealing a pig at Manaia twenty years ago, brought against a plumber now living in Auckland, was dismissed by Mr W.C. Harley SM in the Hawera Court for want of evidence. The court was told that the only living witness cannot recall the facts of the case.

Hemingway could die of envy. It made the front page and earned me three guineas.

Twenty-eight

Seven months of adventure in New Zealand's heartlands seemed enough. I had begun to notice a tremble in my hand, similar to Geoffrey's, when I reached for my first beer of the day. Geoffrey was no longer around; a disturbed doctor had advised him that a month drying out in a sanatorium was desirable. It was fair warning. Sooner than take over Geoffrey's stool in the White Hart I gave in my notice. I set off for a newspaper job in the South Island and got no further than Wellington. There, minutes before the Lyttelton ferry left, I had a message saying Grandmother Kearon was dead. Suddenly I was on a train north rather than a ferry south. Of such ambushes are our lives made. I never went near a daily newspaper again.

I made it to Grandmother Kearon's funeral with an hour to spare. Depleted by cancer, she was small in her coffin. In the chapel members of her strange, musty Welsh family — the Morrises — made their final appearance in our lives. Who were they, what had they been? And who would ever know ? I had a sense of connections broken, stories lost, haze growing. I would never catch up with them now. Near anonymous, they said goodbye and vanished.

Grandmother Kearon's bachelor son, my Uncle Joe, had looked after her in her last years. He was now alone.

'What are you going to do with yourself?' he asked as we walked from the graveside.

I shrugged.

'You've been leading a pretty rackety life,' he said.

'In a way,' I admitted.

'You could do with something healthier,' he diagnosed.

'Like what?'

'A job outdoors,' he said.

I took his point.

After the funeral I took a bed in his Henderson cottage and began labouring alongside him. I confirmed my mother's worst fear by becoming a fully qualified roadman, with bicycle and shovel. When I travel that district now, I still feel a proprietorial pride in roadside ditches. There is pleasure in digging a good ditch, especially with floodwater backed up behind. The need to drain a campsite, to turn swamp into garden, to control unruly streams, may have led to man's first marks on the world. Tools would have been needed and devised, terrain read with care; man in that modest way would have ventured upon mastery of the planet.

Meanwhile my face coloured with sun. The roads we repaired and the verges we trimmed lay among Dalmatian vineyards and orchards. When it rained their owners offered shelter in their wineries. We tidied their drives on the side; and bicycled unsteadily home with gifts of apples and dubious sherry. In the evening we talked politics, philosophy and literature. Stalin had died three months before. Already reports were seeping out of the Soviet Union suggesting that the Saviour of Mankind was as lethal a thug as any in history. Joe was thoughtful. 'Who knows?' he said cautiously, and became uncharacteristically quiet. Sometimes we just read. I made the acquaintance of a compatriot called Katherine Mansfield for the first time, another name hidden from me at school. By way of tribute I wrote one or two sub-Mansfield stories. They were not of a kind one might expect a roadman to write. My fellow adventurers among the ditches and drains and potholes of west Auckland were depression-weary or war-weary men seeing out the last of their working lives; in the fullness of time they would pick up their old age pensions and never, if they could help it, look at a ditch again.

Employed as a roadman I put my twenty-first birthday behind me. As it happened, however, I wasn't finished with Hawera. I had met a tall and lively Australian journalist there named Gillian. Born and brought up in New Guinea, where her British father managed a copra plantation, Gillian had been a wartime evacuee, escaping to Australia with her mother and brother before the Japanese army waded ashore; her father had been taken prisoner and garotted. She had served her apprenticeship as a journalist on Sydney's excitable tabloid press and now worked for a largely sleep-walking local publication named the *Hawera Star*. She had come to New Zealand hoping to ski and to fly. Typing column after column of calf club results for the *Star* — not to speak of reporting Country Women's Institute meetings — didn't leave her time for either. Professional satisfactions were few. She began visiting me in Auckland. Then she found a job as a journalist there. I was again feeling the need for equilibrium. I was also looking for a home I could call mine. This must have been a reaction to the wanderlust of parents. Gillian wasn't averse to the notion of setting up house either. We would marry before the year's end.

After three wholesome months as a roadman, it seemed time to waylay my future. I took a part-time job putting together the local giveaway newsheet, the *Waitakere Gazette*. It was a humble affair, printed in a back shed by its proprietor, and seldom more than a vehicle for advertising. As editor, sub-editor, and sole reporter, I had the chance of making it more. Local government in the *Gazette*'s circulation area was largely in the hands of businessmen and run in their interests rather than that of ratepayers. Tory to a man (there were no women) they nevertheless had no scruple about standing on a Labour Party ticket to better their electoral chances. This in itself was suspicious. I soon encountered a faint but literal reek of corruption. To keep the rates on the commercial district down, sewage was being let loose downhill into low-cost housing and fouling a stream in which local children swam.

I made the acquaintance of critics and wrote a story quoting them in full. The *Gazette*'s proprietor paled. Local businessmen were his bread and butter. I failed to persuade him that a readership ravaged by typhoid might be even poorer for commerce. I resolved this dilemma by furtively alerting the daily *Auckland Star* to the sewage scandal. The chief reporter suggested I provide further stories. I did. With a daily newspaper suddenly and mysteriously publicising the woes of West Auckland, the *Gazette* also had to concede that its circulation area was less than sweet-smelling. That was the leverage I needed. Headlines became banner for the first time in the *Gazette*'s history. Before long policemen were keeping the peace at local body meetings, removing ratepayers who audibly dissented from proceedings or took notes without mayoral permission. And there were queues for the first copies of the *Waitakere Gazette* the day it was printed; impatient citizens couldn't wait for it to be delivered gratis to their letterboxes.

Advertising roared in too. With many more column inches to fill,

I fell still more grievously into the Hawera habit of talking to my typewriter. As a crusading journalist I lost my way; I became capricious, floating absurd notions by way of discovering what the printed word might do. It proved frightening. Britain's newly crowned Queen, on her first visit to New Zealand, was programmed to travel through the district for five minutes. Eminent citizens were puzzling publicly about how best to handle so momentous an occasion. What was fitting? Coloured lights along the way? But the Queen was passing through in daytime. Banners, archways? But every borough and city in New Zealand would have them. Why not, asked the *Gazette*, for many useful column inches, emulate Sir Walter Raleigh's adventures with his cloak, and cast a carpet of the district's lush flora at the Queen's feet? It was so lunatic a proposition that it was bound to be embraced with joy. 'A magnificent idea,' said the mayor, and called on the community to get busy.

Let the record show that on December 28, 1953, the royal entourage hurtled through West Auckland and passed over, without slowing, or Her Majesty knowing, a shimmering rug of summer flowers thirty feet long and eighteen wide. Sir Walter Raleigh's cloak-throwing looked puny; the fragrance of a thousand blooms displaced the district's unhappier smells. For endangering the mental health of the *Gazette's* readership, my talkative typewriter should have been shot. I gave in my notice before I became the Josef Goebbels of suburban Auckland. Local body politics in West Auckland went on their inscrutable way.

They were no less eventful, two or three decades later, when another descendant of Benjamin Shadbolt, cousin Timothy, became mayor of the region. An all-season and frequently arrested student radical in the 1960s, a charismatic commune leader in the 1970s, Timothy thought to build a more conventional political career in the 1980s. Voters were bewitched by his boyish smile, drawling oratory, and amiable impertinence; he wooed little old ladies and kissed babies with style. Even conservatives succumbed. The mayoralty was to be a brief halt on his way to Prime Ministerial office. Things fell apart. His first term was rowdy; his second ignominious. He lost his allies and then, at an animated social function, his mayoral chain. Auditors were called in to inspect the city's finances. Then he lost the mayoralty too. More might be said, but not here. As should be evident by now, the Shadbolts are litigious.

A fetching job offer arrived from the New Zealand National Film Unit. There was no mistaking the cue; my future had come calling. It meant a move to Wellington. Our first dwelling, in the crankily wooden and weathered suburb of Thorndon, was hard by the cluster of workmen's cottages Katherine Mansfield visualised in 'The Garden-Party'. For the first time I felt literature might have some footing in my own land. It was a sunny autumn of surprises. Wellington was exhilarating, infuriating, and liberating.

The National Film Unit fell in the category of infuriating. Founded in the 1930s, in a decade of socially conscious documentary film, it had modest triumphs behind it, and no prospects. It had initially been nourished by the honourable notion that New Zealanders should have a larger sense of themselves and their land. In peace and war it had filled that brief. Now time-servers and bureaucrats had begun to leave the place lifeless. People of talent had left or were packing their bags. The institution, like most institutions, largely existed for itself: to keep managers, executives, secretaries and accountants off the streets. Those who made films, or wanted to, were an inconvenience. Why I should have been recruited was a mystery. Perhaps it was to keep the numbers up, to justify the employment of another accounts clerk.

On my first day I was shown to an empty office. It belonged to a producer on leave. Exploring my new environment, I found several drawers filled with pornography, and long handwritten essays attesting to the virtues of erotica. These were so lavishly detailed that it was a mystery to me how the essayist had ever found time to make movies. His material kept me spellbound for a week. The following week I began borrowing novels from the Wellington Public Library to fill in time more wholesomely. Still no one came near me. I met fellow employees in corridors and in the tea room and tried to introduce myself. I sometimes encountered the executive who had given me the job. 'Ah, yes,' he said, and failed to recall my name or function. When reminded, he promised, 'We'll get you settled somewhere. Don't worry. Any week now.'

Weeks became months. I made myself useful elsewhere. Gillian worked on Wellington's evening paper. At her suggestion the literary editor began sending me books for review.

Perhaps looking for the pornography-loving producer on leave, the senior executive put his head around my door. I looked up from a Norman Mailer novel.

'Ah,' he said. 'You're reading.'

I had to confess that I was.

'You do realise, I suppose, that film is a visual medium?'

I said that something of the sort had been drawn to my attention. Was he telling me that I shouldn't read? I put Mailer aside and listened respectfully.

'Good,' my mentor said. 'Then you'll know that people gifted with words don't necessarily have the talent to put images on the screen.'

I could have replied that there were precious few images being placed on the screen in my vicinity. I didn't.

'Think visually,' he told me, and disappeared. I didn't see him again for a month. I didn't know it then, but that was my apprenticeship in movies.

Attempting to think visually, I got no further than fantasising someone finding me in my temporary office fifty years hence, a cobwebbed skeleton still on the payroll. I began prowling the half-derelict studio to see what others did with their time. There was a kindly producer who invited me into his room to consider his model railway; and talked opera. Though there must have been one, I failed to discover the connection. There was another, with North American accent, reputed to have directed B-grade westerns in the heyday of Hollywood. While putting together inspirational tourist films on beautiful New Zealand, he reeled off anecdotes about his adventures on location with such as Tom Mix and William Boyd in Death Valley. Finally I looked for friends in the laboratory; I might at least learn how film was processed. This strategy proved helpful. I found friends, became less phantasmal, and between one day and the next determined that I was competent to direct films. I dusted off forgotten projects, found cameramen willing to work, and did. No one seemed to object; or even to notice.

Now and then, in the years following, I encountered the executive who had given me the job. He was seldom without a bundle of memos under his arm.

'Keeping yourself busy?' he asked.

'Trying to,' I informed him.

'Good,' he said.

There was a blank moment before he decided who I was. Then he asked, 'Still thinking visually?'

'All the time,' I promised.

'Keep at it,' he urged, and passed on.

In pictorial mode I rode out on high country cattle musters in the Southern Alps; I journeyed through lonely fiords and harbours with fishermen; I played chronicler with a camera in wilderness and city and found my own country. That was the best of it. The worst was having to shape films, or sometimes to shelve them, to accommodate political sensitivities. Anything which might give offence fell to the cutting room floor. Things which might give offence were many. I made a film of a New Zealand painter whose talent thrived on New Zealand colonial architecture in more down at heel rural regions — derelict homesteads and cottages, and historic buildings. Indeed his fascination with such locations was the point of the film. Footage was sent back to Wellington for processing. I received a horrified telegram from the producer after he had looked over the rushes. SHOW NEW HOUSES, he ordered. IF THIS FILM IS SHOWN OUTSIDE NEW ZEALAND THERE MAY BE A SCANDAL. IT COULD BE THOUGHT NEW ZEALANDERS LIVE IN SLUMS. PLEASE CORRECT ANY SUCH IMPRESSION.

I obediently filmed the painter driving past the one recently built house in his region.

Then there was the drama of my documentary on the infant New Zealand wine industry, then dominated by Dalmatians. It was an heroic story, one of impoverished migrants struggling to raise vineyards on inhospitable terrain. It even had a happy ending. Again film was dispatched to Wellington; again the producer was aghast at the rushes. TOO MUCH DRINKING IN THIS FILM, he reported. ALSO TOO MANY DALMATIANS SOME ARE SAID TO BE COMMUNIST. IT MUST NOT BE THOUGHT THAT NEW ZEALANDERS ARE ALL DRUNKS AND DALMATIANS. THE PROJECT IS CANCELLED.

Pen and paper began to seem more to the point than camera and film.

Twenty-nine

There was a puzzling preview of my life. Toward the end of December, 1954, Gillian and I travelled north to Auckland for the Christmas break. There was a family dinner at Grandmother Shadbolt's, largely engineered by aunts. My grandmother had grown vague, no longer able to identify her grandchildren easily. She not only drifted into the past; she floated into the future.

She looked at me. 'It's Maurice, isn't it?' she asked shakily.

'Yes,' I agreed.

'I have just read,' she informed me, 'a short story of yours.'

'Of mine?'

'In the December issue of *Landfall*.'

'*Landfall*?' I said, quite baffled. It was a New Zealand literary magazine she sometimes had in her house.

'In this month's issue,' she repeated.

'This month's?'

'December's,' she confirmed. 'I enjoyed the story very much. I didn't know you were writing.'

'I'm not,' I said, even more mystified.

'Not?' she said.

'I'm making films.'

'So you are,' she said. 'You're very versatile. Making films and writing stories too.'

'I have never,' I protested, 'sent a story to *Landfall*.'

'Of course you have,' she said. To prove her point she began hunting out the December issue of the magazine and, in the material world anyway, failed to locate it.

She was distressed and I was uneasy. A psychic strand in her personality was disconcerting her family more and more. A year or two earlier she had crashed tearfully into my young cousin Kelvin's bedroom at three in the morning to announce that her son Timothy was dead. At roughly that hour Timothy, the baby of her brood, and her most loved son, had flown his jet fighter into an English hillside. It was eight hours before the cablegram arrived confirming his death, which suggests that there are speedier means of communication than man has devised. But what was the message this time? Was it that I *should* be writing stories?

That was my last encounter with her. She died exactly one year later, at the end of 1955. The *Landfall* of *that* December published a story of mine. Was it the one she read twelve months earlier? Or was it a self-fulfilling prophecy? I cannot interpret it. I can only record it. Anyway I am glad she arranged to read the story ahead of publication. She wanted a writer in the family and didn't go to the grave disappointed.

The plausible explanation is that I began writing as disillusion with film set in. But it was also the thing to do in Wellington of the 1950s — as playing guitars in coffee shops would be in the 1960s, and writing television plays in the 1970s. Literature was in the air, and especially poetry. There were bards like James K. Baxter afoot in the city, publishing broadsheets and magazines and giving public readings. Everyone was at it, and not least Kevin Ireland, now resident in Wellington too. We lived a marginally more respectable life on Wellington's steep hillsides. Kevin's poems had become shorter and pithier. Mine were longer and limper.

'They lack something,' Kevin said politely.

'Talent,' I suggested.

'So try a short story or two,' he said.

Or two? With the death-cell gloom of Wellington winter concentrating my mind marvellously, I began writing a story a week and sometimes two a day. Kevin was awed. So was I. I seemed to have tapped a brimming reservoir. New Zealand is a nation of do-it-yourselfers. It turned out that stories I wanted to write were the stories I wanted to read. The New Zealand authors I had read were writing of a society two or three decades gone; not of the New Zealand I knew. Though they protested otherwise, and rather too much, many didn't even seem to *enjoy* their fellow countrymen, or their country. All but a few poets were humourlessly obsessed with the poky, puritan corners of existence. The imagination of disaster — to use Henry James' definition — was there in abundance; the imagination of love was not. It was a literature of limbo: too much in the human spectrum was missing. There was small feeling for the past; and thus less for the present. There was only one thing for it. I would have to write the stories myself. I submitted the first three to editors; they were accepted. Money was pushed in my direction, and I was urged to write more.

My rough introduction to the literary life of my land came when *The New Zealand Listener* published the first of these stories in May 1955. It heralded a more bruising initiation than the one I had survived at high school; more incomprehensible than the one in which I participated to win my licence as a magician. The story refreshed a festering literary feud between the editor of the *Listener*, Monte Holcroft, and the author Frank Sargeson. Sargeson's reputation rested largely on a number of short stories set in the depression and deriving as much from literature — from American writers like Hemingway, William Saroyan and Sherwood Andersen — as from life beyond the high greenery which hedged his misanthrope's retreat in suburban Auckland. He now played the guru of local letters. A vain, preening and rather paranoid man, he held court among a mafia of mediocrities who put down anyone likely to menace his standing. Much has been said elsewhere of Sargeson's generosity, much of it true, by people reluctant to acknowledge the murkier side of the man. His writ didn't run as far as the *Listener*, though Sargeson felt it should; Holcroft had lately been unkind enough to reject one or two Sargeson stories. The appearance of my apprentice work in the *Listener* piqued Sargeson; he used it as the occasion for a pseudonymous and venomous attack on the *Listener*'s judgement, comparing my work unfavourably with his own. He identified unsubtlety, sentimentality and prolixity among my sins. ('One thinks,' he noted modestly, 'of Frank Sargeson's brilliant compression.')

He persuaded a youthful acolyte to serve as hit man and append his name to this communication. It was duly published in the *Listener*, though Holcroft excised a couple of sentences he thought crueller than warranted.

I was twenty-three years old, Sargeson fifty-three. He was the author of two or three books. I had published none. I remain innocently inclined to the view that a man of his age and standing had better things to do than gun after young writers. Not that there was anything personal. He didn't know me and I knew him only by name. It might easily have been someone else: I had just happened to cross his field of fire. Holcroft, in his memoirs, was to puzzle over the episode as one of the odder in his career as editor of the *Listener*. An honourable man, he was at pains not to publish Sargeson again, nor for some years to confirm the identity of my literary knee-capper.

'Think yourself privileged,' Holcroft informed me unconvincingly. 'Young writers attacked at the beginning of their careers are at least taken seriously. So many aren't.' There was a sigh in his voice. He had been a young writer once; no one had noticed.

The affair troubled Sargeson longer than it did me. In conversation with an associate, years afterward, he blamed it on the young acolyte who had functioned as his message boy; he claimed to have been a bystander in the enterprise. Against this, however, it has to be said that Sargeson's character didn't improve. When my first book appeared in London four years later, at a time when he had difficulties finding someone to print his work, he discovered a need to prove he had been right the first time round. He put a couple of compliant cronies to work. Another literary man unwillingly witness to proceedings later described Sargeson's orchestration of their reviews as masterly; he ensured that I would be hit from left and right. One damned me as a neo-fascist bookburner. The other, identified me as a sexually promiscuous beatnik.

Though all but undone by my *Listener* debut, I was in no position to complain that the world was indifferent to my work. One harmless story had won me a reputation. Even at the National Film Unit my cover was blown. 'I hope,' said the chief executive, 'that this doesn't mean you are using your time here to write.'

'Never,' I claimed.

'Think visually,' he warned.

I was. Within a month of the Sargeson denunciation I had written a dozen most visual stories. Sweet are the uses of adversity.

There were unexpected kindnesses. The *Listener* published correspondence — including a lively letter from Kevin Ireland — defending my story. One or two men of letters risked Sargeson's wrath, and literary excommunication, by writing personal letters of sympathy. The poet and editor Louis Johnson was one. James K. Baxter, the *enfant terrible* of New Zealand letters, was another. After a string of baffling aphorisms, half of them in Latin, and largely to the effect that I shouldn't let bastards grind me down, he urged. 'If you're feeling low, come and see me.' I was too awed to take up the invitation.

Meanwhile there was intelligible Kevin. He lived a few hundred yards away from the cottage Gillian and I rented on The Terrace. He shared a flat with Wellington bohemia's most colourful citizen, another novice poet by name of John Kasmin. (He had other names, conspicuously when in difficulty with authorities.) Diminutive, innocent-eyed and exotic Kas was a student of Rimbaud, Villon and Verlaine; he claimed, among other things, to be a Polish count. Sometimes in a cloak, always in a black beret, he liked to mix recklessly with criminals in the bar of Wellington's Grand Hotel. I was inclined to laugh off his claims of intimacy with the underworld.

The patronising smile on my face soon faded. One Saturday afternoon he introduced me to a drinking friend. He was a fair-haired, well-dressed young man. He looked for all the world like a bank teller, and had been. 'This is Percy,' Kas said. 'Percy is going to rob the Lower Hutt branch of the Bank of New Zealand next week.'

'Go on,' I said tolerantly.

'He's showing me his plans,' Kas explained.

There was a map of the Wellington region spread on the bar before them. Here and there were markings in ink, circles drawn, times printed.

'For a bank robbery?' I mocked.

'On Friday,' Kas said.

'That's right,' Percy said.

The bar was crowded. It was a watering hole for Wellington journalists and detectives off duty. Kas and Percy weren't even lowering their voices.

'Pull the other one,' I said.

'Percy is offering me ten pounds if I can pick a flaw in his plan,' Kas explained.

A faint alarm sounded. 'Look,' I said. 'Don't be silly. Someone around here might take this seriously.'

'Ten pounds is very serious,' Kas pointed out.

'Ten years inside too,' I argued.

Finally Kas spied a discrepancy in Percy's timings. Ten pounds, as promised, changed hands. I persuaded myself that I was witness to an implausible charade. That is, until the following Friday, when Percy and two associates were arrested in possession of a sawn-off shotgun in the vicinity of the Lower Hutt branch of the Bank of New Zealand. Kas had failed to detect the largest flaw in the plan. It was ex-bank teller Percy himself. He woke with stage fright that Friday morning, reconsidered, rang the police, and confessed. Promising Percy lenient treatment, the police suggested the robbery proceed as planned. They were in wait at the bank. Percy got four years' prison, his companions eight.

Kas? He had disappeared, as was often his need.

Thirty

*T*oward the end of the year, still subsidised by the National Film Unit, I had a half dozen stories printed or about to be. It seemed time for a novel. I had accumulated four weeks' leave from the unit. If I could write a story in a day, why not a novel in a month? The question was where.

I wrote to Aunt Sis for a suggestion. There was a fast reply from her mangrove-girt realm in the far north. '*War and Peace* has already been written,' she informed me. 'There is now no point in writing anything less. Nevertheless, if you mean to persist with your mad plan of adding to the world's store of mediocre novels, I can find you a cottage up here. It's in a little seaside village, near the mouth of the Hokianga harbour, named Opononi. You should be able to scribble away in romantic isolation to your heart's content. There's so much peace and quiet there it gets on your nerves.'

Opononi? I looked for the name on a map, and found it with a magnifying glass. It was thirty miles from the nearest town, close to two hundred from Auckland. I wrote back to Aunt Sis. 'It sounds perfect,' I said.

First sight of the Hokianga seemed to confirm it. Salmon-coloured sandhills soared up to six hundred feet tall at the mouth of the harbour; sea and sky were spectacularly bright. Pines patched the shore. Dwellings were few, wooden, and modest. There was a pub, post office and store, linked by rickety boardwalk. Gillian and I could pick mussels and pull in fish a dozen yards from our door. There was even a convenient desk. From it I could watch the whole of the Hokianga on parade: fishermen, Maori horsemen, beachcombers. What more could I ask? A novel, perhaps. No more.

There was more. Magically, on our first morning, there was a dolphin leaping a few yards offshore.

'It comes in every day now,' an amiable Maori neighbour reported.

'*Every* day?'

'And gets friendlier every day.'

My scepticism must have been plain.

'It plays with the fishermen,' the neighbour said. 'They tickle it with a mop if they have one, an oar if they haven't, and feed it fresh fish.'

'Every day?'

'For the last week,' the neighbour said.

The dolphin sported up harbour, out of view.

'A nine day wonder,' I announced confidently to Gillian.

I took my breakfast coffee to my typewriter. She set off with a towel and book to swim and sunbathe on the shore.

I was still contemplating the first page of my novel when she returned at noon.

'How was the morning?' I asked.

'Unbelievable,' she reported.

'How?'

'I've been swimming with a dolphin ,' she explained.

'You've what?' I said.

The creature took over the village. First shy, then bold, it was befriending the human race. It not only swam with villagers. It allowed bathers to caress it; small children to mount its back. Soon it was clowning with a rubber ball, or balancing beer bottles empty or full on its nose. Since then we have become familiar with such mammalian feats. But this was no tamed, trained and captive marineland dolphin; it was a creature of the open sea electing human company. Intimacy between dolphin and man had been the stuff of Greek and Roman legend. Until that Opononi summer those old stories had begun to seem rather tall.

Soon there was only one game to play in the village. It was called saying hello to Opo, as the dolphin was soon called. News reports sputtered out to the world. Witty paragraphs grew into three column spreads. Newspapers in London and New York were fast running stories and photographs too. Visitors began arriving by the score, then the hundred; finally there were thousands. Opononi was overnight a twinkling town of tents and dolphin watchers; the pub ran dry. The dolphin's antics were rivalled by the hourly more bizarre behaviour of the human species. People walked fully dressed into the waves to embrace the creature. 'Opo's fans are behaving like hysterical fans of popular crooners,' wrote one breathless journalist. 'They want to get their hands on him (or her). The creature creates a bond between people. Everyone feels better and more friendly for having seen him (or her).' The affair began to take on religious dimension: one imaginative chronicler was to record a 'Biblical scene, with simple believers trying to touch the garment of a holy prophet and gain redemption.' The road beside our cottage grumbled with traffic: with buses, trucks, and queues of cars trying to park. There was dust; there were fumes.

So much for romantic isolation. I was trying to write in New Zealand's noisiest square mile. Anyway how could any novel compete with the narrative shaping outside? In the end I didn't try; I became a neophyte of the dolphin too, swimming with it before breakfast and at dusk when crowds diminished. At the end of three weeks, when we packed to go home, I didn't have even the first page of my first novel finished.

'Fate,' Aunt Sis judged with satisfaction. ' It wasn't meant to be.'

I returned weary to the National Film Unit. 'I believe you've been holidaying in the Hokianga,' a producer said. 'See anything of that dolphin we hear about?'

'A little,' I admitted.

'And it's all true?'

'Mostly,' I said.

'Then you'd better find a cameraman and get back there fast,' he told me.

There was standing room only on the shore when I returned to Opononi. The cameraman and I bunked among empty bottles in the Opononi publican's back shed.

In his *Natural History* Pliny the Younger tells a tale of a wild dolphin bewitching the Roman colonial town of Hippo, in North Africa, two thousand years ago. As at Opononi, people travelled from miles around to partake of a miracle. Roman officials had to be welcomed and entertained. The community lost its peaceful character. Under stress, townsfolk met in secret and agreed to do away with the dolphin. Overnight the deed was done. The parallels were striking. But no one in Opononi was reading Pliny the Younger.

At midnight on a March day in 1956, Opo became protected by decree of the New Zealand government. Hours later it was found dead, its carcass wedged in rocks. Most people believed the dolphin to have died by human hand. Perhaps the hand of a fisherman using dynamite a little too liberally. Perhaps someone resentful of the change Opo had wrought. Anyway it was a replay of events in Hippo. Maoris ritually mourned, children wept, and old soldiers dug Opo's grave six feet deep on the seafront. Through New Zealand flags flew at half mast. I had another novel, if I could fortify myself to write it. That highly coloured summer didn't sit easily with the conventions of fiction. It was also too perfect a parable. Even in outline it left a novelist with little to say. Or so I persuaded myself for most of ten years. I had a dozen versions of an opening chapter done; each expired for lack of imaginative oxygen. Then it happened that I was lunching in a Greek restaurant in Sydney with the Australian novelist Patrick White. Talk turned to Greece, and then to legend. Patrick said, 'There's a New Zealand story that intrigues me.'

'Yes?' I said attentively.

'About that dolphin,' he explained.

My mouth grew dry.

Assuming that I might not know what he was talking about, he reminded me, 'That dolphin which swam into a New Zealand village and changed the lives of its people.'

I began to freeze. I couldn't speak, let alone admit intimacy with the said dolphin.

'There's the shape of a marvellous novel there,' he insisted. 'I've been thinking of it more and more. Of course I should have to set it in Australia.'

'Australia?'

'Of course. I know nothing of New Zealand.'

I sat numb. Bad enough that the tale was slipping from my nerveless hands. It was also to take on Australian colour. It seemed the final indignity. Why? I had no copyright on Opo. Nor had New Zealand. The episode had been waiting a decade for a novelist. Why shouldn't the most majestic novelist in the English speaking world make what he wished of it?

Back from Sydney, my first morning home, I opened a file enigmatically labelled *Dolphin?* I looked through fragments of manuscript, opening paragraphs begun and abandoned. The problem was the same in all; I had committed myself to the story *in situ,* to the salmon-coloured sandhills and transparent tides of the Hokianga. Patrick had identified the difficulty when he spoke of taking the tale to Australia. It had to be parted from its setting and planted elsewhere. In another community, another decade, another setting, imagination might begin to move. It did. Unforeseen characters took shape. So did a novel.

When *This Summer's Dolphin,* was published a year or two later, I had a warm letter from Patrick. There are, after all, gentlemen in the literary world. He was gracious enough not to recall our conversation in that Greek restaurant. Nor could I bring myself to tell him that I was in his debt.

There was more to that summer. While filming the dolphin's last weeks, I persuaded my producer to let me make a short documentary on the New Zealand painter Eric Lee-Johnson, then resident near Opononi. Battling poverty, poor health, and indifference to his work, he was winning a cryptic poetry from the commonplaces of rural New Zealand — from lonely townships, humble farmhouses, raw landscapes, felled forest, drunken telephone poles, leaning letterboxes, cowbails and barns. Working solitary, responding to his own sensitive eye rather than international fashion, he annexed such native subject matter for art. His hope was to make New Zealanders see their country afresh, and with love. He was also telling his fellow countrymen that the largest subject for a painter or writer here was New Zealand itself. For two priceless weeks I had the privilege of seeing the land through his eyes. To lift Paul Klee's phrase, he didn't just render the visible; he rendered visible.

At the least he gave me cause to look twice.

Back in Wellington there were changes. Kevin had gone wandering. Without a flat-mate and protector Kas was in difficulties again. He had lost his job sweeping the floors of the Grand Hotel. Sustenance was lacking, and a reliable bed. Gillian and I fed him on potato soup when he crept bedraggled to our door; he also made use of a mattress spread on the living room floor. But the law was taking an uncomfortable interest in him again. In the wake of a crime, to which he might have been witness, two bulky detectives questioned him vigorously. They examined his possessions, taking particular note of his dog-eared copies of *Ulysses* and *Finegan's Wake*. They carried these suspect volumes off for further study. 'It looks to us like you're in the pornography business,' they judged. 'Who are your associates?'

'Dostoyevsky and Proust,' he informed them.

'Dostoyevsky? He'd be Russian, would he? A Commo?'

'Proust is French,' Kas said helpfully.

'And we know about *them*, don't we?' they said. 'How would you describe yourself?'

'As a poet,' Kas said.

They shook their heads and warned him, 'We don't need your sort here.'

Kas needed no telling. Poetry had become too perilous an occupation in the antipodes. He found a ship, worked his passage to England, became a photographer's agent, took an Armenian mistress, and lived happily ever after as a millionaire art dealer. Kevin took up a more modest occupation. His terse muse at his heels, he began guiding tourists through the Waitomo Caves, providing lyrical commentaries on stalactites, stalagmites, and glow worms.

Bohemia, for better and worse, was astern.

Thirty-one

Eric Lee-Johnson gave me the vocabulary of the land. James K. Baxter helped me read the runes left by Polynesian and pioneer. Jim Baxter, later Hemi Baxter, remains the most enigmatic figure in my life. Now that he has shuffled off into legend I am tempted to leave well alone. Yet without him my life makes no sense.

My first glimpses were inauspicious. I had seen him thunderously drunk at an Auckland poetry reading; I had observed him bawdy at a Wellington student party. He was then in his middle twenties. His reputation was already aweing. The son of New Zealand's most celebrated pacifist in World War I, he had published his first book of verse when he was eighteen. One who read it in manuscript observed prophetically that 'The only thing to stand in the way of his becoming a poet of world stature will be some tragic interior movement in his own soul.' With wind-whipped hair, intense gaze, and sometimes cherubic face, he not only looked a poet; he was also seen to be living his lines. Drink promised to silence him before his soul was put to the test.

I met him finally, at a literary function, in his thirtieth year. He was less flamboyant, tidy, quiet, and a year sober. Before I could utter some commonplace sentiment, such as my respect for his verse, he said 'I liked your last story in the *Listener*.'

The next day, a rainy Sunday, there was a knock on our door. I opened it and found Jim in a grubby garbadine raincoat. He silently walked past me, claimed the nearest chair, and with no social overture, without even shedding his coat, began to talk. It seemed he felt our exchange of the night before unfinished. Since Gillian and I weren't on the phone he had caught a train six miles into the city, and hiked a steep mile to our cottage, to resume conversation. He hadn't been idle. En route he had even written two or three poems. For Jim writing was as natural as breathing. Verse seemed to ooze from him; his pockets were stuffed with drafts and fair copies. Then and later he made me feel a dilettante of letters.

'Do you ask yourself why you write?' he finally asked.

'Often,' I admitted.

'I write because New Zealand is a pain in my gut,' he told me. 'I think you do too.'

While I considered this appraisal of my condition Gillian brought coffee. Jim thirstily emptied his cup in three gulps and, still talking, held it out for more. Without drawing breath, he removed his coat, read several poems, and drew my attention to the mythology at work between the lines. I began to feel giddy.

An hour or two later he said mercifully, 'So let's look at your stories.'

'Now?'

'Now,' he commanded.

They kept him quiet for most of an hour.

'Yes,' he announced finally.

Yes what?

'Because this is a small country,' he explained, 'literature doesn't have to be too.'

I wasn't sure what he meant.

'Everything's here,' he explained. 'All the big things are here,' he argued. 'Love, death, and God. We've got too many bloody miniaturists. Too much backyard writing. No one looks over the fence.'

'And what are you telling me?' I asked.

'Look further,' he said. 'Let life in. Build bigger.'

It must have been ten hours before he left the cottage. Anyway it was two in the morning. Such meetings, largely monologues, became ritual; our cottage became his sounding board. Some may see egocentricity. I saw generosity, a man with a need to share the largesse of his inner life.

Soon after that encounter I wrote the first paragraphs of a manuscript which fifteen years later, in the week of Jim's death, was published as the novel *Strangers and Journeys*. There is a fetching symmetry there, though I still fail to see what it means. Somewhere over the years, in the middle of the journey, I faltered. I claimed, in a letter to Jim, that I couldn't see it through. He used this letter as the occasion for a consolatory sequence of poems. *Whoever can listen/*

Long enough will write again, he advised me in verse. Whether I listened long enough may be argued; the manuscript was long enough. *Strangers and Journeys* was to be the largest New Zealand novel published. If nothing else it had the distinction of giving rise to some of the most luminous lines written by a New Zealander:

> *The man who talks to the masters of Pig Island*
> *About the love they dread*
> *Plaits ropes of sand, yet I was born among them*
> *And will lie some day with their dead.*

He would; he does. When the day came I followed his coffin three hundred miles through rain, mist and mountains, to see him lowered into the land he saw as 'a primeval goddess pitted by sun, earthquake and the waves of the sea'. He had so often anticipated the event — 'for me no sold or rented grave' he declared accurately at the age of twenty — that the reality could easily have been anti-climax. It wasn't. Television cameras peered into his open coffin and thousands of New Zealanders shed tears. A newspaper billboard said: *James K. Baxter, Friend, 1926-1972.*

Which is as much as I can claim. Two decades later I still look for him eloquent at my shoulder when I finish a useful paragraph.

There were other writers. Most were alarmingly dedicated and embattled. In Auckland on a visit, I was ushered into Frank Sargeson's presence. I wasn't then aware of his clandestine blitz of my first short story in the *Listener*. It was some years before I learned of the animosity my name engendered. ('Why doesn't Shadbolt leave me alone?' he was once heard to shout, as if I were shadowing him daily.) At the time I merely noted something odd about the man. He retailed rather tired and smutty stories with a schoolboy snigger. He was also convinced that his suburban neighbours wanted to burn his books and add him to the pyre. Was it his need to think so? I saw kindly people calling in with gifts of fruit and vegetables for their mildly eccentric neighbour. He also had the unlovely facility of speaking ill of friends five minutes gone from his door; especially female well-wishers. Yet at the same time he was sheltering a young woman named Janet Frame — a refugee from a mental hospital — from the worst the outside world could do. With his protection, lodged in a hut to the rear of his dwelling, she was finishing her astonishing first novel *Owls Do Cry*, and a number of short stories soon to shimmer from the pages of *The New Yorker*. Janet sat curled cat-like, quiet and inscrutable on a couch while Sargeson entertained visitors. If she said a word, I never heard it. If her expression changed, I failed to note it. I sensed something remarkable going on. Her novels and autobiographies, which have made her a Nobel Prize candidate, would confirm it; something remarkable, and rather larger than I could imagine, indeed was.

Charles Brasch, poet and editor of the magazine *Landfall*, lamented, 'There are so very few of us.' Us? He meant the enlightened. I wasn't comfortable with the notion of joining a sect.

Denis Glover, stocky poet, ex-boxer and ex-sailor, was more my style. He had survived Arctic convoys to the Soviet Union in World War II, and shepherded soldiers ashore under fire in the D-Day landings. His verse was graceful, resonant, and classical. It was also witty. One of his stanzas meant more to me than most. It urged:

> *Sing all things sweet or harsh upon*
> *These islands in the Pacific sun,*
> *The mountains whitened endlessly*
> *And the white horses of the winter sea.*

We sometimes met at lunchtime in a Molesworth Street pub near the printery where he was sometimes seen busy and more often not. 'If New Zealand writers want to write like Hemingway they should first catch some bloody fish,' he told me. 'Do you catch fish?'

I seemed to be on trial.

'Sometimes,' I admitted.

'Good,' he said. 'That's a start.' Then, 'You've read Jack London?'

'Often,' I said.

'He's lustier company than Katherine Mansfield.'

I said that was my impression too.

'You'll do,' he judged.

Denis was between marriages, often drunk, and also depressed. He confessed that he had seen suicide as a solution to his problems. A gas oven looked the most useful means. He put his head in the oven and turned on the gas. Waiting on oblivion, he felt there must be a more dignified way to die. He heaved mattress and pillow into the kitchen and sealed up windows and doors. He arranged mattress and pillow to his satisfaction. At least this new posture was comfortable. Then he turned on the gas again. It hissed steadily, beginning to fill the kitchen, but taking too long. Boredom set in. Denis found himself in need of a time-killing book. He turned off the gas, unsealed the kitchen and hunted along his bookshelves for a likely volume. Here was a pickle: What was his last book to be? It had to be an old favourite. He was never going to finish it; a fresh story wouldn't do. He fell on *The Pickwick Papers*, bore it off to the kitchen, resealed the room, turned on the gas, and was soon absorbed in the book. Soon he was laughing so much that he reached for cigarettes and matches. On the verge of lighting up he was struck by the thought: If I light this cigarette, I'll kill myself.

Dickens kept Denis writing for another two decades.

Thirty-two

*I*n the 1950s such as Denis Glover and Jim Baxter were still overpoweringly Olympian. In need of contemporaries, Kevin and I thought to invent one or two. High on our list was Maurice Gee. I had known him faintly at Avondale College, largely as a serious scholar, a useful boxer and a rugby back with a neat sidestep. His introspective face suggested that he had business other than in a boxing ring and on the football field. He had. His first published story appeared in the same month as mine.

Kevin and I mounted a successful hunt for Maurice in Auckland. With a crate of beer for company, we sat among tangled pohutukawa trees on Takapuna beach one long summer night. Maurice's stories, seemingly drawn from a deep well of melancholy, might have warned us not to expect high spirits. He had recklessly thrown in a job as a country schoolteacher and returned home to write. Isolated in suburban· Auckland, estranged from his peers, he found words weren't coming. It wasn't that his parents were unsympathetic. It might have been better if they were. His left-wing and literary mother had written one or two children's books; nothing pleased her more than the notion of a novelist son.

Perhaps, I suggested, it was time to cut apron strings. The company of like-minded fellows might help too.

'Like where?' he asked.

'Wellington,' I hinted.

He wasn't sure.

Kevin went to work on his own recipe. He got Maurice drunk. I merely kidnapped him.

Finding the press-ganging of contemporaries too arduous, Kevin returned to his troglodyte life in the Waitomo Caves. Maurice and I meanwhile hitch-hiked to Wellington through sunny January, looking for stories to make sense of our lives. We didn't have to search far. We both had grandfathers filled with cosmic discontent and worth record; we both had fathers with a feeling for racehorses, mothers addicted to poetry; we both had parents who made Marxism their faith in the sullen thirties and whose lives cried out for chroniclers. There was a pact of sorts between us. We were going to tell their stories. No one informed us that this was an improbable proposition; that New Zealand had next to no novelists, and, in the fashionable view, was unlikely to have more. We whittled lines as we waited for rides on dusty roadsides. When a car came we travelled on, past the farms, hills and forests of our unlettered land. I like to think that his marvellous novel *Plumb*, and the trilogy it heralded, was at the end of that journey; I like to think that I might have had a hand in it.

There was no elation to my left. The Krushchev denunciation of Stalin in 1956 had given me the chance to remind old comrades that I had told them so. I had quoted reports from a Soviet Writers' Congress at them in vain; I had read them exerpts of Ilya Ehrenburg's novel *The Thaw* to no purpose. Even after Krushchev blew the whistle they hung on to their faith by their fingertips. Soviet suppression of the Hungarian revolt, six months later, finally persuaded many that Russian socialism, after all, left everything to be desired. Overnight my last friends and acquaintances in the Communist Party were saying their farewells.

Among them was Sid Scott, long the Party's ideologue, a blind, frail and stooped man who had given four decades of his life to interpreting the scriptures of Lenin and Marx. I had known him in Auckland; at the age of eighteen I had sat at his feet and listened to his oracular judgements. When he visited Wellington in early 1957, in the wake of his departure from the Party, Gillian and I had him as a guest. Some thirty or more of his old friends and ex-comrades crowded into our cottage to hear him confess his life a lie. It seemed George Orwell had it right in *Animal Farm* and *1984*; even the renegade Koestler in *Darkness at Noon*. And, for that matter, the despised capitalist press. This was not what his audience wished to hear. They still hoped for a new, purer Party; a new, refurbished Soviet Union. He was telling them not only that the Utopia had been hijacked by criminals, but also that it was in the nature of the beast to be corrupt. Someone protested that Sid was too bitter.

There was a long silence. Sid lifted his head slowly; his face was desolate. 'I have earned the right to be,' he announced.

There was a long silence. I heard the New Zealand Communist Party perish in that minute: the Party to which my parents had given their hopes and often their happiness was as good as gone. It was never a large presence in my life again, or theirs, though for me there was a last purging.

In early 1957, with a few hundred pounds saved, Gillian and I thought to travel. I had no future as a New Zealand film maker; there were next to no New Zealand films being made. In March there was another suggestive sign. The literary magazine *Landfall*, the journal in which Grandmother Shadbolt mistily envisaged my debut, had a short story competition to mark its tenth year. I wrote a story rich with, I thought, the resonances of urban New Zealand in the 1950s; anyway it was a long way from Uncle Bill down on the farm, or sensitive girls growing up in suburbs suspiciously like Katherine Mansfield's Karori, the stuff of most New Zealand fiction. Perhaps I was hearing my own voice for the first time; anyway the story won. There was a cheque for £25 in my pocket to say I might be a professional writer.

We booked sea passage to London in June. Two weeks before our sailing date I met an old leftist friend in the street. 'Why don't you go to Moscow?' he asked.

'Moscow?'

'And Peking.'

I assumed he was joking.

'There's a youth festival in Moscow,' he informed me. 'New Zealanders can go by way of China and the trans-Siberian railway. It's a chance to see how things really are there. Give it a go.'

In June we left for Moscow. The plane carrying us off to Sydney and Hong Kong flew out from Auckland. We had our last view of New Zealand between drifts of cloud. There were ferny hills and, before cloud closed in, a glimpse of a tidal estuary fringed with mangrove forest. For the next three years I talismanically recalled that scrap of New Zealand again and again: the hills of fern, the tangle of tidal channels, the salty mangroves. They were telling me something. Five minutes out of Auckland I had the powerful fear that I might never be back. Precedents were inauspicious. In New Zealand expatriation was still expected of writers and painters who

flew away. Most disappeared forever. London — and sometimes
Oxford and Cambridge, sometimes Paris and Majorca — swallowed
them down. Mine was the first generation of which this was untrue,
but I was not to know it. I was not to know that there were others
who had no intention of losing themselves in the world.

In Hong Kong there was a message at our hotel. Brian Brake, once a
cameraman at the National Film Unit, was staying nearby. We had
not known each other well; he had left the unit soon after I started,
but we had noted each other's existence. Lightly built, red-haired, the
son of a village storekeeper in the Southern Alps, Brian was, among
other things, a considerable climber and skier; a box Brownie given
him as a birthday gift had determined his future. When he quit the
unit he was taken on as a pupil photographer by Henri Cartier-
Bresson. There was no looking back. His sensitive work had begun
winning an international reputation. On assignment for *Life*
magazine, he was just out of China, one of the first Western
photographers allowed access to the country since communists came
to power in 1949; he had even been favoured with an intimate
portrait of Mao Tse-Tung walking in the Forbidden City. Brian
generously told us where to go, what to expect. Things were easier
now, he said. Mao's revolution was seemingly in its spring — 'let a
hundred flowers bloom, let a hundred schools of thought contend'
he had just ordered in one of this century's cruellest hoaxes — and
long-silent Chinese intellectuals were dooming themselves by
expressing reservations about the society Marxists had made.

   Meanwhile Brian was asking, 'What are you going to do with
yourself in London? When you get there?"
   'Film work, perhaps,' I shrugged.
   I didn't quite believe it.
   'Or write,' he said shrewdly.
   'Perhaps,' I allowed.
   'I've been fortunate,' he said.
   'So I gather.'
   He was the most successful expatriate New Zealander of his
generation; and he wasn't yet thirty.
   'I suppose you think I won't be going home again.'
   'Why should you, with your luck?'
   'Then you're wrong,' he informed me. 'When I've finished

photographing the world, I'll be ready for New Zealand. I want New Zealanders to *see* their own country.'

He seemed to mean it.

'Maybe we can work together,' he suggested.

'I'd like that,' I confessed.

With more in common than China, Brian and I parted that night as accomplices. Whatever the world said, we had our own programme.

Next day Gillian and I crossed a little wooden footbridge from Hong Kong to China. On each side of the bridge were uniformed men with firearms. Those on the Chinese side had red stars on their caps. We set down our suitcases and took our first breath of Marxist air.

Thirty-three

*H*oping for the best and fearing the worst, I approached Moscow as a backsliding cradle Catholic might close with the Vatican. The route was fittingly convoluted. There was half China first, and most of Siberia.

The clogs of Canton's people made a steady river of sound outside our hotel window; even at three in the morning it did not diminish. I asked how the hundred flowers were flourishing. Our interpreter professed not to know what I was talking about. I said I wished to meet Chinese writers. He took us to a clothing factory. 'Please criticise if you see any fault,' the interpreter said earnestly. 'We welcome criticism from comrades of the West.' Never having been inside a clothing factory before, I had nothing useful to contribute. I wished to meet writers, I repeated. Our interpreter took us to a kindergarden. 'Please criticise if you see any fault,' he said. I had never seen inside a kindergarten before either.

Canton's writers were not at home. In Shanghai I tried again. Two nervous young men were finally paraded. We drank green tea. They were circumspect, a cultural commissar inches to their rear. What of the hundred flowers, I asked. Were a hundred schools of thought contending? Were poets writing love lyrics again, novelists freely telling their tales?

They looked at each other. They looked at their minder.

'It is difficult for comrades of the West to understand,' one informed me. 'There is no gap between theory and practice here. Nor is there room for idealist philosophy.'

'But the hundred flowers?' I persisted.

The cultural commissar signalled an end to the discussion. It didn't matter. By that time I had decided that though the two might have been good Party men, they were about as literary as the clothing factory.

In Nanking there were museums, parks of culture, and factories and kindergartens again. ('Please criticise, comrades from the west.') Gillian and I took refuge in an Anglican church. The congregation was small, and mostly old; there were old women with bound feet, grotesquely tiny.

The priest was affable, worldly, and bold. Unlike the counterfeit writers seen in Shanghai, he didn't look over his shoulder. He asked how long we were visiting China. Between two and three weeks, we told him.

'Have you seen things that are good?'

'Much that is impressive,' I said politely.

'He who rides the horse sees only the flowers,' he warned with a sweet smile.

Was it Confucius? Never mind. It was a useful proverb that year. But by mid-summer there were barely enough blooms for a credible bouquet.

That afternoon, while Gillian slept, I walked alone through the Nanking market. I had given up making sense of China; I was no longer in search of fellow writers who might help. Yet I met my model there. He was a marketplace storyteller, perhaps seventy, with eloquent hands and a marvellously mobile face. His attentive audience wept sometimes, laughed often, and trembled with fright. With magical ease, and much narrative bravado, he became one character, then another: women, children, warlords and dragons. Bitter armies battled around him; sweet lovers met. Understanding not a word, I was mesmerised. He seemed to be telling all the stories ever told. He was showing me what I should be about.

In Peking our interpreter was excited. 'You have worked in film,' he said, 'and I therefore have invitation for you to visit a film studio. This is particularly splendid.'

The studio was outside the city. At first the afternoon went much as visits to factories and kindergartens had gone. There was a tour of facilities, of processing laboratories, and finally earnest explanations over green tea. We were then shown samples of the studio's documentary work. These samples were not only hysterically propagandist; they were technically abysmal. It was a relief when the screening ended. 'Please criticise if you see fault,' the interpreter said ritually. 'We welcome criticism from comrades of the West.'

I had been unable to offer informed comment on the quality of Chinese clothing; or on the calibre of Chinese kindergartens. This was different. This was my current craft. I left ideology alone and talked of camerawork and editing. I ventured in passing that understatement was desirable in documentary work. Messages, if any, were best left to look after themselves; it was for the audience to put two and two together.

To that point the studio visit had been all smiles. These vanished. Frost formed. A particularly sharp icicle seemed to be hovering above my head. Agitated discourse followed, all in Mandarin. Our interpreter was in distress; it seemed he could not translate what was being said, or refused to. Our visit to the studio was terminated. We were rushed to our car without handshakes or farewells.

'What was that about?' I asked our mute interpreter.

He remained unwilling to say.

'Please,' I said.

Still in turmoil, he reported, 'They say you are an enemy of the Chinese people.'

'Me?'

'And an agent of reactionaries who wishes to slander the people of China. Tell me this is not so.'

'It is not so,' I told him.

'Good,' he said, but did not believe me.

It had not been a splendid day. He never asked for our judgement again. There were comrades from the West and comrades from the West. We were the unenlightened kind. The enlightened knew not to oblige with criticism when requested.

That evening we had dinner with David Chipp, the Reuters correspondent in Peking. We told him of the bewildering visit to the film studio.

'Par for the course,' he said.

Alex Young was a New Zealand-born Chinese. I had known him as a student socialist in Wellington. Soon after Mao's triumph in 1949 he travelled to China, like thousands of other overseas Chinese, and threw in his lot with the revolution. Did he, and they, expect gratitude? If so they were soon disabused. They met derision and distrust. Those with university education were especially suspect. They were given menial work to rid themselves of pernicious outside influences. Many were exiled to remote provinces. Some were given prison cells.

Alex found me at our Peking hotel. We ate together. He looked diminished. His eyes were bleak. He had had his share of cleaning latrines, and humbling himself before sadistic commissars.

'Life in the new China isn't easy,' Alex confided.

'I can see that,' I said.

'Don't say I said so,' he asked.

'Of course not,' I promised.

'Do you know what my trouble is?' he confided. 'I still smell New Zealand trees. I dream New Zealand beaches. When I wake I am in this strange and cruel country called China again.'

He inquired wistfully after friends in Wellington. 'Are their parties still as good?' he asked. 'Are the girls as pretty?' He was not surprised that so many had put Marxism behind them. He had no chance to. Unable to escape China, Alex had the public beatings, dunces' caps and forced confessions of the cultural revolution in his future, and the gunfire of Tiananmen Square; he would survive both to die ridiculously of cancer. Meanwhile his aberrant days were done. He made our lives look shallow. With reminiscing finished, Alex slipped off into the dark and, with a last look over his shoulder, rejoined his eight hundred million compatriots.

Asia became Europe between one mile and the next. Across the Sino-Soviet border faces were suddenly and dourly Russian. Moscow was now a mere six-day journey. Lovely Lake Baikal floated past at sunset. There were knives and forks instead of chopsticks in the dining car, and caviar too. Siberia, a name rich with misery, was colourful in summer — why had no one ever said so? There were forests, sparkling rivers, candy-coloured villages, and ravishing miles of wildflowers. I expected emptiness. There was seldom a vista without dwellings — and, for that matter, innocent of Marxist icons. Even the humblest whistle-stop had its statue of Lenin, and banners and slogans riding the breeze off tundra and taiga. Every horizon and every halt said this was the Soviet Union, the socialist sixth of the world. Hungry for the rhythms of the West, I read Simone de Beauvoir's *The Mandarins*, which was no help in clearing my head. I thought my feverish condition ideological in origin. Meanwhile it was masquerading as Asian flu. Or so it was diagnosed by the muscular woman doctor who rammed a thermometer into my rectum.

As delirium lifted I had my first intelligible glimpse of the Soviet Union at work. Aboard our train were hundreds of young travellers on their way to the festival in Moscow: Vietnamese, Indonesians and Malayans, but mostly Australians and New Zealanders. Wherever our train halted, there were Russian welcome parties. Neatly dressed Komsomols and Pioneers sang patriotic songs, showered us with flowers, and pinned hammer and sickle badges on our chests.

The organisers of these festivities were at pains to make them appear impromptu. At one stop I watched a young man, off to the side of the platform, attempt to join in the welcome to the Western visitors. He bore a spray of flowers and a plainly wrapped parcel. What was inside? A book of Russian verse with Siberian ferns and flowers pressed in its pages, or perhaps a forbidden manuscript? Anyway he was halted by two policemen before he reached us. He argued vehemently. The policemen did too. There was anguish on the young man's face. 'Please,' he was protesting. 'Please.' Two more policemen joined the argument; they appeared to be telling him that he had no business in the vicinity of visitors to the Soviet Union. Who might he have been? An exile, a dissident, or just innocently friendly? That plainly wrapped parcel haunts me. Could it have been the equivalent of some marooned mariner's message corked in a bottle? Anyway it never beached in Western hands. Finally five or six policemen were manhandling him thuggishly, trampling his spray of flowers as they hurled him from view.

Thereafter I seemed to know all I need know about the Soviet Union. I hadn't even reached Moscow.

Thirty-four

Moscow was onion-domed churches, more banners, more statues of Lenin, and boulevards almost empty of traffic. Despite Krushchev's denunciation, Stalin's corpse was on view beside Lenin's in the mausoleum on Red Square, hardly yet cool. One Muscovite story said the apprehensive inhabitants of hell were refusing him admission; that he might be on his way back. Circumspect citizens of the Soviet Union still looked over their shoulders.

Before I left New Zealand a trade union lawyer had given me a mission. He wanted to know what had become of one Len Wincott, a leading figure in Britain's Invergordon naval mutiny of the 1930s. A Party man, Wincott had taken refuge in the Soviet Union. He had been sighted there several times up to the mid 1940s. Then he vanished. Inquiries from Britain and elsewhere produced no result. The presumption was that he had been spirited off to a labour camp, perhaps shot. When I reached Moscow there were letters and some printed material waiting for me from my lawyer friend, with more details likely to be helpful in determining Wincott's fate. It never struck me that my letters might have been opened, and their contents examined by eyes other than mine. Anyway I wasn't optimistic about the mission. Who was I to hunt down a lost Englishman in the Soviet Union? Who was I to knock on the door of the KGB? I was neither a friend nor relative of Wincott; I had no personal stake in the matter. Though in Britain he had been a celebrated hero of the left, a naval rating who once defied admirals of the fleet, Wincott was no more than a name to me.

While reading my correspondence in the lobby of our hostel, that first morning in Moscow, I seemed to hear my surname spoken. There was a stocky man at the reception desk. He looked Russian;

his clothes were shapelessly Soviet; he wore a workingman's cap. Yet his voice suggested that English was his native tongue. 'Shadbolt?' he was asking the Russian girl at the desk. 'A New Zealand visitor?'

I made my way to the desk. 'You're looking for me,' I said.

The man put out a hand. 'Len Wincott,' he said.

With surprise past we sat and drank flavourless lemonade. His was not the most dramatic of stories; I would hear more terrible. In 1947 he had been about to travel from Leningrad to Moscow on an overnight train; his Russian-born wife was waiting at the other end. His train moved off, then halted out of sight of farewelling friends. A posse of policemen boarded his carriage and whisked him off in standard Stalinist style. No one saw him taken. He simply evaporated. Though notified that he was an agent of the imperialist West, that was as far as formalities went; there was no trial. Before long he was behind barbed wire in the penal colony of Vorkuta. In Moscow his wife waited for him in vain; it was five years before she knew what had happened, and most of another five before he was released with apologies.

I liked the man. He was gentle. He seemed honest.

'How did you get my name?' I asked.

'From an English visitor,' he explained. 'He told me you were interested in my case.'

This was possible. My lawyer friend, having made a hobby of the hunt for Wincott, corresponded widely. For all I knew he might have informed someone in England that I was due in Moscow.

'And how do you feel about the Soviet Union now?' I asked.

'The same,' he said.

Naively, perhaps, I thought that impossible.

'Not bitter?'

'Never,' he claimed. 'Mistakes have been made. They are now being corrected. Thank friends in the West interested in my case. Tell them I'm in good health and happy, and don't want any fuss made.'

'It would be better coming from you,' I suggested. 'Why not write yourself and tell them?'

'Perhaps I will,' he said vaguely. He added, 'Is it true that Trotzkyites have been taking up my case to discredit the Soviet Union?'

'Possibly,' I said.

'That does me no good here,' he explained. 'Nor stories in the Western press.'

'I expect not.'

'I don't want anyone to lose faith in the Soviet Union on my account.'

We talked a little longer. I never saw him again. I wanted to believe him. With the best will in the world, I began finding that a problem. What of his appearance magically soon after I picked up correspondence concerning his case? It was less difficult to believe that our meeting had been choreographed. The KGB's attention to detail was infamous. Possibly not even an obscure New Zealand writer was beneath their attention; anyone likely to rake Soviet muck was worth nobbling. Anyway, if this was their hand, they impressed me mightily. There was another question too. Had I met the real Len Wincott?

On balance, I thought so. I reported him found.

Thirty-five

The youth festival meant Muscovites were out in the streets and talking freely to foreigners for the first time in decades. With my own programme, I ducked most formal spectacles. Literary occasions were lively fiascos. One was ambitiously advertised as giving 'the youth of the world' a chance to meet Soviet writers. Youth turned up. Soviet writers of distinction didn't. Some sent unconvincing apologies. Others were unaccountably missing, notably the novelist Ilya Ehrenburg, then in disfavour. Rumour said he had been removed from the panel at the last moment. A carefully culled selection of middle-aged mediocrities, as dour as the doctrine of socialist realism, sat on the platform. Years of repression and compromise, perhaps in penal colonies, had left their faces lined. They protested to their cheated audience that they were not there to represent the Soviet government; no one believed a word. 'Why are we who criticise your fiction,' asked a young Swede, 'called enemies of Soviet literature? We might be right; we might be wrong. But we are not enemies.'

'Would you like to be told that you had been dead since 1930?' one stony-faced man on the platform asked.

He meant since the suicide of the poet Mayakovsky.

Otherwise the occasion was an insult to everyone present. Was this the nation that had perfected show trials? If so, its touch was gone. The affair ended with the youth of the world, first by the dozen, then by the hundred, storming out in disgust. Moscow had never seen anything like it in years.

Next night, less formally, Ilya Ehrenburg took the platform at Moscow university. Short, frail, one of the few notable Soviet writers to have survived Stalin's purges, if not without compromise, he was now purging his conscience and perhaps his soul. Many distinguished dead seemed to keep him company on the platform:

the likes of Osip Mandelstam and Isaac Babel long in unmarked graves. Quietly, sanely, Ehrenburg led his audience through the Soviet maze and, in the end, offered light and a little hope. 'We have to learn to be critical of ourselves,' he pleaded. 'Be patient.'

'For how long?' a voice in the auditorium, perhaps Soviet, asked.

Ehrenburg lifted an arm in a sort of salute. 'You,' he promised, 'will live to see the day.'

The audience ovation lasted five minutes. I managed to find Ehrenburg's hand in the uproar and thank him for his novel *The Thaw*. His smile was weary. He knew he would never live to see the day.

The shock was yet to come. The Soviet press didn't report a word. Not *Pravda*, not *Isvestia*, not the *Literaturnaya Gazeta*. Ehrenburg's masterly performance didn't exist.

Perhaps I could put it on record. I was asked by the editors of the literary journal *Druzba Narodov* for an article on my impressions of literary Moscow. For the most part I was tactful. Then, for a page, I praised Ehrenburg for not treating foreign visitors as fools.

'This is interesting,' said the editor who bore it away. Over his shoulder he added, 'It may be just what we need.'

I wondered. Especially when I was asked for another article by an editor of the English-language *Moscow News*.

'It is unnecessary to say too much about Ehrenburg,' he said, when outlining my brief.

'Unnecessary?' I asked.

'It is not convenient,' he said.

The Soviet Union was a world of weasel words. Stalin's lies were incorrect. His evils were mistakes. His merciless purges were anti-democratic. His massacres were errors. His tyranny was a cult of personality. Anti-Semitism was anti-cosmopolitan. Until Russians learned to call a spade a spade they would never be free of the past. Liberation could only come through language; it would be a long time coming. Sad Ehrenburg seemed to know. But he also knew honesty would outlive lies. Of Boris Pasternak he said, 'If all the world were covered in asphalt, somewhere a crack would appear and grass begin to grow again.'

The crack was soon to appear, and a lone blade of grass. Did he know of, or had he read, *Dr Zhivago*, then still in manuscript?

Pasternak's name surfaced on a boat journey along the Moscow-Volga canal. Soviet writers were entertaining foreign literary people. I spent much of the voyage with Samuel Marshak, essayist, distinguished translator of Shakespeare and Robert Burns, luminous autobiographer, and man who had, perhaps by deft evasion, managed to outlast the Stalin years with serenity. He nodded sympathetically when I talked of the Ehrenburg occasion. There were, he agreed, things to be said. He was grateful to Ehrenburg for saying them. He seemed to be saying that he had missed his own chance. We were joined by Kornei Chukovsky, the most celebrated of Russian children's writers. He liked New Zealanders, having met them as fellow belligerents in World War I; he remembered their hospitality and wanted to return it. 'Why don't you come down to my dacha at Peredelkino for the day?' he asked. 'You can meet my next door neighbour Boris Pasternak.'

I promised to try.

The festival ended. The banners came down, the decorations, and a cool autumn wind gusted down bleak boulevards. Muscovites were monosyllabic again and mostly indoors. Suddenly we were housed in the Hotel Leningradskaya, one of the more lunatic prototypes of Stalinist architecture. There was a limousine on call, guides and interpreters. There were even packets of pocket money. We were, it seemed, honoured guests of the Writers' Union. I didn't look this gift horse in the mouth. My parents' long devotion to the Soviet Union entitled me to a little largesse. Honoured we might have been, but that didn't stop some KGB functionary checking on our whereabouts with telephone calls without fail at 6.30 in the evening. One or two muffled words in Russian. Then silence. After a week we were used to it. We even gave him a name: Charlie. What did Charlie do when we failed to answer? Was another Charlie sent out to ensure that we were meeting only worthy citizens? Did Charlie report our truancy to Charlies in the Writers' Union? Or was it just ancient habit?

I had another mission, this time for a Jewish friend. He wanted to know the fate of forty prominent Jewish cultural figures arrested on Stalin's order during an 'anti-cosmopolitan' purge in 1948. This was best answered by the next of kin of those purged. Helpful Soviet friends steered me to a small Moscow flat to meet Esther Markish, widow of the Yiddish poet Peretz Markish, one of the forty arrested.

222

Her apartment was now a shrine to his memory: there were books, photographs, and paintings of her husband. It was difficult to take it in. Esther Markish was the most beautiful woman I had ever met.

'Forgive my English,' she said. 'I have forgotten how to talk to people from the West.'

'Will my visit cause problems ?' I asked.

She shrugged. 'I do not care,' she said.

When the KGB took Peretz and his colleagues, she and her son Simon had been thrown out of their apartment; they were dependent on friends brave enough to offer beds. After four years in prison, Peretz had been shot without trial in 1952. Esther had not had his death confirmed until 1955. She was also informed that he was innocent of wrongdoing. She was given a new apartment, and monetary compensation. But nothing could repair the evil done. (Esther didn't use weasel words). The arrests and executions had torn the heart out of Jewish culture in the Soviet Union. Yiddish literature had literally been destroyed. Some called it a literature of manuscripts. She called it a literature of the dead.

After an hour or two I felt I was putting her under strain. Tears were always near. I rose to leave. But I heard myself say, 'There is a function at the Writers' Union tonight. Perhaps you would care to keep me company?'

She thought for a moment. 'I have never been there since Peretz was taken,' she said.

'The more reason,' I suggested.

'What did the Writers' Union do for him? Nothing. There will be people there tonight, time servers, who looked the other way when Peretz was arrested. There will be people there who spoke against him or even connived in his arrest. There are also those who once claimed to be friends of Peretz and who have never been near me to convey their regrets, not even with knowledge of his innocence.'

'I understand,' I said.

I should have known better than to suggest it.

'But perhaps it is time,' she said suddenly.

'What does that mean?'

Her eyes were bright. 'I will go with you,' she announced.

That evening we picked Esther up in our limousine and bore her off to 52 Vorovskovy Street, the handsome residence Tolstoy bestowed on the Rostovs in *War and Peace* and now housing the Writers'

Union. There we were party to a vivid moment in Russian literary history. Esther's entry to the function was regal. The silence was aweing. Several writers moved swiftly out of her line of sight, looking for a way to flee the function. Some ostentatiously turned their backs. Others, more kindly, or more penitent, moved to make her welcome; even to embrace her. She was the event of the evening and knew it. With calm eyes, she carried it all off superbly. Before long even many whose first instinct had been to avoid peril were clustering around her. There was even a little laughter.

Toward the evening's end she approached me. 'Thank you for this,' she said. 'I did not know I could be so brave.'

She had been. She also did Peretz proud.

Thirty-six

*T*hat same evening I was waylaid by a friendly Russian journalist. His name was Misha. He wanted an interview.

'On what topic?' I asked.

'You name it,' he said. He added, 'You have an interesting article in the magazine *Druzba Narodov.*'

'You have seen it?' I asked.

I hadn't.

'I have seen it unofficially,' he explained.

'I see.'

'I think you should know,' he continued sotto voce, 'that all reference to Ilya Ehrenburg has been removed from your article.'

'All?'

'He gets not a mention. However, please do not say anything. I am not supposed to know. Nor are you. A meeting of editors was called about publication of your article. Some said it should be published in full. The majority were timid. They wish no trouble.'

'It was my view of Ehrenburg, not theirs.'

'You must understand,' he said impishly. 'Ehrenburg is trouble.'

I liked Misha. We arranged a meeting.

What am I to say? I took Misha to be a genuine dissenter. Perhaps he was. He certainly introduced us to several. I also believed his story as he told it at an outdoor table in Gorki Park. Perhaps it was true. Thirty years on another scenario seems possible.

His father, he told me, had been a good Communist. He was arrested and imprisoned in the purges of the 1930s, while Misha was still at school. Misha had been asked to denounce his father. When he refused to, he was expelled. His father had been released in 1940, in time to be killed fighting the Nazis. Despite ideological unreliability in his background young Misha finally became a national leader in the Komsomol; he wrote, spoke and lectured for the Party. He then worked for the KGB or its predecessor, the NKVD, in Berlin and Vienna in the late 1940s. After two or three years he was recalled to Moscow. Anti-semitism was in business again, and Misha was half Jewish. He wasn't fired. He was assigned to intelligence work within the Soviet Union, especially within the Jewish community. He protested, he said. He informed his superiors that though he was willing to work against his country's enemies, in the Berlin and Vienna stations of the KGB, he was not taken by the notion of working against his own people. At that point he *was* dismissed from the KGB. He went jobless, living on the charity of friends, until after Stalin's death. Finally he found his way into journalism by a side door. His by-line was now regular in several Soviet publications. I saw no reason to be sceptical about his C.V.

I should have been. In the lethal climate of Stalin's last years, could the most principled KGB man have risked making his real feelings known to his superiors? He would have been under suspicion, a man marked.This is not to argue that there were no men of honour in the Soviet apparatus. We know now that there have been, even in the KGB. The KGB could be clumsy, as shown by our nightly telephone caller. It could also be sophisticated. Misha was nothing if not sophisticated. His jesuitical side surfaced when we talked of the recent and very public resignation from the U.S. Communist Party by the novelist Howard Fast.

Though few may remember now, Fast was then the world's best-selling novelist; his novels, due to his standing in the Soviet Union, sold in millions. Hemingway, Fitzgerald and Faulkner were unpublished in the Soviet Union. For most Russian readers, Fast *was* U.S. literature. There was no Western novelist more esteemed; Fast's brief imprisonment, after his clash with the U.S. Un-American Activities Committee, made him even more a hero. The shock of his resignation, of the Soviet Union's most loyal literary ally, was still reverberating in Moscow. Almost overnight the presses stopped rolling on the latest Fast translation. Letters to the novelist from his Soviet readers stopped arriving in weighty mail-bags at his door. His now suspect novels were rumoured to be disappearing from libraries.

'It is madness,' I told Misha. 'One day he is a great novelist, the next he is not. He is the same novelist; the same man. How can the Soviet Union be taken seriously by anyone of intelligence?'

Misha shook his head. 'But he should not have resigned,' he said.

'What else could he have done?' I protested. 'He was lied to. He was betrayed.'

'He could still quarrel with us, and not leave the Party.'

'Not to the same effect,' I argued.

'That is where you are wrong,' Misha insisted. 'Resignation was noble, easy and silly. He would have had influence with us had he remained loyal on the surface. Now he has none.'

I shrugged. 'Are you loyal on the surface?'

'Of course,' he said with a smile. 'If you wish to change an institution, you work within it. That is as true of the communist movement as of anything else. If former friends of the Soviet Union, like Fast for instance, like yourself for instance, were to keep differences in the family to yourselves, and yet make your criticisms heard here, matters might be different. If we are to change things here we need friends in the West.'

So what was he saying? With hindsight I see an amiable sounding out. Family? What family? Might it have three initials? The KGB didn't devote itself only to policing Soviet citizens, to deterring dissent, or to the gathering of raw intelligence. It also liked outside friends, desirably recruited young, who might at some point become prominent in their own societies. Loyal friends. Family friends. There was a name for such friends: agents of influence. People who might be won by a liberal face. Potentially helpful people who might be flattered by the prospect of being privy to the higher theology of the Soviet Union.

There was another clue, though it may have meant nothing, at that first meeting in Gorki Park. Under Misha's arm were English language newspapers. These were a rare sight in the Soviet Union, never on sale. Misha had *The New York Times, The New York Herald Tribune, The Economist,* and the *New Statesman.* I knew that access to such Western publications was reserved to reliable members of the regime. The KGB qualified. Its functionaries were unlikely to suffer ideological confusion.

'My homework,' Misha explained.

Perhaps I was too.

'I would like to visit Kornei Chukovsky in Peredelkino,' I told our guide. 'He wishes me to meet his neighbour Boris Pasternak.'

I didn't know it then, but Pasternak may have been interested in meeting a New Zealander. Manuscripts of his poems had been smuggled out to the West in the New Zealand diplomatic pouch.

Loud telephone calls to the Writers' Union followed, all in Russian.

'It is not convenient today,' our guide reported.

'Kornei Chukovsky said we were welcome at any time,' I objected.

'It is not convenient,' she insisted.

'Why not?'

'Because,' she said, 'I am taking you to Tolstoy's estate at Yasnaya Polyana. You can meet his old secretary who still lives there. You can visit Tolstoy's grave in the woods.'

She made the prospect sound charming. So it proved to be. Who could not be stirred by that lonely grave in the woods? But dead Tolstoy of Yasnaya Polyana was no substitute for live Pasternak of Peredelkino.

Pasternak was mysteriously in the air. Breakfasting at our table in the Leningradskaya was an Italian literary man. He translated Soviet writers including, so he was at pains to add, Pasternak. He was here in Russia to check on the Italian translation of a long novel the poet had lately finished; Pasternak had been working on it for decades and decided the time had come to publish. Our Italian friend predicted that the novel was going to surprise the world.

I had an appointment with the grim Alexei Surkov, the secretary of the Writers' Union, next day. We had already had one meeting on the subject of how much freedom, or how little, Soviet writers now enjoyed. It had not been enlightening. Sitting under a painting which pictured Gorki reading to Stalin, Surkov had been rich in personal anecdotes of the late dictator, but less forthcoming about literary life under his successors. I thought I might ask Surkov about Pasternak's novel. Might its publication herald a new liberalism in Soviet publishing? Pasternak, after all, hadn't been given a hearing in years: it was warming to know that Russians might be reading him again.

I travelled to the house of the Rostovs at 52 Vorovskovy Street to keep the appointment with Surkov. His secretary appeared. She was embarrassed. 'I'm afraid Comrade Surkov can't see you today,' she explained. 'Something urgent has come up. He has had to fly to Milan.'

'To Milan?'

'That is correct. To Italy.'

I didn't make the connection. It was another brush with Russian literary history. 'Something urgent' was *Dr Zhivago*. Publication had been halted in the Soviet Union. But the Italian communist publisher Feltrinelli still held a copy of Pasternak's original manuscript. Surkov had flown to Milan to retrieve it. He had no luck; Feltrinelli went ahead and published. The translator at the breakfast table was right. The world was awed. Within the year there were photographs of Kornei Chukovsky splitting a bottle of champagne with Boris Pasternak, at Peredelkino, in celebration of the Nobel Prize. Were visitors to Peredelkino inconvenient that day too?

I met Misha sometimes in Gorki Park, sometimes on street corners. Often we made our way to the Artists' Cafe on Stanislavsky Street, near the theatre which also carried the famous name. There Misha ordered a Georgian wine of 1953 vintage. 'See?' he said. 'Wine from Stalin's birthplace in the year of his death. It is the most popular wine in Moscow. Let us drink to glorious 1953.'

The toast was premature. In Hungary the executions of Imre Nagy, Pal Maleter, and other leaders of the Hungarian uprising, would soon be announced. In the Soviet Union itself repression would roll on for another thirty years.

'I nearly drank myself to death after Soviet tanks smashed into Budapest,' Misha confided. 'I wasn't the only one. I have an English friend here, a good communist who has thrown in his lot with the Soviet Union, who also drank more than was good for him; he saw all that he believed in, all that he had given his life for, betrayed by those tanks.'

'An Englishman?' I asked. 'Who?'

Misha was untypically reticent. 'I have said too much,' he decided.

He had. Everything he said, and much that he didn't, suggested Guy Burgess or Donald McLean, the Cambridge-educated English diplomats who had flown to the Soviet Union before exposure as spies. They were now safe in Moscow under KGB care. If Misha saw something of them, what did that mean?

Georgia's most popular vintage continued to flow. I cannot recall who picked up the bills. Let us assume it was Misha. And there were mysterious tickets for the ballet, the theatre and the circus. If he was still with the KGB, interesting himself in visitors to Moscow, it was work he enjoyed. For a journalist he spent remarkably little time at his typewriter, or with paperwork, unless perusal of Western magazines counted.

'I will give you a story,' he offered. 'No one has printed it yet. It is yours if you want it.'

'Go on,' I said.

'When Stalin died there was a plan to open his apartment outside Moscow to the public as a museum, exactly as he had left it. It was a revelation for those who saw it — a spartan place, sparsely furnished. He had no more than a handful of books and no paintings on the walls. There was just a solitary photograph of himself in military uniform taking the salute at a May Day parade. There was not even a formal bed. There were two or three couches; the supposition was that he slept on a different one each night because he feared an assassination attempt by someone in his retinue. There was a long bare table on which he ate alone, and on which he planned strategy with his generals during the war. The wardrobe held a meagre collection of uniforms, and one ordinary civilian suit. Those who looked into the wardrobe began the rumour that he had worn this civilian suit when he moved unrecognised among his people. Does that seem likely to you? No? So we will forget the rumour. The important thing is that there were no luxuries at all, but for an old gramophone and a few records of Georgian folk music. Was this the abode of the standard-bearer of mankind, the father of his people? It was more the dwelling place of a hermit, a recluse, a terrified man. It was never opened to the public. It was closed and perhaps cleansed of him. It alarmed visitors too much. It said the most powerful man in the world was also the loneliest man in the world.'

I seemed to have had a surfeit of Georgia's prize wine. Misha too was melancholy.

'I didn't need to tell you that story,' he decided.

'Perhaps not,' I said, puzzled.

'But better it is told,' he suggested. 'Write it down somewhere, print it anywhere, so that one day it can be found and not forgotten. Promise?'

I promised.

'Good,' he said. 'That is what writers are for.'

If he was what I now suspect him to have been, Misha may by this time have decided the cut of my jib unsuitable. Agents of influence were made of more reliable material. That, however, didn't preclude a parting gift — the story of Stalin. Let us allow that he was still in the employ of the KGB. That didn't make him less a Russian. The story was doubly a gift. I now knew what writers were for.

There was an odd sequel. Two or three years later a Soviet diplomat, who later turned out to be the KGB resident in New Zealand, expressed the wish to meet me. I couldn't think why. I had several times made my feelings about the Soviet Union known in print, and they were not of the kind to win the favour of a Soviet diplomat. We met. We talked, mainly of matters of no consequence, for an hour or two. Perhaps I spoke with dismay of the persecution of Pasternak following *Dr Zhivago* and the Nobel Prize. Perhaps I didn't. I cannot recall. The occasion was baffling, full of things unsaid. When we parted, he presented me with Soviet magazines, among them a propagandist journal called *The New Times*. Chance or otherwise arranged it that copies of this magazine featured articles under Misha's name. They expressed the most devout of Soviet sentiments; there was not an unorthodox syllable. I never saw the diplomat again, or heard of Misha. Perhaps those copies of *The New Times*, with Misha's by-line, were meant to provoke an inquiry. If so, I failed to oblige. Was the diplomat checking out Misha or me? If the second, possibly the diplomat was merely confirming Misha's findings in the course of Moscow fieldwork.

Why record this here? That is what writers are for.

A dozen years further on I was commissioned to cover New Zealand's first and only spy trial. The country's most eminent civil servant was charged with passing secrets to the Soviet Union. No evidence was produced of secrets passed. The civil servant in question, an economist and social historian named William Sutch, was nearing the end of a distinguished career, largely in the field of trade and commerce, and now as chairman of the New Zealand Arts Council. Might he have been handing over information of use to the Bolshoi ballet? It was not only like a murder trial without a body; it was like a murder trial with no known victim. Yet it was plain that Sutch's contacts with the KGB had been regular — and prearranged — on wet and windy street corners even in the middle of bitter Wellington winters. Sutch unconvincingly explained that he had been interesting himself in the fate of Soviet writers. But why on wintry street corners? Why not before a log fire in a warm home? No one would have thought it exceptional for the chairman of the New Zealand Arts council to be entertaining a Soviet guest.

Few could make sense of the charge, least of all the jury sitting in judgement. Decency demanded that he be found not guilty, and he was. The jury was never to know that Sutch had spent some months of his youth in the Soviet Union at a time, in the early 1930s, when wandering Westerners were unwelcome, especially in the regions where Russia's recalcitrant peasantry was perishing by the million. Might there have been a Misha in his life? Might there have been Moscow dinners too?

The jury, and perhaps the prosecutor, had never heard of agents of influence. Such agents didn't dirty their hands with state secrets; they gave paternal and largely unwritten advice. They also reported on people of social or cultural eminence who might be receptive to a Soviet approach; who might be, as Sutch himself was, flattered by the attentions of a powerful intelligence agency, so making themselves candidates for blackmail. Documents suggesting this were never placed before the court; reputations of civil servants of stainless character would have been at risk.

Until the KGB surrenders the files, which it may any month now, the verdict is open. Mine on Misha too.

Thirty-seven

Next morning I asked our guide if there was still a chance of visiting Kornei Chukovsky and Boris Pasternak. She professed surprise; she pretended she had never heard the request before. In any case it was impossible. Not just inconvenient. Impossible.

'You are going to Leningrad this afternoon,' she announced, flourishing train tickets. 'All is arranged.'

When we returned from Leningrad I asked again.

Impossible, she said. A visit to Peredelkino was impossible at this time.

'Besides,' she added, this time flourishing air tickets, 'you are going to Georgia this afternoon. All is arranged.'

If I persisted in asking for Peredelkino, for Chukovsky and Pasternak, I might be offered every republic in the Soviet Union.

The Georgian excursion was a package designed for literary visitors, especially for those with difficult requests. When all else failed they could be shunted south to Stalin's sunny birthplace and silenced with wine. We appeared to be bundled together at random — leftovers from the festival, odds and sods no one knew what to do with. Among our companions were Assad, a lanky young novelist from Pakistan; Jorge, a half-Indian poet from Bolivia; Washington, a plump essayist from Peru; Praxita, a fragile young poetess from Chile; Pedro, an exiled poet and academic from Venezuela; and Kazim, a gloomy Persian poet who looked unnervingly like the late Boris Karloff. We got to know each other well at the airport. Again and again our flight was postponed. There were technical problems; there were electrical storms. The hard wooden seats in the waiting room filled with people, mainly peasants with bundles, waiting on grounded aircraft. Afternoon became dusk; dusk became night. At two in the morning I found Assad the Pakistani wandering mournful. 'Mister Maurice,' he said. 'I can no sleep. I think we will no go to Georgia. I think there is no storm. I think our plane is too dangerous to fly and they will no tell us. I think nothing works in the Soviet Union. I can no sleep for thinking. Why are we here? I no wish to go to Georgia. I no ask to go to Georgia. Did you?'

'No,' I admitted.

'It is plot to be rid of us,' he argued. 'I can no sleep for thinking.'

Elsewhere the Latins were tangled and asleep on a couch. Jorge had covered his face with a crumpled copy of the magazine *Soviet Union*. Washington snored. Pretty Praxita slept delicately on Pedro's shoulder.

Nearby was another sleepless individual, not of our party, a Hungarian checking papers in his brief-case. He looked like a Party functionary. 'You must come to Hungary,' he said. 'Our new Government is a fine one. Our problems are past.'

'But you put writers in prison,' I said.

'This is exaggeration,' he claimed. 'Not *all* writers.'

I climbed to the restaurant. There were sleepy waitresses and empty tables. Sinister Kazim sat in a lonely corner, curtains billowing behind him, brooding on a bottle of Georgian wine. I was too tired to notice whether it was 1953 vintage. Planes taxied loudly and pointlessly back and forward over the tarmac outside. Though their noise promised much, none flew.

'I did not ask for this,' he informed me. 'For twelve days I wait with that crazy Pakistani for a plane to Uzbekistan so we may study Muslims in the Soviet Union, and meet Uzbek writers. Now we wait for a plane to Georgia. For what do I want to go to Georgia? I could better stay in Moscow and study vodka. There is nothing for me in Georgia. They say all men look like Stalin. If this is so, I hate Georgia. I wish to study Muslims, and meet Uzbek writers, not study Stalin and wine.'

He beckoned a waitress. She approached nervously. 'These women are afraid of me,' Kazim said. 'I cannot think why. Maybe it is the hate for Georgia which shows in my face. Maybe it is my hate for a land in which all men are as Stalin. What do you think?'

At six we flew. Our rackety aircraft jolted down for intermediary stops at Rostov, then Suomi on the Black Sea, and banged off again. Over the Caucasus we hit air pockets. The aircraft seemed to be heading in several directions, all of them earthward. The Latins grew excitable. They too seemed to feel there was something amiss with the enterprise. Interpreters were ill. Kazim had a more than usually corpse-like colour. Assad fell in love with the English speaking hostess, a slender girl who gave us sweets on take-offs and landings. He recited her sing-song poems in Urdu. 'If you knew what I was saying,' he explained, 'you would never leave me.'

'Will someone kill that crazy Pakistani?' Kazim whispered. The hostess blushed as Assad became affectionate. Sometime in the hot afternoon she unfastened herself from her suitor and announced that we were about to land in Tbilisi, capital of Georgia. Minutes later sunburned land was racing beneath us, then cruelly bouncing us back into the air again. Kazim uttered several oaths, presumably Persian. The Latins also grew loud. 'My spine is no in existence,' Assad disclosed to the hostess. 'I can no leave the plane. I must return to Moscow with you and recite you my poems in Urdu and learn Russian.' The hostess evinced considerable alarm. 'People wait for you,' she protested as we bumped up to the terminal.

Outside in dizzying sunlight were white-suited officials of the Georgian Writers' Union. Bronze and beefy, more like wrestlers than writers, they smiled benignly and shook our feeble hands. Pedro, the Venezuelan, nudged nearer me. 'Who are these people?' he asked blearily. 'Where are we?'

I explained.

'I asked to go to Armenia,' he protested.

'This is Georgia,' I explained.

'Not Armenia?'

'Georgia,' I confirmed.

Now we all knew.

With the wrestler-like writers was a girl from the Georgian Cultural Institute. Her name was Ina. She had high cheekbones and olive skin and was colourfully frocked. She was also rather wonderfully beautiful. The air hostess already forgotten, Assad moved nearer Ina as speeches were made. The most senior Georgian was welcoming fellow writers from Persia, Pakistan, Latin America and New Zealand to the Republic of Georgia. Privately he must have been wondering what to do with so wretched a collection of refugees from literary Moscow.

Limousines sped us through tawny countryside to Tbilisi. There were tremendous cliffs, roaring rivers, and dwellings teetering overhead. It was landscape to make the heart leap and the soul sing. Toward evening we were taken by cable up the great hump-back hill behind the city. Our guide was a bulky but gentle poet named Givi. 'I translate Keats and Shakespeare,' he informed us. Now he tried to interpret Georgia to the best advantage. He was endearingly free of ideology. The Soviet Union was somewhere behind. We passed a picturesque church and graveyard dappled with dusk shadow and sunset light. 'It is where Georgia's greatest poets sleep,' Givi told us. He fondly recited name after name. 'In Georgia every man is born a poet. Therefore one who becomes a poet is a poet twice over. Our great who rest here are indeed great.'

Perhaps Givi himself now sleeps there too. So passionate a patriot, so devout a friend of Georgia's great, deserves to. There was more glory in that graveyard than in the mausoleum under the Kremlin wall. So far Givi hadn't mentioned Stalin. I had the impression he had no wish to.

We clambered from the cable car. The air was exhilarating and the lights of Tbilisi gleamed below.

'You stand on David's hill,' Givi disclosed. 'The hill to which Prometheus was bound.'

Where Prometheus suffered there was now a television mast and a restaurant with sweet violins. The vista was lost on Assad; he was wooing Ina. 'Georgian women are better dressed than Moscow women,' he was telling her.

'Perhaps the climate,' she said.

'Your scarf,' he pointed out, 'has a Picasso design. How can this be?'

'It is a gift from a French delegation,' she said.

'Girls in communist countries can no like Picasso,' Assad insisted. 'In Moscow they say the art of Picasso is reactionary. They say Russians no like the art of Picasso.'

'I am Georgian,' Ina said sweetly. 'This is Georgia.'

That was even more evident next morning. I stood outside our hotel with Kazim, waiting on our limousines. We had been promised a trip into the Caucasus, where we would lunch. 'That means,' Kazim said, 'that we shall drink wine and more wine and remember nothing. Strange we have heard nothing of Stalin yet. Have you seen that Georgian men all wear Stalin moustaches?'

That was true. In the September sunshine it was possible to observe Stalin in many informal poses — buying groceries, walking children, drinking fruit juice, riding a bicycle, and chauffeuring our limousine. 'There is no need of statues,' Kazim said darkly.

We were sped toward the Caucasus. Outside Tbilisi two great rivers meet, the Aragve and the Kura. The poet Lermontov called them two sisters in an embrace. Cradled in this embrace is the 1500-year-old church where Georgia's kings are interred, legend says a shred of Christ's shroud too. The formal atheism of the Soviet Union faded in this Georgian shrine. Guides, interpreters and chauffeurs crossed themselves as we entered. There were brilliantly robed priests about their business, vivid icons, banks of burning candles. Old women in black prostrated themselves on the flagstone floor. Some chanted. It was a place rich in melancholy, filled with the sorrows of a stubborn people. We could not have been further from conspiritorial and paranoid Moscow. .

I wanted to pause there, between the two great rivers, but our programme, possibly as approved in Moscow, precluded loitering. We left the Georgian nation to its griefs and took the old military road into the Caucasus, stopping now and then at derelict churches, crumbling fortresses, and dusty villages. The stony white road grew slender, climbing and dipping; peasant women sold grapes and children sold nuts along the roadside. Suddenly mountains heaved on all sides, huge and white and bleached, scrubby here and rocky there, and patched with distant villages of herdsmen and huntsmen and tiny yellow fields of corn.

The more unpopulated the terrain, the less Assad was impressed. 'We will no be seen again,' he predicted.

We had been joined that day by a lone Englishman, Graham Greene's son, spending his famous father's Soviet royalties on a Georgian excursion. I pointed out to Assad that there would be an international scandal should the son of England's most celebrated novelist disappear in Georgia.

'Then I must stay close to him,' Assad decided.

High in the mountains was a village, a leafy restaurant, food and wine. There was also a smiling deputation of villagers. Then speeches and toasts. Georgian protocol had to be observed. This meant electing the president of the table. Glasses were to be filled on his order and emptied on his order, unless a medical certificate was produced. There was only one candidate for the position; the vote, as in all things Soviet, had to be unanimous. The bacchanalia could only be brought to a close by a dissenter proposing a toast to the president. Dissenters were unwelcome.

Still stunned by travel, we no longer knew where we were or who. Assad, still firmly of the view that no good would come of the day, felt obliged to postpone the evil hour; he meant to go down fighting. His speech began in English and finished most of an hour later in Urdu; no one could tell the difference. He was generously applauded. Still earnestly trying to ensure our survival, Assad began reciting poems in Urdu. By their end people were falling away from the table and remaining prone on the floor of the restaurant. Some simply fell face down into their food. Finally one of our hosts rose to praise Assad's verse. 'Imperialism,' he judged, 'is a terrible thing.'

Resolutely sober Kazim was emptying his wine glass regularly over the verandah. 'Is this all Georgia can give us?' he complained. 'Wine and that crazy Pakistani?'

Pandemonium began. Graham Greene's son was no longer with us. He had taken advantage of Assad's erudite rearguard action to disappear up stony mountainside in hope of sighting Georgian mountain lions. (Mountain lions? That is what memory says.) Guides were aghast. Perhaps they too saw a headline: NOVELIST'S SON DEVOURED BY RED LION. There were shrill voices, recriminations. Villagers drunk, sober and middling were mustered for search parties. The party was over with no need for a presidential toast. Men were scrambling up mountainside and sometimes rolling back again in showers of stone.

'Did you no see him go?' awed Assad said.

'No,' I said.

'He must have been seized,' Assad deduced. 'We must no go to the toilet.'

'The toilet?'

'It is there we might be seized.'

'I have been to the toilet,' grim Kazim said. 'I was seized only by the wish to get out of it fast.'

'I do not believe in these lions,' Assad said. 'That is their excuse.'

An hour or two later Greene junior was located undevoured and returned to our company. Assad was not persuaded by appearances. He made a point of sitting next to the novelist's son in the limousine back to Tbilisi.

The second day, and the third, had much in common. Each was a recipe for delirium tremens. On the fourth we were sped off to Stalin's native village of Gori. It was a dusty, shapeless little place.

The shack where Stalin was born son of the village cobbler now resided under a marble canopy. Local Communist functionaries were our guides in this sensitive region.

'If Stalin were not a great man, he would have been a great poet,' one claimed. To establish this, he read a boyhood poem by the man who in adult life rhymelessly instructed his secret police to 'beat, beat and beat again'.

'Stalin?' Kazim whispered. 'A poet? Is that what they now tell us?'

'For the most part,' I said.

'Let us get out of here,' he said dourly.

Assad was quiet. There were no Urdu poems. 'Do you think we are free now?' he asked.

'If we are not,' Kazim promised, 'I will kill you.'

On the fifth day we were flown out. Perhaps a functionary reported to Moscow that we were no longer a threat to the Soviet Union. He would not have been in error.

Thirty-eight

In Moscow I met a muscular, crop-headed young Bulgarian writer named Vasil Popov. Vasil looked a rebel, and was. Hemingway was his model. Mistaking my standing in Western letters, he asked if I had met the great man.

'Only on the page,' I said.

'Pity,' he said. 'I should like to shake a hand that has shaken his.'

I had shaken one or two that had, I said. Might that do?

'For now,' he said.

He found it difficult to hide contempt for things Soviet, or for literary time-servers.

'Come to Bulgaria,' he urged. 'We do things better.'

Facts didn't support him. Printing of his stories had often been stopped, and a novel had been pulped before publication day; he had been exiled from Sofia and sent to work in coal mines to restore his ideological stability. 'What,' I asked, 'is better about that?'

'I am still alive,' he pointed out.

Walking in Moscow with Vasil, I met a couple with Bulgarian connections named Winter. Paul Winter was public school English, an editor employed in a London publishing house. His Bulgarian-born wife Anna, a journalist, worked as London correspondent for the Sofia press; her communist father, a wartime partisan, was prominent in the regime. Paul was ponderous, and had pretensions as a poet. Anna was dashing, colourfully and expensively dressed.

Vasil was not enthusiastic about the Winters, and subdued in their company. But they were overpoweringly friendly. Anna said to me, 'If you wish to come to Bulgaria, I can arrange it.'

She looked the kind of woman who could arrange anything, at any time. They were, they explained, about to leave for Sofia themselves; they would be there to meet us.

With Bulgarian visas, Gillian and I flew to Sofia in another moody Soviet version of the DC3. The Winters, as promised, were waiting at the airport terminal. So was Vasil. Tension between the Winters and Vasil was even more evident. Vasil had wanted to bed us privately in his Sofia flat so that we might see Bulgaria as humbler citizens did. The Winters had booked a hotel room. I would be able to pay for it by publishing an article or two on New Zealand life and literature, and perhaps some short stories, in Bulgarian journals. Vasil's plan had been overruled: he could offer nothing so grand. Though disgruntled, he said nothing. When he got the chance, however, he whispered, 'The Winters are powerful people. She is a woman with dangerous connections. Do what she says. And do not repeat anything I say.'

This was not auspicious. Dangerous? He seemed to be saying that our benefactor might be more than a journalist.

Vasil caught a bus back into Sofia. The Winters summoned a shiny black car, something less than a limousine, but as good as anything on wheels in Bulgaria of 1957.

I left unease at the airport. After dour Moscow, Sofia was a delight. The KGB, or its local equivalent, didn't make mysterious phone calls to our room. We seemed to be in Europe at last. The autumn weather was warm; there were outdoor cafes with colourful umbrellas. In the Writers' Union restaurant the wine was good, company lively, and conversation seemingly unfettered.

Bulgaria was comprehensible in a way that the Soviet Union could never be. It was a small country; I felt at home in a land only a little more populous than mine, and as minuscule on the world's maps. Its new, iron-faced ruling caste had yet to make itself ostentatious; privilege wasn't especially flaunted. On first sight it seemed as gentle, modest and egalitarian as New Zealand. Before World War II Bulgaria had no ruthless rulers, no conspicuous capitalism. In the countryside there was, with no help from Marx, a sturdy co-operative movement; it was a democratic socialist state masquerading as a monarchy. Exceptionally in Eastern Europe, Bulgaria even acquitted itself with distinction in World War II. No Bulgarian Jew ever perished in a Nazi gas-chamber. Jews, as Bulgarians boast, were never shipped out to Auschwitz; they were interned, to accommodate German sensitivities, and released after the Red Army rolled in.

Soviet tanks heralded the arrival of hard-line communists who had spent the war years in Moscow. Giddied with their new power, owning loyalty only to the Soviet Union, they crushed native tradition to build, as one bold Bulgarian poet put it, a 'Socialist feudalism'. They filled graves and concentration camps with their pre-war political rivals and then with the squeamish in their own ranks. By 1957, twelve years after the war, their grip was more relaxed. Victims of show trials had been posthumously rehabilitated. The original hard-liners had beeen scrapped. Directives from Moscow had grown ambiguous. Perhaps the worst was past. Or so the habitues of Sofia's more civilised cafes and restaurants then hoped.

Anxious that we didn't lose our way in Sofia, and mix with undesirables, the Winters saw that we met helpful people: publishers, editors, translators. I offered a couple of short stories for publication, then two or three articles. In days there was a downpour of money; we were able to pay our own bills in the Writers' Union restaurant.

'Don't believe all you hear there,' Vasil warned. 'Or all you see.'

Vasil took us to meet dissidents, people with poor ideological credentials who had not yet won membership of the Writers' Union and access to privileges. These were considerable. A Writers' Union card could mean dizzying fees from magazines and newspapers, a four-hour day in editorial offices, a large apartment, and eventually country villas, travel outside Bulgaria and even a car. It had taken Vasil five years or more to be admitted; he remained on probation, frequently threatened with expulsion. If he wasn't, it was because of his reputation as a spokesman for the young; literary bureaucrats didn't want a martyr about whom dissidents might gather. Meanwhile Vasil had no villa or vehicle; and his apartment was small.

We found ourselves living two lives. The favoured of the regime, friends of the Winters, entertained us in their handsome villas on the slopes of Mount Vitosha, above the lights of Sofia. Elsewhere, through Vasil, we met up with writers and artists who had no standing in society and few prospects. They lived humbly and worked as translators, proof readers, and publishing house menials. Extraordinarily, both groups were free with anti-communist anecdotes, stories which mocked the pretensions of the regime and its devotion to Moscow. The first group, the privileged, told the stories with elegance and self-mocking irony; the second, the heretics, with bitterness and disgust.

Vasil often took me aside. He wanted me to know his work better; most of his stories existed only in manuscript and none in English translation. So he read aloud, translating slowly, sometimes agonisingly, resorting to a Bulgarian-English dictionary. Meaning arrived from textual murk, shapes, messages. There was the story of a veteran Communist three times imprisoned for political sins — first under the pre-war regime, then under the Nazis, and finally in a prison built by his own Party. 'A parable,' he explained unnecessarily, after referring to his dictionary again. 'You are my only reader. It will never be published.' He threw the manuscript down in mute anguish.

Vasil introduced me to a fellow spirit, the writer Radoi Ralin, the most popular poet in Bulgaria. His irreverent and witty verse had several times got him into trouble with authorities. He therefore had no privileges either. Moreover, he had just published a poem arguing for personal loyalty above public loyalty, and asking for friends who would not betray him when they moved into high places. For friends read fellow writers; the poem said much about the condition of Bulgarian letters. It did him no good, nor the editors who failed to detect impurities in the poem. They were waiting for the axe to fall. I pointed out that an English writer named E.M. Forster had uttered similar sentiments, and that they had been seen as unexceptional.

'And this E.M. Forster,' Radoi asked, 'he still walks free?'

'Of course.'

'And is permitted to publish?'

'As he chooses.'

'He is no Bulgarian,' Radoi sighed.

The good fellowship of the Winters' friends began to pall, their villas, lavish apartments and conspicuous consumption too; all the slivova in Bulgaria didn't disguise corruption. Bulgaria's writers, those who met with official approval, and many who didn't, were becoming the most pampered in the history of literature.

Stalin and his disciples elsewhere in Eastern Europe had used the stick to bring literary men into line. In homely Bulgaria the carrot was more effective. Todor Zhivkov, who had just come to power in the wake of Stalin's demise, and would rule the country for the next three decades, early deduced that the largest threat to his well-being was the literary community. Elsewhere in Eastern Europe — in

Poland and Hungary, and later in Czechoslovakia — it was the writers who asked indelicate questions and heralded upheaval. Rather than imprison them he wooed even the most wilful of their number: he took them walking in the woods, on hunting trips, and entertained them extravagantly at his table. He saw they lacked nothing in comfort; he built them into Bulgaria's new aristocracy.

Aspirant Solzhenitsyns didn't last long. One wave of potential truth-tellers after another succumbed. Nothing was too good for them. The opulent life of Bulgarian writers, even of the mediocre, made even the wealthiest of Western authors seem down at heel. In this devious manner, with considerable personal charm, Zhivkov silenced two generations of Bulgarian writers; and all but levelled a literature. The point of the exercise was not to produce a lapdog literature like the Soviet Union's, desirable though that might be. It was, as the malcontent playwright Georgi Markov brilliantly diagnosed, to stop writers writing altogether. No one knew better than Markov, who after precocious success partook of most of the privileges in wait for Bulgarian writers. He was one of Zhivkov's few failures.

The dictator's interest in Georgi didn't wane even when he fled affluence for impecunious English exile. This time the stick was necessary; hell hath no fury like a spurned tyrant. A poisoned pellet delivered by a lethal umbrella on London's Waterloo Bridge, a decade or two later, was to silence Georgi too. The message wasn't lost on those of Georgi's contemporaries who remained in Bulgaria and may have been tempted to follow his lead. Some would survive with something resembling self-respect by retreating to mountain villages, there to write of traditional peasant life, the natural world, or of the heroic Bulgarian past, regions into which Zhivkov couldn't reach; others merely mouldered in Sofia's flesh-pots and lived off their once flashy reputations as rebels. When their chance came, they joined the literary bureaucracy too. Small wonder that Radoi Ralin prayed for upwardly mobile friends who would not betray him. The complicity of writers in their own demise was astounding: it made for a literary history even sadder than the Soviet Union's. In Zhivkov's tight ship there was no samizdat. When their day of freedom came, Russian writers at least had unpublished manuscripts in their bottom drawers.

In 1957, though, I merely noticed that many of my Bulgarian companions drank rather more than they should; that their hands sometimes shook when sober; that even in their comfortable dwellings they spoke with uneasy discretion. More to the point, their tidy desks did not look much visited. But their liquor cabinets were full.

Unruly Vasil still battled for publication. He had a large, panoramic novel in mind; one which would rove over Bulgaria's recent history. There was no point in writing anything less. There was also no point in writing it yet. He would begin it the day he saw a faint possibility of its publication.

'When will that be?' I asked.

'The day after forever,' he said.

For Vasil forever failed to end. Like Georgi Markov, he was dead before Todor Zhivkov's rancid reign ended in 1989. Vasil's impotence and impatience mounted; stress grew until his heart collapsed. Someone else will have to write his novel.

Thirty-nine

As my stories and articles turned into a rain of money I failed to notice that I had become part of the corruption too. The peasants and proletarians of needy Bulgaria were paying my bills; I was living on their backs, like any indulged Bulgarian writer.

'Perhaps you would like to stay,' Jenny Bojilova said.

Jennny was an editor and translator for the literary press. She had interviewed me for one journal, and translated a story of mine for another. Her questions had been intelligent; she relished anti-authoritarian sentiments, not least when I made the commonplace observation that the best writers were beholden to no doctrine.

'I think I may manage to get that past my editor,' she said. 'But it will be between the lines.' With high Slavic cheekbones, a touch of Turkish in her complexion, eloquent eyes and a bewitching Bulgarian smile, Jenny was easy to fall in love with. Most men did, and I was no exception. She had just ended a long affair with a French philosopher who wanted her to live in Paris. ('He was too much a Marxist for me,' she explained wryly. 'I have enough ideology at home.') Our encounters were affectionate but chaste. They remained so.

'It would be possible, you know,' she said.

'To stay here?'

'Of course,' she said. 'We have cultural institutions which could give you employment. The work would be light — polishing translations, for example. You would have an apartment and all the time you wish for your own writing.'

I was tempted. Not least by the prospect of friends like Vasil and Jenny, people who lived on the century's edge. I had a fascinated envy for their condition. Their concerns made those of most Western writers seem trivial.

'I must think about it,' I said.

'Do,' Jenny teased.

She saw that for me Eastern Europe meant mental upheaval. As son of my parents I was both at home and not in a communist society. I still wished it to be as they wanted it; I still wished good news. Reality rejected me at every turn.

She may also have detected that Gillian and I, when thrown back upon our marital resources, were discovering, after months of travel, less and less there. Nothing was said.

The Winters, especially pious Anna, were disturbed when I uttered mild reservations about the literary life of Bulgaria. They feared that I had been paying too much attention to Vasil and his mutinous friends. There was more to it, of sexual nature. A daughter of Bulgaria's new baronial masters, Anna Winter played the Queen Bee in Sofia on her visits from London; she was seldom without a swarm of admirers while her decently reticent English husband hovered nearby. I was also expected to sit at her feet. She took offence when she saw me converse with other women at restaurants and social functions. She identified Jenny as a rival.

Finally Anna took me aside. 'That woman Bojilova is not reliable,' she reported.

'In what respect?' I asked innocently.

'She has dubious friends. People of the old order. And some of them Jews.'

I could make what I liked of that, though it was difficult. Anna was half-Jewish herself. I was in a strange land.

'Oh?' I said.

'Do you talk politics with her?' Anna asked.

'Not particularly,' I claimed.

This was true. Jenny and I left ideology between the lines.

Anna judged more coddling was in order. Next morning she called at our hotel. 'Are you in a hurry to get to London?' she asked.

'Not especially,' I said.

'Good,' she said. 'I have booked you into an artists' and writers' retreat in the Rila mountains. There you will be at peace with the world, able to get on with your own work.' She looked at Gillian, then at me. 'Also,' she added, 'you can walk in the woods and by mountain streams. You may even see that there is more to Bulgaria than beautiful women.'

I could make what I liked of that too.

('Do what she says,' Vasil had warned me.)

'It sounds splendid,' I said.

'By the way,' Anna added, 'should you wish to remain in Bulgaria, and take a job here, I am the person you should talk to about such matters.'

But who did Anna talk to? How did she know?

Bistritza Palace, in the shadowy woods of the Rila Mountains, among heights 8000 feet tall, had been built as a royal hunting lodge by King Ferdinand. The heads of beasts and birds lined the walls. Small plaques beneath each trophy, some dating back to the nineteenth century, attested to the competence of Europe's crowned heads with firearms. Five generations of aristocrats, monarchs and princes had had the pleasure of the place in the course of killing bear, deer, eagles and any woodland creature that walked or flew. Now writers, artists and musicians made the most of its elegance. To ensure it remained theirs there was even a militiaman on duty downhill, with a presumably efficient submachine gun. It said something for the condition of creative Bulgaria that artists, writers and musicians saw nothing remarkable in a martial presence.

Some days Gillian and I had Bistritza and its staff to ourselves. On weekends it filled, on the whole, with the regime's reliable. One who lingered longer than most was an urbane middle-aged man named Anton. A sometime writer, he had served the old regime and the new as a diplomat. Under Todor Zhivkov he still lived in the manner to which he had long been accustomed. He visited the West on cultural missions. His dress was fashionably Parisian; he smoked Gauloise cigarettes.

Hadn't it troubled him, I asked, to serve masters so different? The last Czar, and then such as Zhivkov?

'Not at all,' he explained. 'I became a Party member.'

'As a writer,' I suggested, 'you have seen interesting contrasts.'

'As a writer,' he said, 'I see no reason to contradict the Party.'

That conversation was at an end.

He claimed to be staying at Bistritza to further the writing of his memoirs. He may have been; but he seemed in no haste to put pen to paper after we breakfasted together. In the afternoon we fished mountain pools or walked in autumnally misty woods. If we passed the militiaman on guard Anton looked through the man; he wasn't there. I couldn't keep my eyes off the fellow, or his well-polished weapon. He was a dissonant note in the wilderness. Out of nervous friendliness, however, I often gave the sentry a smile and polite salute.

'Why,' I finally ventured, 'should he be here?'

'This country has enemies,' Anton said.

'Within or without?'

'Who knows?'

'No enemy in his right mind would see Bistritza of importance,' I argued.

'You are being difficult,' Anton said.

The fact of the matter is that the only enemies in sight were the burdened and beleaguered Bulgarian people, those who paid for the upkeep of the place. Anton knew it.

We walked a winding road down to the village of Borovets. It was not a happy or affluent place. A threadbare banner, with a slogan in Cyrillic, and a hammer and sickle, fluttered above the village centre. Dwellings were squalid, shops lacklustre, and villagers watched us with suspicion. Perhaps we looked like new bureacrats here to tell them how to live their comfortless lives. We took a slivova in a dismal tavern; conversation at the bar ended when we walked in. Anton struggled to revive it, presumably for my benefit. Possibly he was too fluent for local liking. One or two drinkers pulled on sheepskin jackets and slipped surly out the door. Those remaining did not seem much impressed when Anton informed them that I was a friendly visitor from the West; they looked even more deeply into their glasses. They knew who was paying my bills.

Anton and I began walking home.

'Ignorant people, of course,' he observed.

I shrugged tactfully.

'There are still dark patches in our beautiful life,' he said without irony.

'I notice,' I said.

We walked in silence for a time.

'If given the choice,' Anton mused, 'would you choose a communist hell or a capitalist hell?'

'Must I choose?'

'The communist hell is much to be preferred,' he explained. 'The boiling pitch is bound to be lukewarm, the brimstone unreliable, and there is certain to be a shortage of pitchforks. As for the devils, they will be most of their day attending Party meetings to better productivity.'

I could make what I liked of that. Anton gave me an untypically bleak look and lit a Gauloise.

Anton had reason to be slow with his memoirs. Taking Krushchev's denunciation of Stalin as his cue, he had uttered sentiments of a prematurely anti-totalitarian character in the course of the Party coup which brought Zhivkov to power. This had been a mistake. Zhivkov had no more use for Lazarus-like liberals than his murderous predecessors had for peasant democrats. Having backed the right horse when the Red Army arrived in 1944, this time Anton found his money was on an also-ran. He found it better to keep a distance from Sofia. He was in Bistritza for his health.

Another longer-staying resident of Bistritza was an illustrator of children's books, a sweet and elderly woman named Sonia. She fearlessly confided in us when Anton was out of earshot. She listed the atrocities, the show trials, the beatings and executions which went into the shaping of a Soviet satellite. Some of her relatives had disappeared. Others had returned skeletal after years in prison camps. That had been bad enough. But it was still going on.

Still?

Still, she assured us. A cousin of hers had been arrested on an obscure charge only that year for speaking his mind. He was now resident in the dreaded island prison of Belene, on the Danube. It was possible he would never be seen again. Nothing had changed, or was likely to. She was fortunate in that her work was not political; she retained a peaceful niche in the horror.

Anton was wrong. There was no shortage of pitchforks.

He was unhappy when he saw us in conversation with Sonia. 'That woman is unwise,' he informed us. 'What has she been telling you?'

Nothing, we insisted.

All the same, Sonia disappeared from Bistritza between one day and the next. There was no explanation. No farewell. Anton may have had nothing to do with her departure. But he was distinctly on the side of wisdom: it meant, among other things, French cigarettes.

I began a novel. In the Balkan forest life as lived in my free and affluent land seemed microscopic; I failed to make it lift off the page.

Bulgarian authors, on the other hand, would have envied such a writer's block.

Back in Sofia, before we left Bulgaria, I met Jenny Bojilova in the Ulitsa Russki. We took coffee and brandy in a warm bar and watched promenaders weave past the window. Most were young: sullen students in check shirts and black berets, slender girls with sulky Slav features. Did I see bewilderment and despair or was I wishing it upon them? Never mind; I saw bewilderment and despair. Their faces said they weren't going anywhere.

'Our hooligans,' Jenny said wryly.

I thought that judgement harsh. Jenny, however, meant it kindly.

'In another age,' Jenny explained, 'we called them haidouks.'

The haidouks were the young Bulgarians — bandits to some, patriots to others — who lived outside Ottoman law in the mountains and plundered the caravans of their Turkish overlords. Hristo Botev, Bulgaria's national poet, had been one. Jenny quoted:

> *Do not weep, Mother, or sorrow*
> *That I have become a haidouk*
> *A haidouk, Mother, or brigand,*
> *Leaving you lone and unhappy,*
> *Mourning the first of your children*
> *But, Mother, blast with your curses*
> *This black oppression*
> *That sends young men into exile*
> *To a strange land's desolation.*

I got Jenny's message. She had more on the theme.

'Do you hear people tell the truth here?' she asked.

'When they know it,' I said.

'Can I tell you a story?'

'Please,' I said.

'There was once an old, weary and rather terrifying mathematics teacher,' she said. 'When he died a bright young teacher took his place. He was horrified to discover that his esteemed predecessor had been teaching children that two plus two equalled ten. He therefore called a meeting of the school committee to explain his problem. The committee divided on what best to do. Some said that it was better to keep the children happy by telling them that two plus two equalled ten. Others thought it better to tell the children immediately that two plus two equalled four. These people were expelled from the committee. The majority decided that it would be best to admit the facts slowly. So the new teacher returned to his pupils. He told them that their old teacher, though a fine man in many respects, had been incorrect in detail. For example, their old teacher had informed them that two plus two equalled ten. This was not so. Two plus two equalled eight.

'The teacher returned to the committee. What now? Proceed as planned, the committee ordered; reveal the truth by stages. So he went back to his pupils and told them that though their old teacher had been a great man, he was sometimes incorrect in detail. For example, two plus two did not equal ten. In fact it equalled six.

'The children groaned. They were tired of the game, having long known the answer anyway. One child, braver than the rest, rushed up to the blackboard, grabbed a piece of chalk, and there wrote — for all the world to see — that two plus two equalled four. And that child was, of course, expelled for hooliganism.'

I saw the faces outside the window differently. It did not seem likely that they had difficulty in adding two and two. When we left the cafe Jenny walked quickly through the parading crowd of young people.

'We must not loiter here,' she said impishly. 'I cannot afford to be mistaken for a hooligan too.'

Two days later we took a train west. Jenny was at the station to farewell us together with Vasil and several of his friends. The Winters were there too, but at a seemly distance from the rest. We shook hands, kissed, and were overwhelmed by gifts. It has never been fashionable to celebrate Bulgaria and its people. But a little of both would live in me for the rest of my life. It was as if I had found another homeland. I still go into retreat there, in my imagination, and sometimes in dream. But never to Bistritza. Todor Zhivkov in the end decided the place was too good for writers and artists; he emptied them out and made it his own.

Forty

Paris was autumnal, London wintry. After five months in unfamiliar lands, steering through ideological shoals, I went into slump. There were no guides now, no interpreters, no limousines. We fended for ourselves in late October gloom and early November fog.

Our first nights were spent with a former Wellington friend, a journalist and aspirant novelist named Howard. In London less than a year, Howard had established himself comfortably as sub-editor on a respectable Sunday paper. He was no longer the Howard I recalled. His antipodean vowels were already subdued; he looked like an Englishman. He had a flat in Baron's Court, and was hoping for better. He was out to impress me, and did: he needed me to see how far he had come.

'New Zealand?' he said with an eloquent shudder. 'No. I'll never go back.'

I must have said something.

'Let's face it,' Howard said. He lit a black Turkish cigarette and opened a bottle of Beaujolais. 'You're here forever too.'

This was not what I wanted to hear. I begged to differ.

'Come on,' he said. 'Don't fool yourself.' He added, 'Still writing?'

'A little,' I confessed.

'About New Zealand, I imagine.'

'For the most part.'

'Forget it,' he advised.

'New Zealand?'

'It's on the dark side of the moon.' He leaned forward confidentially. 'Look at it this way. You're a lucky bastard.'

I didn't feel like one. And I didn't need a New Zealander telling me I was of no account here. I could discover that for myself.

'Lucky?' I asked.

'Look at all this travel, the people you've met. You want my advice? Turn out a cold war thriller. That could go down big.'

Though I envied Howard his urbanity, his way with French wine and Turkish cigarettes, I was no longer easy in his company. I was to meet many Howards in London. Some were fellow countrymen. Others were Australian, Canadian, and South African. Many were writers, or hoping to be. All were cultural chameleons. They imagined they were doing the world a favour by shaking the dust of home from their feet. They were not even doing themselves a kindness. England had a surfeit of Englishmen; it had no need of counterfeits. Nor, as it turned out, did London publishers.

It was years before we resumed contact. By then I was a decade back in New Zealand. I began getting curious telephone calls at midnight London time and something like noon in New Zealand; Howard was invariably drunk and I was too sober. First he wanted to know what the weather was like.

'Fine,' I would say even if it wasn't.

'So the grass still grows green in the antipodes?'

'As advertised.'

'Can you see the sea from where you're standing?'

'The tide's in,' I told him.

'Any more children?'

'Another one,' I allowed.

'And you're writing another novel?'

'As usual,' I said.

There would be a long silence.

'All right, you bugger,' he said. 'You don't have to rub it in.'

'Rub what in?'

'You know,' he said, and crashed his receiver down.

That was how it went for years. He never missed a year; he tended to mumble and meander more as time passed. But the receiver never failed to crash.

Sometimes I saw reviews he had written for *The Observer*, *The Sunday Times*, and *The Statesman*; and heard him on the BBC World Service. He could still turn an elegant phrase. He wrote magisterially about most subjects. His authoritative voice suggested a man of whom much might be expected.

In 1974 my novel *A Touch of Clay* was published in England. In London for the first time in fifteen years, I invited Howard to the launch at New Zealand House. It was a mistake. He was not only drunk; he was grey, shrivelled and seedy in a singularly London literary way. He also had a sour curl to his mouth. He insulted my publisher, my agent, and several harmless bystanders. Then it was my turn.

'Written the Great New Zealand Novel at last, have you?' he asked belligerently.

'Not so you'd notice,' I said.

He stormed off, shouting over his shoulder, 'Who do you think you're fooling? Who?'

Six months or more later he rang me in New Zealand with an apology. 'Been through a bad patch,' he explained tersely.

'So I gathered,' I said.

'My time's coming,' he announced enigmatically.

'Good,' I said.

'I'll do all you've done and better,' he promised.

'I'm glad to hear it,' I said.

He mistook this for mockery.

'You'll laugh on the other side of your face,' he predicted.

The receiver crashed down for the last time. As I reconstructed it, there had been a legacy. Howard severed his London literary connections and travelled to Greece with a typewriter, more or less as I had to Spain twenty years before. There, on the island of Skyros, presumably with no telephone to hand, he lived for a year. Perhaps there was a manuscript; perhaps there wasn't. There would certainly have been retsina and ouzo. The legacy dwindled. He returned to London, failed to pick up where he had left off, and succumbed to a mix of whisky and barbiturates on a winter evening.

Literature has much to answer for. Literary ambition even more.

We left Howard's apartment for a small flat in Ealing, across the way from the Ealing film studios. It was in a block called Byron House, presumably built by a poetry-lover. By then we were into November. Trees were leafless. Black branches dripped. London's Dickensian pea-soupers had begun. Bruising ourselves on abandoned vehicles, it took us an hour to negotiate the hundred yards between tube station and home. I longed for green and got white. I fingered snow for the first time in my life. No longer the stuff of literature, of Charles Dickens and Emily Bronte, it made even dour Ealing festive and fascinating. Overnight it shrank to sooty sludge. So did my spirits.

Literature had never warned of the sludge.

London should have been the climax of our journey. All else — China, Russia, Bulgaria, France — should have been overture. Instead, with Howard's help, it was as uplifting as a toppled garbage can. It took me time to identify my exhaustion. It wasn't just emotional, spiritual or ideological depression. It was physical too. A spinal growth, which surgeons had twice attacked in New Zealand, was flourishing again; I was in need of an enlightened knife. A kindly man named Ian Aird, famous for having separated Siamese twins, insisted that my condition was curable too; that I could be parted from the growth. I went on to his waiting list.

There was a play I imagined I needed to see. 'There aren't any big brave causes left,' cried Jimmy Porter from the stage of the Royal Court. *Look Back in Anger* was electrifying and demoralising. It seemed John Osborne had left my generation with no more to say. I was quiet on the tube ride home, quieter still the next day. It was a week before I argued myself back to my typewriter with a faint heart.

Within a month I knew that reaction extravagant. Even Tolstoy, alas for Aunt Sis, hadn't said it all: Osborne's ranting and randy hero with the sweet stall certainly hadn't. The play also began to seem the last gasp of a literary culture losing its resonance. In that first post-imperial decade, with India gone, colony after colony going, English concerns were shrinking. Introspection was again the name of the game. Class was its mysterious code. Such liveliness as English literature had now was often the work of outsiders.

So circumstances determined that I continued to write. My spinal growth prevented me looking for work; at least until it was removed. I wrote until my name rose the top of the waiting list. There were scraps of journalism for New Zealand, essays, a short story or two. I sent off several stories, old and new, to English magazines: one after another these manuscripts thumped back into our Byron House letter-box; I fantasised that they were beginning to breed there. Some letters of rejection were pleasantly worded; most were routinely terse. All tended to confirm Howard's diagnosis: no one in the metropolis was interested in New Zealand. Gillian found work as a waitress in a Lyons' Corner House, then on Lord Beaverbrook's *Sunday Express*.

Sometimes with Gillian, often alone, I groped my way around London, not with large success. Starting from identifiable Trafalgar Square, I spent a fruitless afternoon looking for Soho, hiking up

Regent Street, along Oxford Street, and down Charing Cross Road to Trafalgar Square again. I could well have been the first person ever to circumnavigate Soho without actually seeing it: it had seldom been more than five yards from my right shoulder.

Others as lost in London began to find their way to Byron House. Some were New Zealanders; others had been met in travel. The New Zealanders were of a lame dog kind. There was Olga, an actress we had known in Wellington. Of Russian ancestry, born in Berlin but reared in New Zealand, she was blessed — or in this case cursed — with a hybrid accent, a medley of kiwi and kulak: in temperament too. She didn't need a Howard, or some theatrical equivalent, to inform her that she had no future in London. After two desperate terms at drama school she struggled with, and walked out on, a small role at Leatherhead Repertory. At some point in this period Simon, another borderline case of disillusion, wandered into our lives. He had finished university in New Zealand with honours in philosophy. Unable to make sense of this qualification, or of himself, he failed to find a post-graduate scholarship at Oxford helpful either. He had spent a humble year in Europe imitating George Orwell's *Down and Out in Paris and London* without having read the book. He had slept rough on Parisian park benches and under London arches. When lucky he worked as a waiter. Currently he was tending doomed rabbits and mice in a research laboratory. Piquant as this was, it seemed unlikely that he was going to put the experience to use. His literary ambitions were growing faint. He said that at least he now had philosophy in perspective; the world had no surprises left. Between bouts of despair — in the end to multiply them — Simon fell disconsolately in love with Olga.

So did Pedro Duno. Pedro was the Venezuelan poet we had met in Soviet Georgia: a poet and sometime university lecturer, and a political exile. Months after we had last seen him, we found him knocking on our door. It should have been no surprise: Pedro had been footloose in the world for years, after leading an unsuccessful student strike in Caracas which finished with blood in the streets. On the run since, he had camped in Buenos Aires, Mexico City, Berlin and Paris; especially and recently Paris. Small, heartfelt volumes of poems, published by Spanish-language presses in Mexico or Argentina, marked his passage from country to country. Now he was experimenting with exile in London. He was still waiting on an overdue revolution to allow him to return home. He was short, dark and vivid-eyed; his laugh was reverberant. He was never shy about playing the romantic revolutionary in company. 'Sometimes,' he said, 'I think I would be better learning to use a gun than interesting myself in literature. Combining the gun and literature is one big problem.'

'The gun?' Simon said in alarm.

'And literature,' Pedro agreed amiably.

Olga and Simon were wide-eyed. Simon stuttered, 'What is so wrong with pacifism?'

'My pacifist friends are dead,' Pedro explained.

We were an improbable mix. Added to Olga, Simon and Pedro were other Latin Americans, East Europeans, Asians and West Indians. If nothing else, they attested to London's potency as a clearing house for the human species: it was a salad of personalities seldom to be seen elsewhere. Some were sighted once or twice, and never again. Others never missed a weekly rendezvous. We met in a nearby pub on Sundays and afterwards gathered around cheap Spanish wine, a mountain of bread and cheese and a pot of Gillian's potato soup. There had to be a story in this, and was. I wrote it after ten weeks in London. A year or two later the story was singled out by a bleakly nationalist New Zealand critic as symptomatic of cosmopolitan corruption in my work. In failing to pay my respects to realism, he added damningly, I demonstrated that I had been too long in London. My characters — derived rather too literally from the likes of Olga, Simon and Pedro — were, he claimed, people not to be met with in the real world. Anyway that was what this authoritative voice said: I didn't dwell in the real world. Ten weeks in London had depraved me.

Forty-one

There was revolution in Venezuela. The American-sponsored dictator Perez Jimenez had been deposed by a coalition of liberals and left-wingers; his troops and tanks were in surly retreat. Pedro was jubilant. After a decade of melancholy exile he could go home. He arrived at our door with champagne. Then he sprang a surprise: How did I feel about a few days in Paris? He had to go back there, to pack up his poems and possessions and celebrate with fellow emigres before catching a boat to Caracas. His friends were all interesting people, he argued; people I should meet. It would be good for me as a writer to meet real revolutionaries — not the corrupt and bureaucratic pro-Soviet kind. Meeting up with Latin American insurrectionists in Paris looked to be more enlivening than another week waiting for my name to rise to the top of Ian Aird's list.

A day or two later I was walking alongside the Seine with Pedro. Open-air booksellers were unwrapping their stalls and arranging their ageing volumes in pale morning sunlight. It was winter in Paris, but no matter; it was spring in Caracas. He picked up a cache of unforwarded mail from his old Parisian pension informing him so. We walked from the Quai St Michel up to Saint Germain. There, in a warm cafe, he leafed through his letters. Sometimes he read me extracts. Their contents did not vary. They listed dramatic events in Caracas and urged his early return. His first jubilation was gone. There was even a sigh or two.

'What is it?' I asked.

'To tell the truth,' Pedro confided, 'I am terrified.'

'Terrified?' I asked.

'I know only how to be an exile,' Pedro explained. 'How to be a peaceful citizen now?'

Paris was a problem too on so splendid a morning. He was reluctant to farewell Europe, and particularly Paris. He would also be farewelling his youth. The tragedy of the exile, he explained, was that he found new loves. He could foresee some future poem on that theme, written in Caracas. His poetry would enter another phase, perhaps; anyway it was bound to be different.

Then he opened a fat letter from Mexico. Newspaper cuttings fell over our croissants. They were reviews of his latest book of verse, most by fellow exiles. There was no love lost in Venezuela's literary community either. The best were lukewarm about his work. The rest were rabid. They denounced Pedro as a poseur, a poet who had forgotten his native land and, worse, one who traded shamelessly on his unwarranted reputation as a revolutionary. He was not, in short, a poet needed by a new and democratic Venezuela. (Along the way it was also pointed out that Pedro was brazenly derivative of Lorca and Pablo Neruda.)

Pedro, after translating these reprimands, slumped low in his chair. I suggested another coffee. Pedro needed cognac.

'What am I going back to?' he asked gloomily.

All expatriates, all exiles willing or unwilling, ask the same question. My day would come.

Pedro sought out old comrades. His fellow Venezuelans were busy stowing canvases and manuscripts into trunks, stripping their dim little rooms in the Latin Quarter. Cubans and Guatemalans looked on with envy. Pedro and I scrambled through the debris of departure to find his fellow countrymen. There they were, among the accoutrements of exile — dingy wallpaper, cracked mirrors, discoloured washbasins and dripping taps. Yes, they said joyfully, it was time to go home. After all, there might be a counter-revolution. The ruthless Jimenez might at this moment be mustering arms and American money for his return. They might be needed to repel him. To envious Cubans, Columbians and Guatemalans they said, 'Your day will dawn.'

For some, not least the Cubans, dusk would follow hard on dawn. How many of them saw out the next decade alongside Fidel Castro? How many failed to last the distance, or finished in Castro's prisons? As for the Columbians, the Guatemalans, did they end despairingly in lethal guerrilla bands? Or as revered servants of right-wing regimes?

For one long night we hunted through the bars of Pigalle for a Venezuelan painter who had scuttled himself somewhere in the vicinity. Once a revolutionary comrade of Pedro's, he had disappeared in the mire of Parisian low life. Last report placed him in a bar, doing lightning sketches of customers. Pedro was determined to tell him of the new day in Caracas and urge him home too, for the sake of his soul. Bartenders shook their heads. Prostitutes and strippers hadn't seen him in months either. Pedro was soon in despair.

'He is crazy but great,' Pedro informed me. 'We need him for the new Venezuela.'

But by the evening's end it was plain that the new Venezuela was going to manage without one distinguished expatriate. He had to be counted a casualty of exile. 'If he is not dead in one way he is dead in another,' Pedro decided. 'This night has been boring for you, no?'

'No,' I insisted.

He had given me a new opening chapter for the novel I would call *Strangers and Journeys*. The cast-list would differ only in respect of nationality. We may have been strangers; our journeys were much the same.

The next day, and for three days, winter returned to Paris. Snow drifted across parked cars and turned to foul slush on the pavements. Our shoes leaked as we plodded through the city. We stopped to reinforce our footwear with carefully folded sheets of *Le Monde*, which seasoned Pedro pronounced superior in absorbent quality to *Figaro* and *L'Humanité*.

Pedro's gloom was not altogether due to dismal weather and damp feet. It had its origin in the uncertainties ahead. These were multiplying. Did he really, to be honest, want the revolution? Life at least had been full of surprise as an exiled revolutionary. He might never live so richly again. It was possible his verse would wither. He might even be a gauche stranger in his own land. His sighs grew frequent.

'Then don't go home,' I suggested.

'That is impossible,' he said stiffly.

As of course it was.

Our last day in Paris turned sunny. The dry pavements shone; buildings were vivid with light. Coatless crowds dawdled beneath the bare trees. We walked along the Seine and finished on Saint Germain again. Pedro had shed some of his melancholy.

'Yes,' he announced suddenly. 'There will be new poems. I will turn these mixed feelings into verse. They will be my treasure. My work will never again be mistaken for Neruda's or Lorca's.'

A young man at our cafe table lowered his copy of the *New York Times* half an inch as Pedro talked. As Pedro continued to talk the newspaper descended another half inch. We were under surveillance. Taking advantage of a pause in Pedro's flow, the stranger finally collapsed his newspaper and leaned toward us. His waistcoat was bright yellow; his accent gently American.

'Am I to understand,' he asked, 'that you two are writers?'

We said he understood right.

'Marvellous,' he said.

What, Pedro asked, was so marvellous about that? In Saint Germain one should expect to encounter writers.

Jake, for that was his name, hadn't. He had been two weeks in Paris trying to eavesdrop on literary conversation. We were the first to oblige with anything of interest. He had heard a little talk of film, and much of politics. Of literature, nothing. 'Do you mind if I buy you pernod?' Jake asked.

We didn't. He waved for a waiter.

'What is your interest?' Pedro asked. 'Are you a writer also?'

That, Jake admitted, was the case. At least he was trying to be. He had taken a course in creative writing.

'At university?' Pedro asked with awe.

That, Jake agreed, was the fact of the matter.

'Lorca learned with the gypsies,' Pedro objected.

Jake had studied Faulkner's symbolism, Carson McCullers' cadences, and Henry James' sentences. He had done class exercises in the manner of all three.

'And now you write?' Pedro said.

There was a pause.

'As a matter of fact, no,' Jake said.

Pedro tried to come to grips with this. 'What,' he asked, 'is the problem?'

'Finding what to write about,' Jake said.

'And you hope Paris might help?'

'I guess,' Jake said.

'Then here is your story,' Pedro suggested. 'A lonely American in Paris, waiting for sight of Sartre in the Cafe de Flore, meets instead a Venezuelan poet and a New Zealand storyteller.'

'Then what?' Jake asked.

Pedro shrugged. 'It is your story.'

Jake thought for a time. 'It doesn't sound right,' he decided.

'You mean,' Pedro said, 'it doesn't sound like stories already written?'

'If you put it like that,' Jake said.

'What other way is there to put it?' Pedro asked.

Jake looked into his pernod.

'Write stories that haven't been written,' Pedro urged.

'That is easy to say,' Jake said.

'But true for me to say,' Pedro insisted. 'It helps to be rebel.'

Now it was Jake's turn to be disconcerted. 'A what?'

'A rebel,' Pedro informed him.

Jake had reason to feel that he might be in deep water. Pedro was looking passionate again.

'A rebel,' Pedro went on, 'sees things differently. He takes nothing for granted.'

'And riots?'

'Revolts,' Pedro said.

'Against what?'

Pedro shrugged again. 'Your parents,' he suggested. 'Your father.'

'But my father,' Jake protested, 'is a most tolerant man.'

It seemed that when Jake informed his father that he didn't want to go into the family business, and wanted to be a writer, his father thought that a reasonable idea. Everyone knew that the proper course for a father would have been to heave Jake out of the house. Instead, he gave Jake an allowance. Having failed to ruffle his father, Jake announced that he was deserting the United States for civilised Europe. His father took this serenely too. He allowed that life in the United States had limitations, that Europe would do Jake no harm. Now a number of uncivilised US dollars crossed the Atlantic for Jake monthly. If Jake needed more, his father said, he had only to ask.

'You see?' Jake said. 'He's impossible.'

Even Pedro had to agree. 'Terrible,' he said. 'There is only one thing for it.'

'What is that?' Jake asked.

'You must rebel against your government.'

Jake looked alarmed.

'Against your President,' Pedro explained.

Jake looked even more alarmed. 'Against President Eisenhower?'

'And Vice President Nixon too,' Pedro proposed.

'But what would I want to do that for?' Jake asked.

Pedro despaired. 'Do you wish it said that only Venezuelans and Hungarians rebel?'

'So I guess you must be lucky,' Jake decided. 'Another round of pernod?'

Pedro was himself again. Jake's situation had persuaded him that there were others worse off than he. From that point, until he took ship for Caracas a week later, Pedro didn't utter a syllable of foreboding about his future. He wrote once or twice after his return. The first said things were difficult but getting better. The second said things were difficult. Then there was silence. Did he despair of a democratic Venezuela and join Marxist guerrillas in the jungle? Or did he settle for something more commonplace? I can imagine him as a grey and serene professor lecturing to large assemblies of docile students. Either way I hope his poetry flourished.

As for Jake, there may be a story, perhaps in a small and discreet volume from an academic press, about a lone young American, an apprentice writer in Paris, meeting up with a wild Venezuelan poet and a suspiciously silent New Zealander. There are stories stranger.

With Pedro gone, our Sunday gatherings lost their verve; and fellow expatriates their nerve. Simon cabled his parents for passage money and sailed home to New Zealand. There he became a newspaper columnist given to weekly reflections on wildlife and wilderness, a commentator on the cadences of the natural world. Sandor, the gentle Hungarian journalist, sheltering in England since Soviet tanks stormed into Budapest, decided to risk going home too, possibly to prison. 'Exile is prison anyway,' he explained. 'At least my guards will speak Hungarian.' Olga wasn't to be left out of this diaspora. She tactfully ended an unpromising affair with a journalist on the communist *Daily Worker* and went home to New Zealand to marry a stockbroker.

My name climbed to the top of Dr Ian Aird's surgery list. On the operating table, before the anaesthetic began work, I heard him say, 'I'm sorry for the wait.'

How explain that no weeks of my life had been more therapeutic? His knife was an anti-climax.

Forty-two

*A*fter two months and four operations, Ian Aird pronounced my rear refurbished; I was ready for the world again. I limped feebly about Ealing Common to confirm this finding and then, more ambitiously, across the Thames to Kew. These excursions did more than loosen my legs; they allowed me to think. Thought of some sort was desirable.

Letters from Bulgaria told me that Jenny Bojilova was holding a door wide. I could return to Bulgaria. There was a job in a publishing house. My salary would be handsome. And I would have friends. Above all, I would have time to concentrate on my own work; Bistritza would always be available for my use. There was more to it. Jenny's letters were passionate. And my marriage was faltering. Late in the day, I tried to behave honorably, as people then did. I wrote to Jenny to say that I couldn't come; that I might be a liability to Bulgarian friends. I would certainly find it difficult to keep quiet in Eastern Europe about such events as the execution of Imre Nagy and Pal Maleter.

Was this genuine? Though it sounded a serviceable excuse, it possibly was. A day or two after writing to Jenny I tried to get it down in a story. A Westerner like myself and an Easterner like Jenny sit at a cafe table in Sofia — or Prague, Budapest, Bucharest, perhaps even Moscow. He is leaving on a train in an hour; she is not. In any other time, any other place, they would be together. But the bulk of a bitter world is between them. She cannot leave her land; he cannot stay. It is their parting. I titled it 'Thank You Goodbye'. Was it a good story? That was not the point.

There is only one reason to write, and it is not to serve literary fashion or scholarly fads. It is, as it was in the beginning, to get a grip on our existence. Or to flag it down for a moment as it flies past. If we also win a little harmony from the human bedlam, that is serendipity.

Beginning again, Gillian and I were in luck. We found a basement in Chelsea for four guineas a week. Servants' quarters in another era, its one distinguishing feature was a bathtub based in the kitchen. We moved from Byron House to Shelley Court. The contemporary critical view of the romantics suggested this a step down. Otherwise it was a step up. In Tite Street, Shelley Court was a few yards from the Thames, and a few doors from Oscar Wilde's onetime residence. Whistler had left his mark there too, and Sargent. Dante Gabriel Rossetti had lived around the corner. The pubs were friendly. Our landlord was a retired Indian Army colonel, of the kind mostly to be found in fiction, named Roy. With the demise of the Raj Colonel Roy looked after his ageing mother and sold advertising for a suburban newspaper. He was a gentle, kindly and in most respects a decent man. His politics, however, were alarming. He loathed Irishmen without exception ('they smell of treason') and barely tolerated blacks ('sons of Ham, hewers of wood and drawers of water'). Indians might have had something to be said for them, or the loyal thousand he had commanded in his time. Chinese too had to be numbered worthy, since they were due to inherit the earth.

'The Chinese?' I said with surprise.

'They'll make sense of the world,' he promised.

Roy's mother looked in frequently. She fancied the idea of a writer in her basement. Though it surely wasn't true, she claimed that the last of my kind in the neighbourhood had been Oscar Wilde. She had been a young girl and then a young woman when Oscar was resident. She could remember him coming and going from Tite Street — arriving or leaving in hansom cabs — in the days of his glory. The great man had once even tipped his hat to her. 'Such a fuss,' she said of his downfall. On second thought, she added, 'Don't *you* go doing anything silly, will you?'

I promised not. An oath sworn on a copy of *The Importance of Being Earnest* might have been fitting. Oscar's was a hard act to follow. I may have been the first writer in years to be obliged to declare his sexual bona fides to win residence in Tite Street.

'He was really Irish,' she observed.

Yes, I said. I knew.

'So being a New Zealander will be no excuse,' she announced.

She had seen change, not of a desirable kind. In the war, during the blitz, refugees from the beleaguered East End had been billeted in Tite Street — God knew why, because the Battersea Power Station, a target of Nazi bombers, sat just across the river. Anyway there they were, the refugees. Standards fell, she said.

'In what way?' I asked, expecting coal-in-the-bath stories, and underwear drying on balconies.

'There were children playing in the street,' she said.

'Children?'

'And perambulators.'

Affliction could go no further. Tite Street, surviving the blitz, East Enders and socialists, was sedate once more.

Luck struck again. In New Zealand the committee of the State Literary Fund, with £2000 at its annual disposal, had just met to consider hand-outs to deserving writers. Someone miscalculated; perhaps some candidate was judged undesirable. After doing its sums the committee was left with £200 in its purse. What to do with it?

'Throw it at a young writer,' someone suggested.

'Who, then?' someone asked.

'This fellow Shadbolt,' the poet Denis Glover proposed.

'Shadbolt? Who is he?'

'Throw the money at him and you might find out.'

A week later our telephone rang. It was New Zealand's high commissioner in London. 'I have some largesse here, apparently for you,' he said. 'How would you like it paid out?'

I felt dizzy. Money? The man was talking about half a year's income: that is, when I last had an income. In New Zealand there had been debate about the dangers of state patronage of literature. Some saw it as paving the way for lapdog writers. Some pictured pigs at the state trough. I discovered no strong feelings. Jim Baxter put it succinctly: 'Taking a ride on the gravy train doesn't mean you have to take off your hat to the driver.' The money might keep me alive and writing in a climate more amiable than London's sullen, saturating summer. And my remodelled rump — not to speak of still angrily red legs, where skin had been stripped for grafts — might heal faster with sea and sun. That suggested the Mediterranean or the Adriatic. The money might buy health; it might mean my first book.

'By the way,' the high commisioner added, 'you are expected to do something worthy with it. But that's rather over to you. No one's going to notice if you don't. Except you, of course.'

Wavering, I first booked a rail ticket to Yugoslavia. A Columbian writer friend was renting a cottage outside Dubrovnik for the summer. There were rooms to spare. The outlines, however, were vague.

There was nothing indistinct about the postcard I received from a pair of painter friends, Pat Hanly and Gil Taverner. Looking for somewhere to lodge for the summer, they had enterprisingly discovered Ibiza before mass tourism ended its innocence. They rented a room for the English equivalent of two pounds monthly. Food cost them less than one pound a week. 'Come,' they urged. They had a convincing case. My £200 might last a lifetime.

I went to British Rail to change my ticket. 'You want Barcelona now, not Belgrade?' a puzzled clerk said.

'That's right,' I said. 'Barcelona, not Belgrade.'

'They're in different countries,' he warned. 'But it's not for me to tell you your business.'

'Thanks,' I said. Everyone else, everything else, seemed to be.

I would stay on Ibiza until I had something identifiable as a volume of stories. Gillian would join me for her summer holidays. With the book off my back, I might consider some legitimate livelihood.

Forty-three

The plan promised to come apart within hours of leaving London. Paris was hot, stuffy and rowdy with armed police and military patrols. General De Gaulle, backed by the army, and particularly the elite *paras*, had just deposed a civilian government. Before he disclosed his own programme and emasculated his allies, he seemed another General Franco in the making, and France another Spain.

At Saint Lazare station I made the mistake of behaving gallantly to an Englishwoman with a robust accumulation of baggage and a repellent child. His name was Nigel; hers was Edith. Edith was refusing to pay boorish porters or to parley in French; the porters played deaf. 'Wretches,' she said. 'They know perfectly well what I am saying.' Nigel was pulling faces at the porters and experimentally kicking their shins. 'The French,' Edith was announcing, 'are a squalid race.' The porters got that message. Uproar mounted. The military, with this British offensive in progress, might have to establish its proficiency. I eased myself between belligerents and picked up a couple of her suitcases. The surly porters stomped away.

'So you're going to the Baleares,' Edith said. 'How marvellous. So am I. Which way are you going? Through Port Bou? Absurd. That route is impossible at this time of year. Come with me through the Pyrenees, through Puigcerda. No one travels that way. It's cool and uncrowded travelling through the mountains. If you come with me you'll just have time to make the connection. Hurry.'

Edith needed another unpaid porter.

'My ticket is through Port Bou,' I pointed out.

'A guard can fix that in seconds,' she said dismissively. 'Come along now.'

A bus carried us through hot and lustreless Paris to Austerlitz station.

'Canadian, are you?' Edith asked.

'New Zealander,' I said.

'I suppose it's the same thing.'

'Not altogether,' I began.

Nigel kicked out at his mother. With the authority of his eight years, he said, 'New Zealand isn't in America.'

'No?' said his mother.

'No,' Nigel said. 'It's in Africa.'

Pointed at the Pyrenees, our train steamed out of Paris. 'It is rather slower this way,' Edith disclosed. 'But one gets to Spain eventually.'

That was unpromising.

'You're a good chap,' Nigel said. 'Have a chocolate. Where did you learn to speak English?'

The suburbs of Paris drifted behind. The guard looked sternly at my ticket. 'You are on the wrong train,' he announced. 'For Port Bou you must change at Toulouse.'

'I no longer wish to go through Port Bou.'

'You must,' he said decisively.

'This is absurd,' Edith announced. 'This young man wishes to travel with me. Understand?'

The guard shrugged. 'Impossible,' he said. 'You must leave this train.'

'Talk to him in African,' Nigel suggested.

'Can't someone help?' Edith cried. 'Can't *someone* help with this uniformed fool?'

Commotion grew. Suddenly everyone was trying to help. The guard was overwhelmed by Frenchmen doing their best to oblige Edith and keep me on the train. Finally he retreated. 'It is all right,' he said. 'You may remain.'

'You see?' Edith said. 'Simple. The French can't stand up to a good talking to. They don't have the stamina.'

'I'm hungry,' Nigel said. 'You going to eat now, old chap?'

Beyond the windows of the dining car there was darkening farmland patched with mist.

'Why aren't you black?' Nigel asked. 'Is it because there isn't any sun in England? Did you just go pale in England?'

There was a new bout of noise. Drunken paratroopers were battering on the locked door of the dining car and demanding liquor. We were in a besieged fort. Waiters tried to pacify them. 'Drink,' they explained, 'will be served after the meal. First you must allow people to eat. You must wait.'

Having just humbled a government, the soldiery was in no mood to be detained by waiters. With a little more bashing, the dining car door shuddered inward. Waiters were brushed aside. '*Vive De Gaulle*,' someone shouted. Hot, heavy young men in uniform were crowding the carriage, blocking aisles, and making it impossible for waiters to serve. 'Drink,' the paratroopers demanded.

'You must wait,' an old and weary waiter insisted.

He was knocked to the floor. Food sprayed over our table. A flick-knife snapped open. There was no more discussion. Paratroopers occupied empty seats in the dining car and lounged thick in the aisle. 'Drink,' they demanded menacingly and this time got it.

We fled the dining car and fell into our seats.

'That was interesting,' Nigel concluded. 'Do you think they'll kill anyone?'

'Thank God for Spain,' Edith said.

'Why?' Nigel asked.

'It is peaceful,' his mother explained. 'It is decent. General Franco would never permit such goings on.'

A new passenger in our compartment, a short aloof man with a long moustache, lowered his copy of *L'Express*; he smiled wryly and lifted it again. Nothing was said.

The train rushed south. Escaping Nigel and Edith, I found myself in the corridor with the new passenger. His name was Carlos. We talked in fragments of English, French, Spanish, and Russian. When in doubt we drew pictures on a misty window. Anyway he was Spanish. 'No longer do I live there,' he said. 'Not in twenty years.'

'The war?' I said.

'The civil war,' he agreed.

'You fought?'

'Against Franco. Against fascism. In the 41st Brigade.'

'Were you ever wounded?' I asked.

'Twice.'

'Perhaps my aunt nursed you.'

He was incredulous.

'A woman from New Zealand? All that way to help Spaniards?'

'True,' I assured him.

That won his heart. He embraced me.

271

The war had ended for Carlos as it had for thousands of his comrades. Flight over the Pyrenees into France; exile in France, Mexico or the Soviet Union. Many of the 41st who went to the Soviet Union perished in service with the Red Army. Others disappeared between the cracks in the twentieth century.

'But not you,' I said.

'Luck,' he claimed.

He had been in Russia for a time, then Yugoslavia, not comfortable in either. He now lived in Paris.

'What do you do in Paris?'

'I work,' he said with some reticence.

I didn't inquire further. 'Until you can go back to Spain?'

'Franco cannot live a hundred years,' he said.

We talked of Russia, Yugoslavia, France and Spain; and of the heroic 41st. The last man I had met from the 41st was a shell-shocked cripple who worked shining tourist shoes in a Pigalle bar.

'Those are the saddest,' Carlos said. 'Those for whom return will be too late.'

'But not you.'

'I have made up my mind to live long enough to spit on Franco's grave,' he explained. 'Even God cannot cheat me of that.'

It was late. We returned to our compartment and slept. At four in the morning we halted at Toulouse. De Gaulle's paratroopers clamoured on to the platform, boarded waiting vehicles, and rumbled off into the dark. Did they have a mission? And, for that matter, did Carlos? I slept again.

I woke to sunrise over the Pyrenees, the valleys of Andorra wide and green beyond train windows. There was a new guard asking for my ticket. 'This is no good,' he announced. 'You must return to Toulouse to travel to Port Bou.'

'But,' I began.

This time it was not Edith who intervened; it was Carlos.

'Are you a good union man?' he asked the guard.

The guard claimed he was.

'A socialist?'

'A good socialist,' the guard insisted.

'And against De Gaulle?'

'Of course.'

'So would you throw a good union man and a socialist — someone against De Gaulle — off your train?'

The guard allowed that he preferred not to. He returned my ticket, shook my hand with apologies, and moved on.

'That is the way the world should be,' Carlos judged. 'We are comrades in this life.'

Edith, who had lost track of me through the night, hurried heavy-lidded Nigel off to the toilet. There was precious silence in our compartment. Beyond our window the sun was colouring the mountains. French mountains or Spanish? Either way they were splendid in the morning.

'We are near Spain,' Carlos said. 'I must leave the train.'

'You are here on business?'

'That could be said,' he admitted.

He preferred to talk poetry. 'You know Lorca?' he asked. 'Our poet who was shot by the fascists in 1936? You read his poems?'

As a matter of fact I did. I even had a bilingual book of his verse in my haversack at this moment; I fancied reading Lorca in Spain and learning his lines in Spanish.

'Show me,' Carlos said. I fetched the book. He turned the pages slowly. Then he read the Spanish.

> *Y que yo me la lieve al rio* . . .
> So I took her to the river
> believing she was a maiden
> but she already had a husband . . .

Edith, back in the compartment with Nigel, grew fidgety. 'That is not particularly palatable,' she said.

'It is *great*,' Carlos said.

It was not the voice of a man inclined to tolerate argument. Even noxious Nigel was silent. Carlos read on, his voice gathering even more authority.

> *Puede el hombre, si quiere, conducir su deseo*
> Man can, if he wishes, lead his desire
> *por vena de coral o celeste desnudo*
> through vein of coral or celestial nude
> *Manana los amores seran rocas y el Tiempo*
> tomorrow love will be rocks and Time
> *una brise que viene dormida por las ramas*
> a breeze which comes sleeping through the branches.

273

Carlos grew thoughtful, looking out on mountains I took to be Spain's. The train slowed for the last halt before Puigcerda. He removed a single suitcase from the overhead rack. 'Nearly Spain,' he announced. 'I must leave you here. Give my love to the land of Lorca.'

We jolted into a small mountain town. Carlos shook my hand and left the train stiffly. For the first time I noticed he walked with a limp. Another legacy of his service with the 41st ? Possibly. And did he make this pilgrimage — to look out into Spain — often?

'*Adios!*' I called through the window.

He raised an arm. '*Salud!*' he replied.

The London *Times* came up with a postscript a fortnight later. I was sunbathing among thyme-scented Ibizan rocks; the world was distant, and this copy of the *Times* several days' old. An item in the cable page took my eye. Franco's Falangist government had been making arrests in Madrid and Barcelona. Three wanted students — one of them the rebellious son of a Falangist politician — had been hunted across northern Spain by police and militia. They avoided capture by escaping across the Pyrenees into France, at a point near Puigcerda.

It may have been coincidence that Carlos was located at a point near Puigcerda at that time, possibly on the day the students made their crossing. It may have been. It may also have been my imagination at work. Carlos might not have been there to welcome them out of the mountains. He might have been holidaying in the Pyrenees for his health.

But I remember he read Lorca well.

Forty-four

*B*arcelona was stifling in the siesta hour. Dockside cafes were filled with young American males sporting beards and straw hats and talking in terse Hemingway prose. Many had been running with the bulls in the streets of Pamplona, living *The Sun Also Rises* to the letter. Life now held no surprises. And a hundred courses in American literature were thus enriched.

'You're off to Ibiza?' one asked.

I was, I agreed.

'That place is *dead*, man. Dead, dead, dead. What do you want to do with yourself there?'

In present company my reply was bound to be immodest.

'Write,' I said.

'About Spain?'

'New Zealand,' I told him.

'Like what? Like all of it?'

'Like most of it,' I said.

My interrogator tipped back his hat. 'Wow,' he said.

The overnight ferry to Ibiza reeked of diesel and burnt cooking oil. In the morning there was rocky shore, bleached hills and scrubby cliffs. Then, beyond a curving breakwater and a lighthouse, the town of Ibiza heaved suddenly and theatrically into sight: terraces of spellbindingly white cube houses climbed to the tall city wall and a taller cathedral. What was I doing in this neighbourhood? I had no more than a month or two to find out.

Wow.

For a pound a week I had a house in the fishermen's quarter. It was at the end of a cliffside cul de sac called the Calle Miranda. I slept through the beat of the sea, the cathedral bell chiming the hours, fishing boats throbbing out of the harbour at three in the morning. There were two omens, one auspicious and the other not. The Calle Miranda had already been home to two New Zealand writers. A year earlier Janet Frame had lived there, scrupulously shunning the cosmopolitan life of Ibiza's cafes and inconspicuously finishing a novel. (*Her* Ibiza is to be found in her autobiography *An Angel at My Table*, and as memorably in a much-honoured movie of the same name.) Another aspirant novelist named Fassett Burnett had also just moved out. Fassett too had been labouring on a novel. Then, around page 300, after an over-long night in Ibizan bars, he hurled his manuscript into the Mediterranean. That obliged him to return to New Zealand and distinguish himself as a painter and print-maker instead. There was a warning here, largely to the effect that moderation was desirable. I had no prospects as painter or print-maker.

I inherited a difficulty. Until rehabilitated by the Guardia Civil, my residence had recently been in business as a two-cubicle bordello. News of its closure hadn't reached the hinterland of the island. I was roused by young villagers, in town for the night, battering on my door at midnight or after. I had to climb blearily out on to my balcony and proclaim 'No *senoritas acqui.*' They seldom believed me. Incomprehensible protest followed, possibly to the effect that I was selfish, that one cubicle was enough for any man. I appeared to be in tune with William Faulkner's prescription for young writers. Live in a brothel, he advised; nights might be noisy but mornings were quiet.

Otherwise the place was luxurious by Ibizan measure. There was flickering electric light; there was sometimes a gush of water from a tap. The plumbing was inventive. With strategic footholds over a sewer outlet my shower also served as a latrine.

There were neighbours. A blonde Danish teacher of languages, moonlighting as a prostitute for the summer, ensured that the Calle Miranda retained its x-rated character. There were painters and writers. There was a solemn and bearded American novelist with a powerful sense of literary history in the making. At waterside cafes he boomed out his belief that we — the writers resident on Ibiza that summer — were the harbingers of a new lost generation, destined to be even more mislaid than Hemingway's. 'People,' he predicted, 'are going to look at us with wonder when we let slip that we lived on Ibiza in 1958. Were you, they'll ask, really there that summer? Were you?'

Was I? I have been waiting half a lifetime for someone to ask. If there had been an *annus mirabilis* I would be a poor witness. I was elsewhere, trying to trap a distant land in my typewriter, trying to whittle a score of stories down to a dozen and make even those leaner. Trying to master the manuscript, and counting my pounds, I puritanically kept my head down while others banged on in cafes about their destined place in literary history. I envied them their visionary approach to letters. After tea and an Ibizan pastry, I worked through the cool hours, lunched with the Hanlys, then took a siesta and swam.

Friendships grew. There was Denis Chesworth, a talented young painter from Manchester; there was Ernest Mondorf, a refugee from an advertising agency in Manhattan. In the evenings we took station at a cafe we styled the Bitter End. Later still we looked in on the Casa de Pepe. Pepe de Madrid was a lean, melancholy and half-crippled guitarist. When his audience thinned, toward midnight, he played and sang songs of the Spanish Republic. He left the impression that he had fought on the republican side and possibly had. But it also happened to be the case that he was an informer for the Guardia Civil, and reported on foreigners expressing themselves freely on General Franco. Pepe used republican songs to draw out indiscreet utterances. Those who spoke up found themselves deported.

Trust the song and not the singer.

Most of those writing and painting on Ibiza that summer were discovering that they were not writers and painters. They were to travel home with their unfinished manuscripts and unfilled sketchbooks; they were to become stockbrokers, lawyers and academics. As summer cooled so would illusion. Black-bearded and boisterous Duff Daniels, noting the end near, began cabling his parents to sell his shares in the family business. He was unsuccessful. Before another month was out he would shave off his beard, burn his action paintings in the manner of Jackson Pollock, and fly home to Iowa to become Vice President of his father's company.

Some made the most of their situation. Irish Eddie had gone to Ibiza to write a novel which picked up on Dublin where James Joyce left off. When he located his limitations as a novelist, and found Dublin an unwilling partner in the enterprise, he wasn't dismayed. He trimmed sail and wrote a lurid piece of romantic fiction (*Ibizan Sunrise*) to keep boredom at bay. It was pure wish fulfilment: it told the the tale of a rich and beautiful American girl falling in love with a young Irish writer. He sold it with ease, and then wrote another (*Moon over the Balearics*). The story was essentially the same. Since life notoriously imitates art the American girl soon turned up, and then a few more as a bonus. He now sold a novel a month to Mills and Boon at £100 a time. He wrote a chapter a morning, never more than two hours at his typewriter, and dawdled away the rest of the day in Dirty Domingo's or Clean Domingo's, whichever cafe was in favour. (Broiled squid was best at Dirty Domingo's, and cognac cheaper.) Eddie may still roost high in the town with a library of love stories. But never one to rival Paulo's; his story would never make a Mills and Boon list.

Paulo was a restless, frequently sleepless Italian painter. I came to expect his thunderous knocking on my door day or night. He was a shambling, shapeless giant of a man with a surprisingly soft voice. But his work was never slight. To enter his pension room, above the city wall, was to walk into an aquarium swimming with exquisitely coloured shapes. His paintings were neither naturalist nor abstract: they were just the world Paulo saw. The problem was that he always saw more than he could persuade his paintbrush to say. Between aspiration and achievement there were fretful nights.

'It is so with you also, when you write,' he pointed out.

'Sometimes,' I admitted.

Toward the end of the war Paulo had been a partisan. He fought Germans and fellow Italians. Most of one winter was spent hiding high in the hills. It was a bad winter. They lost contact with their leaders. Some of his comrades died; others were captured, tortured and killed by Mussolini's ruthless *Brigate Nere*. Survivors were thin and ill. If it was not sickness of the body, Paulo said, it was sickness of the heart. There was fighting in the south, however, and the Germans, even the fascists of the *Brigate Nere*, were less apparent. With spring the partisans moved warily out of the hills. Paulo's band finally emerged from dark forest into bright sunlight. Before them was a small mountain village. Its inhabitants raced to welcome the partisans and help the lame and the wounded to safety. Villagers offered wine and such food as they had and the priest gave them his church to sleep in. Some were sick again, with the food and the wine; their stomachs had shrunken in the hills. Guards were posted lest the enemy come again from the south. For days, weeks, Paulo's band rested and healed in that village. Time passed sweetly; another day of peace meant another less of war.

'And there was a girl,' Paulo admitted.

'Ah,' I said.

'She came every day with food and fresh bandages,' he explained. 'She was a thin little girl, barefoot, with the eyes of a forest creature. She was always serious, never smiling. I was seventeen, but already I held myself as a man, spoke with the voice of a man, had the scars of a man. The partisans every day teased her, and teased me, so that we could not look at each other. I held myself as a man, but I was still a shy boy.'

'So?' I asked.

'There was nothing,' he said.

'Nothing?'

'A German patrol was seen moving toward the hills. We had to leave. Otherwise we would endanger the villagers. As we marched into the forest again I heard running feet behind me. Bare feet. It was of course the girl to whom I never spoke. She had a mountain flower in her hand. She fastened it to my tunic while my comrades laughed. Yet we looked at each other for the first time. I looked into her eyes and she into mine.'

Paulo did not seem to wish to push the narrative further.

'And?' I asked impatiently.

'We waited for the patrol, by a path at the edge of the stream, and shot them as they came. We put bullets in the heads of those who still moved. We took their boots, their rations, their guns and ammunition and ran back into the mist and forest. It was our last bad winter; soon the war was over.'

It was, nevertheless, an unsatisfying close.

'Did you see that village again?' I asked. 'That girl?'

'Never.'

'Did you wish to?'

'That country was strange to us,' he protested. 'The place might have been difficult to find again. There could be many such villages, many such girls.'

This was not true, of course. For Paulo there was just one such village, just one such girl. He reached for the cognac with a shaky hand and filled our glasses. From our table at Clean Domingo's we watched townsfolk flow past in their evening *paseo*.

'How was your work today?' Paulo asked.

'I tell myself tomorrow will be better.'

'Sometimes,' he said, 'I wish I could write.'

'Sometimes I wish I could paint,' I said.

'But it will not happen,' he observed sadly. 'You will not paint. I will not write.'

'Probably not,' I admitted.

'So you will tell, perhaps, my partisan story.'

'Perhaps.'

'Good,' he said. 'Then I have no further wish to write.'

'What of my wish to paint?'

'That,' he pointed out, 'is your problem.'

That night it was impossible to sleep. It was hot, and mosquitoes were noisy. My casa was messy with crumpled pages of manuscript. Outside there was a faint breeze on offer. I sat out on the sea wall, sipped cold tea, and attempted to make sense of some Spanish tobacco with the consistency of seaweed. Finally I walked across town — with bats flickering overhead — to Paulo's pension; his light was still burning. His giant hand wrapped around a tiny brush, he was trying to bring another large undersea canvas under control. I stood marvelling. I didn't understand then that the telling of his war story was the overture to another painting: there was a seventeen-year-old partisan somewhere in those magic shapes, and a mountain girl.

'Never wait on tomorrow,' he said fiercely. 'There is only today.'

A cognac later I went home and slept. I failed to notice heat or mosquitoes. I didn't even have a hangover next morning. I was at my typewriter till noon.

Forty-five

July passed, and August. By September my manuscript began to have a professional look. There was an epigraph and a dedication, everything but a title. Gillian turned up on Ibiza for her promised holiday. Now a seasoned native of the island, I showed her around with authority; we bicycled up to San Antonio and Santa Eulalia; we went netting with my fisherman friend Lorenzo. Lorenzo had been exiled on the island by the Franco government after a last-minute reprieve from the firing squad. Sometimes he took us to a bar where fellow exiles gathered; and the Italian republican song *Bandierra Rossa* was sung for the benefit of approved guests. My family connection with the International Brigade earned us honorary membership of Lorenzo's sad and ageing circle. Each had his own story; their eyes and scars told it best. When Franco died, two decades later, their remembered faces filled my mind. Did they perish, one by one, before walking mainland Spain again?

Meanwhile I was suffering a foggy condition I finally identified as folktale fatigue. I'd had my fill of Europe's: of those of Bulgaria, Russia, Georgia, Italy and now Spain too. It made those of my own tribe more imperative. I saw what I might be up to at last. My manuscript was still missing a title. I discovered it. By way of nailing my colours to the mast I called the book *The New Zealanders*. That title hadn't been used since the 1850s, and then meant Maoris. It seemed to make my point — that there was a new Pacific race in the making — more piquant. There was a literary echo too. Hadn't James Joyce called his first book of stories *Dubliners*?

That was back in London, in late summer or early autumn. Title found, I bundled the manuscript into a cupboard and closed the door. I was resigned to it finding no publisher in the northern hemisphere. I might take it back to New Zealand and interest some small press.

I took a train to Aberdeen to stay with an mariner friend who had forsaken the sea and had begun turning himself into a geographer of distinction. We hiked across Scottish highland, and a good deal of lowland, until his academic year began. I had a sense of life at a standstill. Was I waiting on fate?

'What's happened to your book?' Alistair finally asked.

'A good question,' I said.

I was pleased that he did not persist in asking it.

On our return to Aberdeen he announced, 'We're invited to dinner tonight. 'You should find our hostess interesting.'

'Oh?'

'Her name's Jean Cockburn. Once the wife of Claude Cockburn, the left-wing journalist, editor of *The Week* before the war.'

I knew of Claude Cockburn and *The Week*. Anyone who knew anything about England in the 1930s knew of both. *The Week* had dedicated itself to disclosing scandal, corruption and sympathy for fascism in high places.

'Jean is still very political,' Alistair explained. 'She also knew a lot of literary people. You'll like her.'

I did. Jean Cockburn was a lean, handsome and warm-eyed woman. Though most of her friends of the 1930s had surrendered the Soviet Union as a cause, Jean was still a heartfelt Communist; she sold *The Daily Worker* on street corners. Yet she was surprisingly undogmatic. Her taste in literature was catholic. Table talk turned to English writers of the 1930s. She spoke of them with familiarity and sometimes fondness: Wystan Auden, Stephen Spender, Cecil Day Lewis, Rex Warner, Edward Upward, Christopher Isherwood; especially Isherwood. I should, perhaps, have been suspicious. There was more here than met the ear.

At length she looked across the table at me. 'I believe you're a writer too,' she said.

'Of sorts,' I agreed.

'Alistair tells me you have finished a book. When can we expect to see it?'

'Perhaps never,' I said. 'It's very regional.'

'Regional?'

'Local. New Zealand.'

'What's wrong with that?'

I shrugged, hoping the subject might change.

'Most good writing is local,' she said. 'It's just that some localities are more fashionable than others.'

'New Zealand's day hasn't come,' I argued.

'Who knows?' she said. 'Where is the manuscript now?'

'In a cupboard,' I confessed.

'Dig it out,' she said. 'Dust it off. Try it on a London publisher. On Victor Gollancz, say. You know who I mean?'

'I know the books he publishes.' I had grown up with Victor Gollancz's red Left Book Club editions. With the change in ideological temperature his publications now sported yellow jackets.

'Victor has an eye for fresh writing,' she went on. 'He might be the answer to your prayers.'

'I'm not praying that hard,' I protested.

'Come,' she said. 'Try him.'

Back in London winter closed in. I wrote travel sketches and book reviews. I four times read and three times reviewed *Dr Zhivago* for journals in Britain, Australia and New Zealand. In Australia one review became a cause celebre. Stephen Murray-Smith, the editor of a left-wing literary magazine called *Overland*, proposed to print it. Stalinists on the editorial board argued otherwise; they wheeled out the ageing novelist Katherine Susannah Pritchard, and more than a few other Party veterans, to denounce both Boris Pasternak and the sentiments expressed in my review. It finished with Murray-Smith, and a few others, being expelled from the Communist Party. Others resigned. Half Australia's literary left wasn't speaking to the other half; there was everything but blood on the floor. I was unaware of the mayhem until, months later, I had a letter from Murray-Smith in Melbourne apologising for the delay in printing my piece. There had been a few difficulties, he explained, and went on to list them. I couldn't believe it. To reassure myself I went on to read *Dr Zhivago* a fifth time. It confirmed my bearings. *Strangers and Journeys*, published a dozen years later, became my genuflexion to Pasternak.

1958 drifted into 1959. The manuscript cheekily titled *The New Zealanders* was still domiciled bashfully in the cupboard of a Chelsea basement. Six months had gone. I wasn't tempted to look at it again.

A young writer, someone I had known faintly in Wellington, appeared on our doorstep. He was shy and nervous and looking for a bed. He stayed a night or two before disappearing in London; I never saw or heard of him again and nor did anyone I knew. Before he left he showed me the manuscript of a novel he meant to hawk around London publishers. Would I care to read a chapter or two? I found that no problem. I read three or four. His manuscript seemed no more flawed than *The New Zealanders*. If he had the nerve to try, why shouldn't I? Five minutes after he vanished I opened the cupboard. The corners of my manuscript had begun to curl up in the chronic damp of a Thameside basement. There actually *was* a fine film of dust on it. I blew it off and retyped the title page.

Then I took a walk along the King's Road, peering into bookshop windows. Victor Gollancz was still in business. Better still, he appeared to publish more volumes of stories than most of his kind. As it happened, this was in error; most of the storytellers on his list had been market-tested in New York. Scribbling down the address of his firm, I met a neighbour, the Portuguese poet in exile; he bought me a pint of bitter in the Chelsea Potter. 'So what are you up to?' he asked.

'Looking for a publisher,' I explained.

In sympathy he insisted on buying my next drink too.

Mail rustled through our door on a sunny Saturday morning in March. There were letters from New Zealand, from Australia, from Bulgaria. There was also one with a London postmark; from the firm of Victor Gollancz. It was too thin to be more than a terse rejection. I put it aside and read other mail. Dennis Chesworth, the young artist from Manchester, was staying. We breakfasted and read through *The Times* and *The Guardian*. Finally Gillian said, 'At least you could see what he says.'

'Who?'

'Victor Gollancz.'

'Why spoil a good weekend?' I asked.

Then Dennis suggested, 'There's something odd about it.'

'Odd?'

'No manuscript,' he pointed out. 'Shouldn't they have returned it?'

'Parcels take longer.'

'All the same,' he said.

I opened the letter warily. In some form or another, over one signature or another, I had scripted it in my imagination for years. It was to the effect that a distinguished publishing house not only wanted my manuscript; it was even prepared to pay me £75 in advance royalties. The print blurred. My hands were shaking. That wasn't in the script. God knows what my face was saying. Anyway my silence was impressive. Particularly when I reeled down the page to a paragraph saying that Victor Gollancz was travelling to the United States the following week and wanted my permission to interest the *The New Yorker* and a New York publishing house in the stories. My *permission*?

'Come on,' Gillian said. 'Tell us what's in it. It can't be all bad.'

'It isn't,' I said.

Judging us in need of a party, Dennis hurtled out to an off-licence for champagne. To fetch up some New Zealand friends at World's End for more extensive celebration, I walked the Chelsea embankment. The Thames brimmed with light; London glowed. The paving stones underfoot were queerly vivid. How many heady first-time authors had walked this way before? The day had one imperfection. Kevin Ireland, friend, mentor, wasn't around; he was beyond reach of a letter. A note from his mother said that in the wake of an unhappy love affair he had quit shepherding tourists through the Waitomo Caves and disappeared in the direction of the Australian outback. Where was he? Driving a camel train through the desert beyond Alice Springs? Hunting crocodiles in Queensland? I had no literary shoulder to lean on. I walked the embankment alone.

Other writers tell me that what happened then is not uncommon. Though the morning was unseasonally warm, my shaking turned to shivering. It had been too easy. It was also improbable. The letter must have been meant for some other author. By the time I reached World's End I had all but convinced myself. There was another, more sobering reaction. I was the perpetrator of a confidence trick. After hoodwinking readers, editors and fellow writers for years, I was now misrepresenting myself to a London publishing house too. I was no author. Aunt Sis had known it all along. But I managed to go through the motions, rousing New Zealand friends and inviting them to the party. On the way back through Chelsea I found a post office and cabled my parents. Confidence trick or not, I had to see it through now.

An alarm bell rang when I telephoned friends, and in particular a

New Zealand contemporary named Marcus. A witty, occasionally wise and always acid essayist, a poet and literary critic, Marcus had a manuscript novel on the move from one London publishing house to another; editors' letters of rejection had been kindly but many. Too clever to see that the race isn't necessarily to the clever, or at least to vendors of elegant pastiche, Marcus failed to understand the refusals. Flushed by the Gollancz letter, I foolishly forgot his situation. To this point he had been closer to me than most New Zealanders camped in literary London; we had taken in plays together, galleries and concerts. Even when he was at his most provocative, or disagreeable, I enjoyed his company more than he might have noticed; he gave life an edge. It was natural to give him the news early.

On the telephone, though, there was a long silence. The silence lengthened. I sensed disbelief, which was reasonable. But it went on. I could hear him breathing. Then words finally formed.

'That's marvellous,' he said. 'Marvellous.'

I didn't believe a word, though there were only three spoken, and one of them twice. Intuition told me a friendship had expired. It was confirmed when his manuscript found no publisher. Before another year was out *The New Zealanders* was dismantled by my late friend. He proved comprehensively that it did not exist; or that, if it did, it shouldn't. I had it coming: the review was of the stylishly malicious kind which, when about the work of others, had often left me laughing. Later Marcus urged a literary editor to give my work still more rigorous scrutiny and offered a list of approved reviewers. I no longer laughed. I was learning. The storyteller has a longer shelf life. I banished Marcus to a comic novel where he resides inoffensively, even rather likeably, to this day.

Is there a postscript? It took most of thirty years to arrive. In the 1980s Christopher Isherwood died. There were long obituaries, not least in London's *Observer*. On a sunny morning in New Zealand I was reading my six-week-old copy of that newspaper. I heard a loud cry. It was mine.

The obituary for Isherwood recalled his precocious success as a novelist, and named the original of Sally Bowles, the dizzy butterfly of 1930s Berlin; the heroine of his novel *Goodbye to Berlin*, of the movie *I Am a Camera*, and the musical *Cabaret*. According to the *Observer* the model for Sally Bowles was a woman named Jean

Cockburn. Jean Cockburn? The warm-eyed woman of Aberdeen? The obituary informed me that she had predeceased Isherwood by several years.

There it was, then.

In *Goodbye to Berlin* Sally Bowles tells Herr Issyvoo: 'I think it must be marvellous to be a novelist. You're frightfully dreamy and unpractical and unbusinesslike, and people imagine they can swindle you as much as they want — and then you sit down and write a book about them which fairly shows them what swine they all are, and it's the most terrific success and you make pots of money.'

So who steered me to a publisher? Jean Cockburn? Or Sally Bowles? It sounds suspiciously like Sally. As it happens I have been dreamy and unpractical and unbusinesslike and have sometimes been swindled. But it has been fairly marvellous, these past thirty years, even with the pots of money missing.

Isherwood ends his story: 'When you read this, Sally — if you ever do — please accept it as a tribute, the sincerest I can pay, to yourself and to our friendship.'

My gratitude is sincere too. Jean Cockburn is no longer around to thank. As long as *Goodbye to Berlin* is read, and *Cabaret* staged, Sally Bowles is.

Forty-six

*P*atrick White once said something like this to me: 'Until his first book, a young writer flirts with the muses. His life may be of interest. His work is not. Thereafter he is just another tradesman. Everything important has happened to him. His work may be of interest. His life is not.'

I thought that an unduly austere notion, disproved by his own life. Yet I saw what he meant. On this view the slow months before the appearance of a first book allows a writer a last liaison with life before the heady honeymoon of publication and then humdrum marriage to his craft.

In anticipation of a printers' strike Gollancz wanted to push *The New Zealanders* through quickly; a proof copy of the book was with me in weeks. Even more magically, Kevin Ireland appeared bedraggled at our door. There had been more heartbreak in Sydney. He had put it behind him by boarding a ship bound for Britain.

Between love affairs and travel he hadn't heard my news. 'Where can I buy you a drink?' he said.

There was generosity here, not jealousy. My second thoughts were dispersed by his delight. He shared our Chelsea basement until he had found a bed and a job. I argued that it was time for his first book too.

'Why?' he asked.

'Why not?' I said.

He grew thoughtful.

While I laboured on proofs in the living room, he arranged a plank cover over our kitchen-based bathtub and sifted through his poems. We fashioned those we deemed unworthy into paper boats. In the late afternoon we floated them off in flimsy flotilla down the Thames, each with a cargo of words discharged from duty. There were enough left over. In a fortnight he had his first book too.

John Kasmin, now legitimate in the art world, materialised benevolently in our lives again. First he found Kevin a job as a handyman in Soho's lively Gallery One. Then he took us to parties and gallery openings to demonstrate that his police-ridden past was behind him, that he no longer needed to sweep sodden cigarette butts from bar floors or serve as technical adviser to dilettante bank robbers. He was now repaying old debts: those who had fed him potato soup for survival were paid back with caviar.

Kas was doing his sober best to marry into an old and distinguished English family with impressive connections in art, in literature, in politics and publishing. The Nicholsons, in short. There were difficulties. Who was this Kasmin, the family was asking, what were his credentials? Prospective bride Jane was spirited off to New Mexico in an attempt to make her think again about the marriage — and, better still, forget Kasmin. This was unproductive. Bored by New Mexico, Jane was unable to think of anything but Kas. Stalemate ensued, with battle lines firm.

Kas called on me, looking more owlish than usual.

'I need you,' he said.

'What for?'

'I need a respectable friend,' he explained.

'Me?' I said, bewildered.

'You're the only one I can fetch up.'

'In all London?' I didn't believe it.

'I need someone who's known me for years. Also someone to talk to Jane's family and tell them what a reliable fellow I am.'

'You can do better than me,' I argued. 'What about Kevin?'

Kevin wouldn't do. He still had the taint of bohemia. Kas needed someone who mightn't look uncomfortable in suit and tie. It had to be me. So I shook the wrinkles from a vintage suit, knotted my one tie, and went out to do battle for Kas, or at least to persuade Jane's mother that her imminent son-in-law would prove a jewel in the crown of her illustrious family. This was in a Bloomsbury restaurant. There were several such meetings. Mrs Nicholson, a woman of much charm, paid most bills; otherwise anxious Kas covered expenses.

Not only did I argue that Kas was of impeccable character. I made the point that Kas's departure from New Zealand had been a loss to art and letters in that land.

'You surprise me,' she said coolly.

I was surprising myself. In for a penny, in for a pound.

'If his future was so promising there,' she asked, 'why did he leave?'

I had to think on that answer.

'New Zealand was too small a stage,' I informed her with no word of lie. 'Kas needed somewhere larger.'

'Like London?' she said.

'Exactly.'

She mused on that. 'You wouldn't see him as a fortune hunter, then.'

'Never,' I said. 'If Kas ever has a fortune, it will be his own.'

'Well,' she said, and thought.

One tete a tete, all ostensibly concerned with Kas and his character, followed another. Mrs Nicholson enjoyed them. After a month she appeared to be enjoying them too much. In dutifully wooing Jane's family I was to all appearances wooing Mrs Nicholson. She was not averse to being courted. Gifts made an appearance. Somewhat in advance of publication, she ordered a dozen copies of *The New Zealanders* from her bookseller. She meant to distribute them to her closest friends and draw their attention to her young man from New Zealand. Kas observed a thaw on the family front.

'Things are going well,' he reported.

I dissented. 'At this rate,' I pointed out, '*I* could finish up in the Nicholson family.'

Kas raced Jane off to a registry office. Within a year or two he was rather grander than the Nicholsons and entertaining the good and the great in his country house. As for his first million, that was his own. So was his second. He determined the market value of Francis Bacon and discovered David Hockney.

Summer came. So did the printers' strike. *The New Zealanders* languished with other books on the Gollancz summer list. I began writing a novel set in Eastern Europe but never got further than the first sentence. It read, 'I have never been able to believe in frontiers.'

I put this to the test. In Vienna there was another youth festival, more or less on Moscow's model, but in a non-communist country. This time Americans were descending on it in number. Thousands of East Europeans would be at liberty in a western society for the first time. Uproar was probable and defections expected. A commission came my way to cover the event. For want of compatriots I joined friends in the Indian delegation. Before leaving London I had a letter from Vasil Popov urging me to visit Bulgaria when the festival finished. 'Why don't you come too?' I asked Kevin. Increasingly restive, he looked in need of another bout of heartbreak. We agreed on a rendezvous with Vasil in Sofia.

Vienna was all that publicity promised. There were anguished debates on street corners, brawls and blood noses as rival demonstrators clashed. Delegations split right and left: first the Indians, then the British, and even the Americans. Their problem was that ideological fervour was lacking on the other side. There to argue the case for liberal democracy or democratic socialism, Westerners found themselves shouting into a sour void. The Chinese were preoccupied with the perfidy of the Russians. The Russians were being made miserable by prickly Poles. More confusingly some Hungarian emigres, there to persuade fellow countrymen of the virtues of the West, were defecting homesick to their native country.

Escaping assault and battery, I took refuge in a literary seminar. Soviet apologists presented the case against *Dr Zhivago*, which was no large surprise. Their morose and monotone speeches lacked all conviction. I could see a long-winded *Pravda* headline in the making: *Progressive Youth of the World Condemn Pasternak*. Applause was weak and mainly from the undistinguished Soviet delegation. Other East Europeans sat on their hands. I discovered myself on my feet in rage. The seminar chairman signalled me to speak. 'The New Zealand writer has the floor,' he said.

Words were slow coming. If in doubt, go for the underbelly.

Were the Soviet representatives, I asked, writers themselves?

Yes, they claimed.

How could they be, I asked.

They were, they insisted. Two of their number were even Stalin prizewinners.

Then how countenance a fellow writer being hounded? How approve of his book being banned? They were betraying their brotherhood; they were betraying their calling.

It was helpfully melodramatic. One by one the Soviets looked uncomfortably at each other and then grimly into space. This allowed Americans on my right and left flank to press a more considered attack. There was applause from both sides of the political divide. We might have ensured that there would be no Moscow headline. On the other hand, it was probably already written.

The dividend of the day came at the seminar's end while I stood talking to the American speakers. A blonde girl from Kiev bravely broke ranks, crossed the conference floor, and thanked us for defending Pasternak. 'Ignore what our official speakers said today,' she told us. 'They do not speak for the people of the Soviet Union. They speak only for themselves, their privileges and their dachas.' Then, with a toss of the head, she returned to her delegation; I was left speculating on what her act might have cost her. There would be no privileges for her, no dachas.

Then there was a Polish writer shaking my hand. 'Have you thought of visiting Poland?' he asked.

I hadn't, I said.

'Consider yourself invited,' he said.

I cabled Kevin in London and Vasil in Sofia to rearrange our Bulgarian rendezvous. DELAYED, I informed them. AMBUSHED BY POLES.

There was a guide and interpreter waiting for me when my train shunted into Poland. His name was Jerzy Szkup. He was a translator, university lecturer, and literary critic. He had been at pains to get the job of guiding me through Poland. He was completing a doctoral thesis on Katherine Mansfield; he needed a New Zealander in his life. Meanwhile I needed a Pole. 'Welcome to the socialist paradise,' he said sardonically.

I seemed in good hands. I needed a reliable companion to get through a long day in Auschwitz. We walked a wasteland of rusting wire, sagging watch-towers and abandoned crematoria. Here and there human remains still whitened the ground, testifying to the last feverish slaughter before the Red Army arrived. The crematoria couldn't cope with the output of corpses; heaped bodies had to be burned outdoors, the last of the four million to perish there.

'The Russians may have been brutal,' Jerzy said. 'But brutal in the way of children. No one but the Nazis has made an industry of murder.'

I didn't need elucidation. I wanted to escape the place and knew I never would.

'So let us get to Warsaw fast,' Jerzy said.

292

On the way we stopped in Poznan. Two years earlier the workers in that city had marched against their Stalinist masters; sixty had been shot down. But there were other dead remembered here too: there was a vast war cemetery mostly devoted to the fallen of the Red Army. It was impossible not to be moved by it. But there was more. Something familiar lodged in my eye, just outside my line of vision. I stopped and looked back. It wasn't. It was. Among the graves with Cyrillic script was a cluster of headstones marked with a New Zealand fern leaf. Who were these young men from familiar places? Perhaps crashed pilots. Perhaps captives who escaped internment to die with Poland's partisans. All that mattered was that they were dust of my tribe; clay of my clan.

'I'm sorry,' I said to Jerzy. 'I have to sit down.'

We found a bench.

'What is the matter?' Jerzy asked.

'I'm a long way from home,' I confided.

How explain that I had found who I was in a Polish cemetery?

A day or two later I woke in Warsaw. Jerzy and I had both been twelve years old in 1944. That was the year of the Warsaw uprising. It was a beautiful summer, Jerzy recalled. It seemed to go on and on. The Red Army advanced through the eastern suburbs of Warsaw, all the way to the Vistula, with the old and new towns of Warsaw, the historic heart of the city, just across the water.

Scenting liberation at last, the people of Warsaw rose and battled their Nazi masters. The Red Army did nothing. On instruction from Stalin, a man whose hatred of Polish patriots was matched only by Hitler's, the Russians stood off and watched dust and smoke rise as the old and new towns shook with explosions and fires blazed. One hundred thousand Poles died. Stalin's hope was that the flame of Polish nationalism would be extinguished by blonde Aryan executioners, thus sparing him the task. The slaughter went on without a Soviet shot fired. There wasn't even a feint to divert the killers. Jerzy saw the makeshift German firing squads dispatching partisans at the end of his street. The Nazis finally drove resistance down into Warsaw's sewers. Jerzy remembered the sewers. Running to safety with his father, a stray bullet caught him in the leg. The wound turned septic and he became delirious as his father dragged and carried him through the subterranean maze. The clammy sewers were turning into a graveyard. In moments of lucidity he saw bodies

293

floating, the survivors of the uprising bracing for a last stand in the foul gloom, the earth shaking as Hitler's departing legions dynamited Warsaw building by building, carrying out Hitler's order to expunge the city from the map of Europe. And with Stalin's apparent acquiesence.

Jerzy couldn't recall how his war finished, other than in a bed in some relative's dwelling to the west of the city. But he remembered helping clear rubble after Nazi rule ended and Russian occupation began; he remembered Warsaw rising again. (While I sledded down a green New Zealand hillside, fought make-believe battles with wooden weapons, and wondered if the war would go on long enough for me to join the army.)

'Here,' Jerzy explained, 'is where the two tyrants met. Here is where the two most powerful men in history agreed Poland should die.'

It was difficult to believe now. The resurrected spires and towers of the old town glowed once more, its lanes and cafes lively and colourful again. It looked much as it might have in the Middle Ages, when it was born. Warsaw had outlived those who would level it.

'Shall I tell you something?' Jerzy said.

'Please,' I asked.

'You know I loathe this regime.'

'You make it no secret.'

'I have been to England,' he said. 'I have been to France. I could have put Poland behind me. I could have defected.'

'I expect you could have.'

'Ask me why not,' he suggested.

'So why not?' I asked.

His eyes were shrewd and melancholy.

'Because I am Warsaw,' he said. 'Because Warsaw is me.'

As Warsaw's old town fades in memory, as its churches, squares and cafes dim, I still recall Jerzy vivid and tousle-haired that summer morning — a summer already as long and hot as any since 1944.

'How could I defect?' he said.

There was silence for a time.

'You are thinking,' he said.

'Yes,' I said.

'And of your own country.'

'Perhaps,' I agreed.

'And that you will not defect either.'

'London tempts me. Europe does.'

'That is not an answer.'

'No,' I had to admit.

We walked on to the headquarters of the Polish Writers' Union. I had an appointment with the poet, editor and veteran liberal Antoni Slominski. He was a grey and weary man. He had seen out Stalin's years precariously; he had survived to win a few freedoms for Polish writers, especially the young.

'I believe you had something to say about Boris Pasternak in Vienna,' he said quietly.

'Others too,' I informed him.

'Then welcome to Poland,' he said. 'Such protest may keep Pasternak safe.' He explained, 'I wrote him a poem of sympathy. It was to appear in the literary journal *Nowa Kultura*. Then it was banned. So we published instead a discreet article on his translations from Polish literature. It was the best we could do to show support. There was no reference to *Dr Zhivago*, to the Nobel Prize, nor to his expulsion from the Soviet Writers' Union. If we couldn't write honestly about such matters it was better to say nothing at all. Does this seem cowardice to you?'

'No,' I insisted.

'It is,' he sighed. 'My hope is that the future will forgive us.'

The future is here, and has.

The Writers' Union was a busy and casual place, full of loud and eloquent literary Poles. I saw a notice board, letters for visitors pinned to it. I had no reason to expect anything there. But there was. A letter with an English stamp, a London postmark. It was from Gillian. There were two items of news. The largest was that I was to become a father in seven or eight months. The lesser was that there was a $1200 cheque in the mail from *The New Yorker*. It would buy us passage home, with a useful sum left over. In a PS she said she supposed the question was whether we wanted our child born in England or New Zealand. She left it to me to decide; she couldn't begin to think about it.

So I had to.

Jerzy judged a large vodka might steady me. Beyond a cafe window on the Nowy Swiat Poles passed back and forward in the warm August sun. But who were they? Who was I? I was suddenly blank. I looked at Jerzy. He looked at me.

'I think you have already decided,' he said.

'I think I have,' I agreed.

He raised his glass. 'Permit me to be godfather,' he said.

Forty-seven

*E*verything said I should speed back to London. The difficulty was that Kevin was on his way to Sofia. He knew no one there; he didn't have a syllable of Bulgarian. He might already be marooned in a sea of unfamiliar Slav faces. I was in difficulty myself. There were four frontiers and five languages in the way of our Sofia rendezvous. I negotiated Czechoslovakia, crossed Hungary, and on a cool morning left a train in Belgrade. Checking my passport, I found my Bulgarian visa had expired. To get another I battled across the city, dodging snarling Fiats, double-decker buses and horse-drawn peasant wagons, to the Bulgarian embassy. The embassy was busy and bureaucratic, reluctant to part with visas except as a last resort. There was a comfortless waiting room filled with frustrated Americans, baffled Scandinavians and angry Frenchmen. Some had been two days there already. Most were merely trying to win a way through to Turkey; I was one of the few bound for Bulgaria itself. That was unpromising: it might mean my application required more extensive checking. I had a train to catch that night; it seemed unlikely I would be on it.

Bouncing among sweaty travellers — conveying reassurances in one language after another — was a short, darkish, middle-aged and jokey man. At first I took this fluent fellow to be an official. But his eyes were too lively. 'Who,' he asked, 'are you?'

I tried to account for myself.

'A lover of Bulgaria?' he said.

'Of Bulgarians.'

'So what is your problem?'

I explained how my visa had expired while making an unplanned visit to Poland.

'I can fix that,' he promised.

He pushed me to the head of the queue and spoke to an official in

an authoritative tone; and in Bulgarian. The man was a marvel. I
estimated that he must have at least six languages. 'This man is a
writer,' he appeared to be saying, 'and a friend of Bulgaria.'

The Bulgarians were impressed. They took my passport away.

'Call me Fred,' my acquaintance said. 'I am also waiting on a
visitor's visa.'

'You seem to know Bulgarian well.'

'I grew up in Sofia,' he said.

Otherwise he was an Italian from West Germany. He had
escaped Bulgaria after the Russian tanks pushed into Sofia in 1944.
Others of his family were less lucky. He left a slow-moving brother
behind; a brother he was trying to visit.

Our names were called from the desk. Our visas were ready.

'Can I give you a ride through to Sofia?' Fred asked.

'I have a train tonight. Even a ticket for it.'

'Forget the train,' he said. 'Forget the ticket. I like company. We
will eat well and drink well on the way. My car is a wonder, a Ford,
the greatest in the world.'

I followed him from the embassy. There was a 1935 Ford, dusty
with Yugoslav roads, parked carelessly across a pavement. Fred
slapped his vehicle affectionately; it creaked in response.

'Well?' he asked. 'Coming?'

The problem was climbing aboard with my typewriter and pack.
There were suitcases stacked to the roof; the boot was bulging too,
and tied down with rope. Finally I wedged in.

'How long are you staying in Bulgaria?' I asked.

'A week or two.'

'A lot of baggage for a short stay,' I observed.

'That is true,' he said, but did not explain.

The car coughed into motion. On open road it hiccuped along at
thirty miles an hour. Belgrade's industrial suburbs drifted behind.
Soon we were in open country, among Serbian fields, with mountains
hazy ahead.

Fred talked. His business took him everywhere, he informed me.
Thus his command of languages. At last count he had ten.

What business? He was still wasn't saying.

Two hours out of Belgrade he became more forthcoming.

'In Bulgaria,' he said, 'good shoes fetch a high price. They can
cost a man a month's wages or more.'

He paused while I took this in.

'In the back,' he added, 'I have sixty pairs of good shoes.'

I was impressed.

'In Bulgaria,' he went on, 'nylon stockings are rare and very expensive. A Bulgar woman will do anything for nylon stockings.'

He let me consider this.

'I have,' he explained, 'two hundred pairs of nylons.'

I also had a dozen pairs aboard, as gifts for friends, along with other merchandise scarce in Bulgaria. But I wasn't in Fred's class. He continued listing his cargo of contraband proudly: women's dresses, drip-dry shirts, cans of instant coffee. But the piece de resistance was his Ford; he meant to sell that off too. With the money he would holiday on the Black Sea. Such Bulgarian currency as he had left over would go to his impoverished brother. He would then fly back to Frankfurt unencumbered.

I grew uneasy. 'What about the frontier?' I asked. 'What about customs?'

'Never a problem,' he said.

'You mean you've done this before?'

'Often,' he said. 'Bulgaria is my favourite country.'

I began to sweat. It wasn't the weather. If Fred were picked up as a smuggler, who would see me as an harmless hitch-hiker? In Bulgaria, a land of few motor vehicles, there were no hitch-hikers. And I had clandestine goods too. The frontier was ten hours away, lurching nearer every minute. On corrugated Yugoslav highways his Ford was showing its form. We careered breathtakingly from pothole to pothole, leaving Volkswagens, Renaults, Simcas and Chevrolets stuttering to our rear. Breakdowns were frequent along the way. Motorists gazed blankly into steaming engines or lamented broken axles. Fred often stopped to commiserate, to give helpful advice, to lend tools or a jack.

We lunched in a vine-greened village restaurant. Over schnitzel and white wine, I realised, rather late in the day, that I might be in even more peril than Fred. In my pack was a bundle of books forbidden in Bulgaria and meant for Vasil Popov and his fellow dissidents: Orwell's *1984* and *Animal Farm*; Koestler's *Darkness at Noon*; and not least *Dr Zhivago*. They presented rather more of a menace to the Bulgarian regime than sturdy shoes, instant coffee and drip-dry shirts. Fred's freight might suggest that we were up to no good; my books would confirm it. They could ensure a longer prison sentence. If arrested as a smuggler Fred might get months. I could get years.

We hurtled on again.

'How far to the frontier now?' I asked.

'Who cares?' he said, wind blowing wildly through his hair.

I did. I could leave Fred here and now and hike back to Belgrade. I could also dump my dangerous books before the frontier. Incomprehensibly I did neither. Perhaps it was lethargy. Perhaps I was numbed by travel. Perhaps I was tempting fate. There was sweet watermelon from a roadside stall. There was a swim in an icy river. We arrived at Nis toward evening. Ahead was a long drive through the mountains to the frontier. Following the Nisava river, we laboured up the pass through which Alexander's Macedonians travelled to subdue Thrace; through which crusader and infidel had marched. The road was winding and difficult. Surprising villages loomed from the dusk. We threaded through the old pottery town of Bela Palanka, weaved among the populace of Pirot on evening parade. Then our headlights were feeble in the Balkan dark again.

'How long now?' I asked Fred.

'Not allowing for refreshment?'

'Not allowing for refreshment.'

'An hour or two,' he claimed.

His eyes were on the road.

'You are nervous,' he judged.

'A little,' I agreed.

'No need,' he insisted. 'After midnight the frontier is quiet and the guards are sleepy. They like a visitor with a few stories, a few jokes, and some American cigarettes. They will be so busy listening and laughing they will forget to look in our baggage.'

I found this difficult to credit.

The road was empty. Finally there were the lights of Dimitrovgrad, the last Yugoslav town before the frontier. We stopped at a cafe and had a leisurely supper. Perhaps our last. 'Take your time,' Fred said. 'It is not midnight yet. The guards will not be tired.'

A man in a corner of the cafe played an accordion and sang melancholy ballads. He was a week unshaven and had bloodshot eyes. Fred invited him to drink at our table. The fellow instantly burst into tears. With no urging he told Fred his life story. A Bulgarian, he had once been a musician in Sofia's best cafes. Then his father was arrested, his mother, finally his brother. He fled into Yugoslavia. He lived close to the frontier so that he could look out on his homeland every day. When his story sputtered out, there were more tears. Fred gripped the man's shoulder and freshened his glass.

'One day it will be different,' Fred assured him.

'My day has gone,' the man said, and favoured us with another tragic melody.

Midnight passed. It was time to face the frontier. We didn't have far to drive. In a yellow lake of light there were two barriers, one Yugoslav, one Bulgarian, with a no-man's-land of thirty yards between. The Yugoslavs dismissed us quickly. A few friendly questions, a rubber stamp, and the first barrier rose. As the second lifted we drove on to Bulgarian earth.

The Iron Curtain was no robust Churchillian euphemism. It may have been soundless, it may have been invisible, but there was metal in the atmosphere. Bulgarian guards with humourless faces shuffled around the vehicle with automatic rifles. We were ordered to climb out. Then, with a couple of guards apiece, we were ushered into a reception room for questions and form-filling.

Fred flipped a Lucky Strike cigarette conspicuously into his mouth. Then he passed the packet around. Guard after guard lit up. Bulgarian faces began looking less stern. Always amiable Fred told stories, made jokes. Soon there were smiles. The questions, the filling of forms, went on agreeably.

After an hour we were ushered into the night again. For an optimistic moment I thought we were free.

'Now they must look at the car,' Fred explained.

The Bulgarians were connoisseurs of old cars. They patted Fred's Ford, stroked it. They probed its murky recesses with screw drivers; they jacked it up to consider its underside at length. Presumably in quest of contraband, they kicked tyres and lifted lining and looked under seats, Fred's stories became longer and rambling. Did I detect desperation? There were now at least a dozen Bulgarians, including a couple of braided officers, pawing over the vehicle. They looked around our baggage, under our baggage; they lifted baggage from the boot and returned baggage to the boot. They looked everywhere, in fact, but in our baggage. Meanwhile more Lucky Strike cigarettes were smoked and more hilarious tales told. Fred finally offered them the car provided we were allowed to walk into Bulgaria with our bags. This proposition was received riotously; even the officers grinned. By now most had glazed eyes. Fred's tactic was not only to humour inquisitors; it was also to wear them down.

At length the Ford was pronounced free of contagion. Hostilities ended. This time cigarettes were passed around by the packet. Our passports were stamped and we were waved on. I couldn't believe it. Had Fred been free with more than cigarettes? Possibly. But I hadn't seen anything resembling money change hands.

The rest of our run was on fast road. Dim suburbs of Sofia grew around. The streets were without traffic and, aside from guards pacing outside state buildings, without people. Then we arrived at his brother's door. It was in an old and slummy quarter of the city strange to me. I was more familiar with the Sofia of the privileged, of those wooed and won by the state: the Sofia of writers, artists, musicians, journalists and academics. This was the Sofia of factory workers, shop assistants, clerks. This was not the city foreigners knew. This was the Sofia where people worked twelve hours a day and lived ten to a room.

Fred's brother Luigi, a beefy man with a cherubic smile, welcomed us in. The household was roused. Children were rubbing their eyes. Women were bustling. Men were slapping Fred's back and shaking his hand. Liugi's family shared a two room flat with another. There was room for beds, but little for living: five beds in one room, four in another.

Downing a slivova by way of preliminary, Fred went into a conjurer's routine — opening up suitcases, and spilling out commodities of most shapes and sizes. There were sighs and shouts of delight. The apartment resembled a department store. Women were pulling on nylons and trying Italian fashions for size. The men experimented with shoes and shirts. Children were munching Swiss chocolate. Neighbours arrived to join in festivities, and to choose gifts. Anything left over, Fred explained, would be disposed of on Sofia's black market by brother Luigi. Meanwhile he sat back and laughed with delight. 'This,' he said to me, 'is worth a little trouble at the frontier, no?'

Who was I to argue? For the first time I saw Fred as more than a mercenary smuggler. I had hitch-hiked into Bulgaria with Santa Claus himself. Contrary to folklore, he rode no sleigh; he drove a 1935 Ford.

Later that morning I arrived red-eyed at Vasil Popov's apartment in central Sofia. Vasil was not impressed by the manner of my arrival in Bulgaria.

'With a criminal?' he said.

'No more than me,' I claimed.

'I think you should not see this man Fred again,' he judged. 'Sooner or later he could be watched by our secret police. Who knows? You may be too.'

With that show of virtue he grabbed up my literary contraband and hid book after forbidden book from view. *Dr Zhivago* received especially reverential treatment; he slid it under his pillow. Vasil didn't call in neighbours to celebrate. In any case one was a secret policeman; another a judge famed for handing out long sentences.

Kevin Ireland was arriving by train from Belgrade that night. In the afternoon Vasil and I went swimming in a public pool. Sunning herself there was a friend of Vasil's, a blonde and strikingly attractive theatrical designer named Donna. Others joined us. We drank Czech beer. Wistful Donna wanted to know about London and New Zealand; what was life like for theatre designers in the West? Others wished word on *Dr Zhivago*. Was it as great a novel as rumoured? I said I thought it a pity Bulgarians, like Russians, had no chance to judge for themselves. That left a silence. Vasil smiled slyly, but said nothing. Sofia was as amiable as I remembered. At the afternoon's end I had several new friends. Then it was time to rescue travel-worn Kevin from his train.

Next morning I left Vasil deep in *Dr Zhivago* and walked Kevin through the yellow-cobbled streets of central Sofia. Cafes were open, the summer sun warm. In the course of impressing Kevin with local knowledge, I sighted Donna, Vasil's designer friend. She was reading under a cafe awning on the Ulitsa Russki.

'I know her,' I claimed.

Kevin gazed. 'You do?'

'Her name is Donna,' I informed him.

'She's beautiful,' he said.

'Hang on,' I said. 'You've only just got here.'

We walked on a few paces. Then Kevin halted. He was never slow to identify fate.

'I need to meet her,' he announced.

We turned back.

There were difficulties. Donna spoke next to no English, and little French. Kevin spoke no Bulgarian and his French was worse. The rapport they established was remarkable for its extra-lingual nature. By the morning's end Kevin was more than merely in love again. He was as good as married, though the ceremony would have to wait another two weeks.

'Impossible,' Jenny Bojilova laughed. 'Do New Zealanders come to Bulgaria only to fall in love?'

We met in the cafe where I had set our story.

'There are two tables free,' Jenny pointed out. 'One is the table in the middle of the cafe where we actually sat when we said goodbye. The other is the window table where you imagined us sitting in your story. Which table is it to be?'

I didn't think long. 'The window table,' I said.

'As I thought,' she said.

She wasn't really laughing. Nor was I. Lunch was quiet and introspective. We didn't dwell on the details of our fiasco. They were in the story with the window table.

'We would not have been happy,' she said. 'Could you have been here? Could I have been in New Zealand?'

'We never tried,' I said.

'You never,' she pointed out.

Jenny was about to share her life with a talented Bulgarian novelist named Nikolai instead of a New Zealander named Maurice. Nikolai lived in the Rhodope mountains and wrote on gentle peasant themes. Perhaps Nikolai would not have chosen the window table. 'I will be safe with him,' Jenny said. 'I will be happy.'

She was, and is.

There was a literary dinner in the Balkan hotel, Sofia's best. The guest of honour was the Scottish poet Hugh McDiarmid. Expelled from the Communist Party twice in the 1930s, he had joined again in 1956, after the Krushchev denunciation of Stalin and the Soviet invasion of Hungary, when all but fools were bidding the Party goodbye. McDiarmid may not have been a fool, but he was possibly the last distinguished Western writer left with loyalty to the Party, the last who could be feted with safety in Eastern Europe. In celebration of the bicentenary of Robert Burns' birth he had been making regal progress through Czechoslovakia, Romania, and finally Bulgaria. His idiosyncracies and past ideological wavering were forgotten. Bulgaria's literary bureaucrats had been wining and dining him for a month or more. Their hope was that McDiarmid might come up with fresh English versions of Bulgaria's national poet Hristo Botev

(1848-1876); versions which would not only establish Botev as a great if neglected Balkan poet, but also give Bulgaria larger standing in world literature. It was a tense time. His hosts were anxious. After some weeks perusing prose cribs of Botev provided by a team of translators, McDiarmid hadn't come up with a line. He was still being primed for the task. There were toasts to Scottish literature, to Bulgarian literature, to the memory of Hristo Botev and Robert Burns and Scotland's reigning bard.

Kevin and I sat opposite McDiarmid, Vasil Popov between us. I leaned across the table to McDiarmid and asked how he was finding Hristo Botev.

'You really want to know?' he asked.

I said I did.

'Well, for one thing,' he said, 'he's no bloody good.'

'Botev?' I said faintly. I hoped my question had been misunderstood.

'Who else?' he said. In case I hadn't heard right the first time, he said, 'No bloody good at all.'

Most Bulgarians at the table didn't hear or didn't understand McDiarmid's Scottish accent; riot was a possibility. Vasil, however, had understood enough to be suspicious.

'What is that Scottish man saying?' he asked me.

'I think he is saying that past translations of Botev have been no good,' I lied.

'He said more,' Vasil argued.

'Only that he is in difficulty with Botev,' I said.

'Because Botev is no good?'

'Because he is afraid he cannot do Botev justice.'

Vasil was not to be placated. 'Botev was a great, great poet,' he said. 'Greater than Robert Burns. Greater than this ridiculous Scotsman too.'

That might have ended the matter. McDiarmid, however, hadn't finished. He leaned confidentially across the table and said to me, 'It's no use telling Bulgarians, of course.'

'Telling Bulgarians what?' I asked.

'That the bugger's no bloody good. He's a national icon, not a poet.'

This time Vasil heard every word. The honour of his homeland was at risk. Botev, after all, wasn't just a poet. He had been a nationalist, a revolutionary, and had died in the fight to free his countrymen from Turkish rule. With this and much else in mind, Vasil began to rise belligerently above the table. His large fists were clenched, but McDiarmid was oblivious to peril. Kevin and I rose too, more or less pinioning Vasil between us. With his free hand Kevin raised his glass. With great poise he proposed, 'To Bulgarian and Scottish friendship.'

Diners rose enthusiastically to the toast. We persuaded Vasil to resume his seat. Sight of McDiarmid, however, only produced a new head of steam.

'This Scotsman is shit,' he said. 'He must be thrown out of Bulgaria.'

'Not tonight,' I suggested.

'Why not tonight?' he said.

'Come,' I pleaded.

Vasil again stood with grievous bodily harm in mind. As before Kevin and I rose too, wedging him tight between us and cramping his style. While our trio held firm Kevin lifted his glass. 'To Bulgarian and New Zealand friendship,' he suggested.

No one was willing to gainsay that either. We manoeuvered Vasil to a seat at a distance from Scotland's living treasure. The evening passed with no further drama. Unaware that his brush with Bulgarian letters had been all but terminal, McDiarmid had to be helped home. So did almost everyone else.

The night had a serendipitous sequel. McDiarmid was never to produce fresh English versions of Botev. Kevin would. His lean, elegant lines suggest that Botev was indeed a poet of power and distinction. Perhaps not a great European poet, but better than most. Something the same might be said of Hugh McDiarmid.

There was a letter from Gillian. She was past morning sickness. The printers' strike was over. *The New Zealanders* was set down for publication on October 26. A New York publisher was now interested. The Book Society had recommended it to its members. The *Statesman* had placed it in its autumn selection. An insistent journalist wanted to interview me for *The Bookman*. The book was almost in business. I bought a rail ticket to London. Jenny was again there to farewell me on Sofia station. We parted less dramatically this time; there would be no short story. Vasil, never to be seen again, embraced me. Then Kevin too. It would be a decade and more before I saw Kevin. He was to recall the event in verse:

*. . . he then remembered more than fifteen years ago
an express train hauling Shadders out of Sofia station —
leaving him abandoned to private ridicule and conflict.*

Who abandoned? Him? Me?
Both.

Forty-eight

Staying in a Chinese hotel in the Malayan city of Malacca once, I found a riddling and seemingly metaphysical message on my bedroom wall: 'The management apologise to guest for disobedience on the part of the days.' I trust the management remains remorseful. This guest, in this life, has never found it easy to persuade his days to behave in submissive fashion.

Up to publication day I might have been other. The future was still flexible. I might have found my way back to a film studio and become a competent maker of television commercials. I might have waited around for the 1960s to begin, joined the counter culture, found a guru or become one, smoked pot benignly, and grown comfrey in an organic garden. It didn't happen. Instead of opening out, life closed in.

I didn't see it. I soon would. In the six months between my first book and my first child, my life ceased to be distinguishable from that of others in service to the printed page. Rites of passage were past: I was a neophyte in the largely reclusive calling of letters.

On the face of it, it wasn't to be a conspicuously monkish life. I would marry and divorce more than was good for me, and father five children. Nor was it to be colourless. I would swim with pearl-divers and sharks among equatorial reefs; paddle up Borneo rivers with recently retired headhunters; bounce on a copra boat through mid-Pacific hurricane; clamber into long-hidden Macedonian tombs with Greek archaeologists; descend with Icelandic scientists into the crater of the world's steamy new island of Surtsey; travel on pirate patrol with Gurkhas on the South China Sea; help crew a protest yacht into a French Polynesia fouled by nuclear testing.

Yet little of this had meaning until I was back at my desk again; it was there the thrills were.

Gillian and I wavered for a week or two when I arrived back from Bulgaria in September. Decision wasn't easy. Doors had begun opening in England; doors on which I had never knocked. *The New Zealanders* had been widely read in proof. There were commendations from respectable authors. I was asked to review for *The Sunday Times*. The economics of return to New Zealand were unpromising; I could at least earn a living at the Grub Street end of literary London. But the test wasn't there. Nor the sustenance. The book had already been released in New Zealand. Among the earliest to buy it was Jim Baxter. His was my first fan letter. It was a blessing and a confirmation. It also delivered a stern warning: Don't become something you aren't.

His letter arrived on a sunny autumn morning. So did a complimentary review in *The New Zealand Listener*, the first and one of the few of its kind in New Zealand. That afternoon we booked our passage home. Sailing day was November 26.

Publication day arrived first. That Monday morning I walked through the Chelsea bookshops I had visited to win intelligence of the publishing world seven months earlier. No longer a collection of coffee-flecked pages, *The New Zealanders* was now magically virginal in yellow jacket.

There were friends to be farewelled. Kevin was the most conspicuous absentee. I had picked up his possessions and crated them off to Bulgaria. Now a married man of sober habits, he was repairing prose translations for a Sofia publishing house.

November 26 came. Our voyage was postponed a day. English reviews of *The New Zealanders* had been pleasant, but few and slight. It seemed the Jeremiahs were right: London literary editors weren't interested. This dispelled last-minute doubts about the wisdom of leaving.

The day's delay meant I could pick up a copy of the latest *Times Literary Supplement* before we climbed aboard ship. We watched the docks of Tilbury disappear astern, then the last of wintry England grow faint in mist. We went down to the bar for a brandy apiece. I opened the *TLS*, and there it was. A review of *The New Zealanders* headed the fiction page. The anonymous reviewer raced on for a column. A find indeed, he or she said: I was to be mentioned in the same breath as Australia's Patrick White. 'So this is how it feels to be a New Zealander,' the reviewer mused. 'It is an exciting glimpse of national identity and destiny.'

Too good to be true, and it was.

I passed it to Gillian.

'What if you'd read it a month sooner?' she asked.

'Meaning?'

'Would you have wanted to stay?'

The ship was meeting heavy sea; there was already a faint roll.

'Let's take a walk on deck,' I said.

But England was gone.

Other English reviews caught up with us in Port Said, Colombo, and Perth. There was praise from Alan Sillitoe in *The Bookman*; Stevie Smith had kind words in the *Daily Telegraph*; Muriel Spark was dazzling in *The Observer*; Naomi Lewis extravagant in *The Statesman*. There was also word from Gollancz that the book had gone into second and third printings; that rights had been sold in New York, Hamburg and Milan. There was more such mail in Sydney. I was soon to need good news from far places.

On New Year's Day, 1960, we sighted those outlying lumps of New Zealand rock, all but whittled away by the Pacific, which Dutch voyager Abel Tasman named The Three Kings. As dusk came we were cruising past sandy Cape Maria Van Diemen, then dramatic Cape Reinga. Next morning we woke to the green islands of the Hauraki Gulf. By breakfast we were sailing into Auckland harbour. Sunlit Auckland seemed a strange, rather raffish tropical city: all palm trees, spiky pines, pale houses, red rooftops and white beaches. A reporter climbed aboard from the pilot's launch and asked for an interview. English reviews of *The New Zealanders* had been cabled from London. Was I, he asked, the successor to Katherine Mansfield? (At this time any New Zealander who had written a respectable sentence was said to be the new Mansfield, regardless of gender.) No, I said. I was merely the successor to my parents, my grandparents, and my great-grandparents. The man looked baffled. Were they writers too? No, I explained, but I wrote to fill the silences they left, the silences I knew as New Zealand's.

It was not a successful interview. The bemused journalist had hardly taken a note. There was one more earnest question: Was this just a visit back to New Zealand or was I home to stay?

On that score I managed to make myself understood. WRITER RETURNS, the story was headed next day.

Native ground might be exhilarating, but there were home truths too. Local journals of a literary kind informed me that I was, much as I suspected, a literary impostor. One implied that I should be shipped back to unenlightened London. Credible rumour said I had bribed an impoverished Victor Gollancz to publish *The New Zealanders*, seduced such as Stevie Smith and Muriel Spark to win their approval, and written the anonymous review in the *TLS* myself. The book was damned in lecture rooms, denounced from the pulpit. In at least one community it was removed from library shelves. Elsewhere bookshops declined to stock it.

Though some literary friendships became stronger still, others ended. Writing a book was one thing; publishing conspicuously was another. The vanities of the village were at risk; I was an unauthorised author. A familiar story, but I was not familiar with it then. Patrick White turned up in New Zealand and brought on heartburn at a soiree in his honour by saying that he found my work interesting; and taking me aside to tell me so. 'You should have seen what they did to me in Australia,' he told me. Looking back, I fail to see what the tantrums were about. It was the first book of a twenty-six-year-old.

I needed an angel, and one winged in. A week back in New Zealand, I had a telegram from Brian Brake. Wreathed with even more international honours — the American Society of Magazine Photographers was about to give him an award of merit for a photo-essay on India's monsoon — he was home on assignment for *National Geographic*. He recalled our pact, made in a Hong Kong hotel, to work together when we had the chance. We now had the chance. With *National Geographic* picking up the bills, we could rediscover New Zealand together.

The invitation was seductive. It meant escape from literary din. It would put Europe behind me. For most of three months we worked our way through New Zealand. We tramped with musterers under the Southern Alps; we walked wild West Coast beaches; we lived with lighthouse keepers and fishermen in lonely recesses of the land. We picked mushrooms under autumnal maples about the old gold mining town of Arrowtown, caught fat fish in the Bay of Islands, and gathered tuatua and toheroa from the sand of Ninety Mile Beach. New Zealand's champion shearer Godfrey Bowen taught me how to part a sheep from its fleece. I learned how to pan for gold from a grizzled prospector. And an old Maori under waterside willows told me the legends of the Waikato River.

I was due to join Gillian in Wellington. Our child was a week away. There was just time for another chore. On an autumn afternoon Brian and I took the winding road from Christchurch to Banks Peninsula, where the Shadbolts began, where my pioneer kin were buried. It was my first meeting with ancestral earth. As we drove out of the hills Akaroa harbour unfurled below, as shapely as family legend said. The road descended sharply to sea. Left and right were the hills Benjamin cleared, the paddocks where the Hertfordshire peasant trained his horses. There was lumpy Onawe peninsula where Ernest farmed. There were the waters my father fished.

At the tiny settlement of Duvauchelle the Shadbolt-built pub was still open for business. We stopped for a beer and a sandwich. We were the only customers. While Brian and I talked, the barman, a lifelong local, scrutinised me warily while pretending to mop the bar.

'You'd be a Shadbolt,' he concluded.

'That's right,' I agreed.

He gave my face further consideration.

'And one of Ben's,' he decided.

'How would you know?'

'Ben's people keep coming back,' he explained.

He talked with familiarity of Benjamin and Elizabeth, as if they had been around the Tuesday before last.

We left the pub, paused at the diminutive Shadbolt church, and walked land once Benjamin's. Hertford Farm had disappeared into a dozen less heroic holdings; sheep grazed most of the land now. His mansion, with an unpromising lean, now served a farmer as a haybarn. There was little left of its surrounds. The iron gates were gone, the drive, the lily ponds and flower beds. The homestead, after ten decades, wouldn't see out another.

Uphill, in the cemetery, I picked my way among pioneer graves. Half the headstone names seemed to be French; almost as many bore my family name. Counting William and Annie Shaw too, I could tally four great-grandparents serenely resident in the vicinity. I halted longest at the grave Elizabeth and Benjamin shared. *Highly esteemed by all who knew him*, the inscription for Benjamin asserted. A queer and surely needless claim. So what was the inscription trying to say? Certainly more than it said.

Brian pretended to be busy with his camera while I waited on the grave to tell me more. Without my willing it, without even my knowledge, a story was taking form, a story to fill the silence, to seed further stories, and soon novels too. Continuities, however, were most on my mind, and my first child. Understudy years were ending. I was a candidate ancestor.

'Finished?' Brian asked. We had a ferry to catch from Lyttelton to Wellington, to all that might be. Might? Would.

'Almost,' I said.

I had come empty-handed. I picked wild roses and scattered them on the grave.

One of Ben's?

And Elizabeth's. Not to name William and Annie, Ernest and Ada, Arklow Joe and Louisa, or Frank and Violet. Spinster Amelia, bachelor Joe, and childless Sis had demands on me too. Their uncelebrated lives were mysteriously mine; their land likewise. One of Ben's? Who was I to argue? The answer could never be no.

•